PENGUIN BOOKS

THE TEATIME ISLANDS

Ben Fogle took part in the BBC's hit series *Castaway 2000*. He now presents BBC1's *Countryfile*, and his writing has appeared in numerous newspapers and magazines, including the *Sunday Times*, the *Daily Telegraph* and the *Guardian*. *The Teatime Islands* is his first book – and the fulfilment of a lifetime's ambition. He lives in London.

The Teatime Islands

Adventures in Britain's Faraway Outposts

BEN FOGLE

PENGUIN BOOKS

PENGUIN BOOKS

Published by the Penguin Group
Penguin Books Ltd, 80 Strand, London WC2R ORL, England
Penguin Group (USA) Inc., 375 Hudson Street, New York, New York 10014, USA
Penguin Books Australia Ltd, 250 Camberwell Road, Camberwell, Victoria 3124, Australia
Penguin Books Canada Ltd, 10 Alcorn Avenue, Toronto, Ontario, Canada M4V 3B2
Penguin Books India (P) Ltd, 11 Community Centre, Panchsheel Park, New Delhi – 110 017, India
Penguin Group (NZ), cnr Airborne and Rosedale Roads, Albany, Auckland 1310, New Zealand
Penguin Books (South Africa) (Pty) Ltd, 24 Sturdee Avenue, Rosebank 2196, South Africa

Penguin Books Ltd, Registered Offices: 80 Strand, London WC2R ORL, England

www.penguin.com

First published by Michael Joseph 2003
Published in Penguin Books 2004
7

Copyright © Ben Fogle, 2003
All rights reserved

The moral right of the author has been asserted

Set by Rowland Phototypesetting Ltd, Bury St Edmunds, Suffolk
Printed in England by Clays Ltd, St Ives plc

ISBN-13: 978–0–141–01046–5
ISBN-10: 0–141–01046–0

Contents

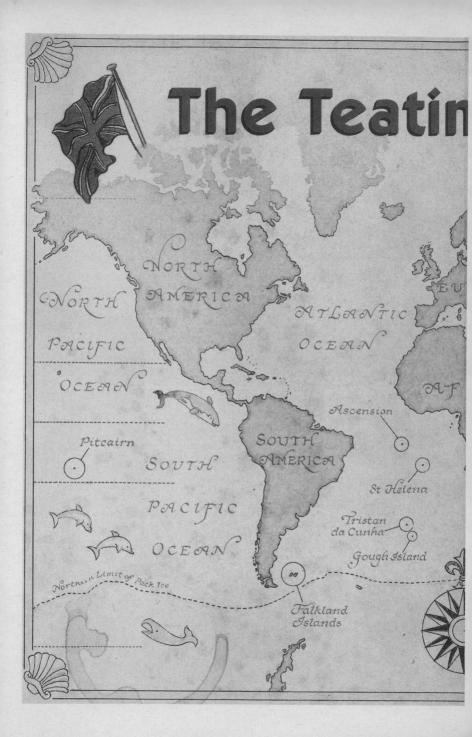

The Teatin

NORTH AMERICA

NORTH PACIFIC OCEAN

SOUTH AMERICA

SOUTH PACIFIC OCEAN

ATLANTIC OCEAN

EU

AF

Pitcairn

Ascension

St Helena

Tristan da Cunha

Gough Island

Northern Limit of Pack Ice

Falkland Islands

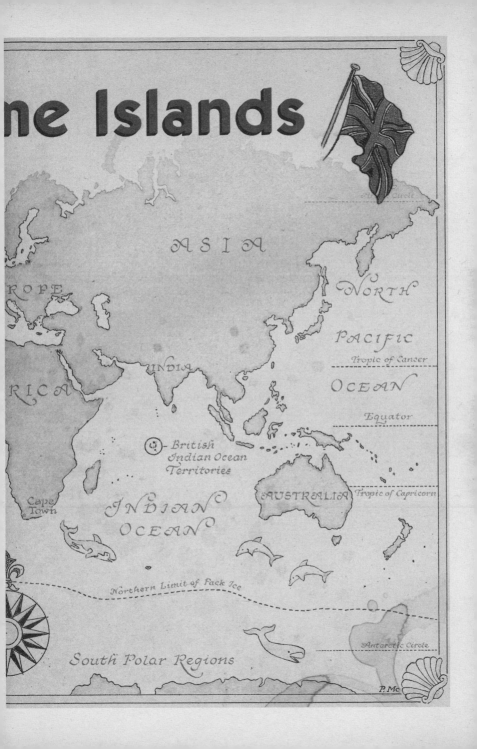

To my family, for letting me be a dreamer

Acknowledgements

Thanks to Sukey Cameron and everyone at FIGO for all their hard work planning, organizing and hosting me twice, Becky Ingham, Debbie Summers, Councillor Richard Cockwell, Hattie Lee for her hospitality, Karen Taylor, Rob McGill, Neil Watson, Ken Greenland, Tex and Mandy at Port Edgar for their time, HM Governor Donald Lamont and Lynda Lamont, HMS *Endurance*, HH Administrator Geoffrey Fairhurst and Wendy Fairhurst, Chief Islander James 'Jimmy' Glass, Constable Conrad Glass, Yvonne and Lewis Glass for their hospitality, HH Administrator Bill Dickson and Trisha Daniels, HM Governor David Hollamby and Mrs Hollamby, Captain Roberts and the crew of the RMS *St Helena* with particular thanks to Purser Geoff for his humour during the long passages, Linda Butler at Andrew Weir Shipping for coping with my disorganization, Didier Wattrelot and the *Sauvage* for getting me to Pitcairn against the elements, Johnny Hobson for all his kind help both on and off Ascension, Adam Hensham and Buffalo, the crew of the *Dream Voyager*, Jeff Shea, Ted Cookson, Brian Appleby, Dick Benson, Bill Woodward, Doug Patterson and family, Dulcie and Bobby Robertson, Shelco and Bryan Jones, Basil George, Michael Swales for his indispensable knowledge, Anne and Frank Dakin for their wonderful story, Air New Zealand for the comfy seats, Ken Lennox for his photographs and all those trips, Lucy Irvine for the inspiration, the Taransay castaways, Colin Cameron, Chris Kelly, Jeremy Mills and everyone at Lion Television for the opportunity, Sheila Jowers for her artwork and Roger Stephenson for all his helpful advice. A hearty thanks to Charles Veley; good luck to you, sir — you have made the world a very small place. And finally, to everyone who helped me along the way, thank you.

Julian Alexander and all at LAW, Ginette Chalmers and Kathryn

Fleming at PFD for the transition, to Ed Bettison, Clare Pollock, Georgina Atsiaris and all at Michael Joseph and Penguin for helping me steer a course through the publishing ocean, and for allowing me to fulfil my dream, and thanks to Peter McClure for the maps. Special thanks to my editor Rowland White for his enthusiasm and zeal throughout.

To Mum and Dad for their unfailing support and encouragement throughout the years, and to friends and work colleagues who have put up with incessant 'book talk' for so long. Thank you all for putting up with me, and sticking around.

To my darling Kinvara: thank you for an understanding and patience way beyond the call of duty and for always being there for me. You will always be special to me, x.

Toby Grimwood and Linford Casenove, two friends and fellow dreamers, their lives cut tragically short, you are not forgotten.

To the people of Tristan da Cunha, Pitcairn, Ascension, St Helena, the Falklands and the British Indian Ocean Territories: this book is about you and for you. Thanks, guys.

Introduction

A milky Corn Flake fell on to the kitchen table as I spluttered over my bowl of breakfast cereal. 'NAVAL OFFICER FINDS ISLAND', read the small article in the *Daily Telegraph*. My eyes strained as I read the news story hidden in the depths of the broadsheet: 'A Royal Navy petty officer who discovered an island in the South Atlantic which did not appear on any charts may have the rocky outcrop named after him.' The article went on to explain that 'Mark Robinson, 28, a medical assistant, was serving on HMS *Endurance* when he saw the island, which is a quarter of a square mile in size with a peak of 18 feet.'

I was flabbergasted, mesmerized and, quite frankly, very, very envious. What was an island doing hanging about undiscovered – this was 2002 not 1702 – and, more to the point, where were all the other officers looking? It certainly didn't inspire my confidence in the Royal Navy, although the visual acuity of their medical assistants was reassuring.

That an island could remain undiscovered in the twenty-first century seemed inconceivable. I dusted off my world map and scanned the South Atlantic. I had forgotten how vast that great South Atlantic ocean is, and as I searched across it I reacquainted myself with some old friends, the Teatime Islands.

I have been fascinated by islands and travel since I was a young boy. I went on my first expedition when I was just six. It was teatime and I had just finished a milk chocolate digestive. I decided to visit Ostrov Kotel'Nyj in the Arctic Ocean above the former Soviet Union. A bitterly cold island chain highlighted by an assortment of fallen biscuit crumbs and inhabited, I imagined, by a lost tribe of brown-jumper-wearing Latin teachers, it seemed a suitably remote place to begin my 'daydream' travels.

The trip had been a success, and over the next few years these

teatime expeditions took me to some of the most remote corners
of the earth: from the South Sandwich Islands (if I told you they
were giant floating ham and cheese sandwiches you wouldn't
believe me) to Christmas Island (inhabited by a whole tribe of
Father Christmases). I was the 'Teatime Traveller'. The world was
at my knees (my mother actually made me some special cushioned
kneepads for comfort, and because I wore through so many trousers)
and I embarked on some serious finger-walking.

The school became so concerned about my lack of attention that I
was eventually sent to a number of specialist doctors who examined
everything from my hearing to my sight, and all because I was busy
daydreaming down the Amazon. I can still remember thinking how
useful the ear doctor's little torch would be for night-time trips.

I found a map of Britain's former empire in an old *National
Geographic*. I was dazzled by the vast tracts of colour that streaked
the globe pink. It seemed incredible that this small rainy island in
Western Europe once governed nearly a quarter of the world's
population and about the same proportion of the earth's land. The
British Empire was the biggest empire ever, encompassing 1,000
territories, but how had we done it?

Rapid decolonization after the Second World War left only a
handful of dependent territories – now politically classified more
correctly as overseas territories – including Hong Kong and Gibraltar, but it was a series of tiny islands that captured my imagination
more than anywhere else: St Helena, Tristan da Cunha, Gough,
Ascension, the Falkland Islands, the Pitcairn islands and the Chagos
Archipelago. It wasn't just the remoteness of these tiny places that
lay predominantly in the South Atlantic, nor was it their exotic
names – what intrigued me most was the tiny '(UK)' that appeared
next to each name. These few places were all that remained of that
great empire. Why did Britain insist on retaining this flotsam and
jetsam?

There were other islands of course with equally evocative names,
such as Anguilla, Grand Cayman and Turks and Caicos, but they
were all in the Caribbean, a tamed playground for the rich and
famous and a well-documented hotchpotch of cultures and races. I

was more intrigued by the remoteness and anonymity of these other strange places. Apart from the fact that they seemed barely large enough to appear on most maps, they were thousands of miles from the nearest land, and many more from the UK.

I became infatuated by these islands, and the people that lived there. What did they look like? Did they look like me? Or were they more like my friend William? I would spend hours staring at my map hoping somehow to learn more about these remote places.

I had friends who had lived in Bermuda and even Gibraltar, but I had certainly never met anyone from Tristan da Cunha. I had a friend called Tristan so I asked him, but he was unsure. I asked my geography teacher (daydream co-ordinator), who was also uncertain.

On close inspection of a larger-scale map I noticed that Tristan da Cunha's main settlement (I wasn't even sure if it was a capital) was called Edinburgh. This was certainly a new lead, but now I wondered: was it anything like Scotland? Did they wear kilts and eat haggis? If they were British did they drink tea? Did they have a branch of Boots? And, most important of all, where was their local Marks & Spencer's? The more I discovered, the more questions there were.

Within a few months of leaving school, my teatime expeditions left the realms of fantasy and became reality as I found myself on a cargo boat of biscuits sailing 3,000 miles up the Amazon from Belém to Iquitos in Peru. I couldn't help but wonder whether my being aboard with this biscuity cargo was somehow the effect of one of those early childhood crumbs.

I spent the rest of the year living in Quito, Ecuador, where I taught English in a primary school and helped out in an orphanage. The year had a profound effect on me. I relished the freedom afforded me, and the rich sights that flooded my mind. I decided to spend a second year in Central America, where I sought the location of one of my literary heroes, Paul Theroux, and travelled to the Mosquito Coast of Honduras, where I worked on a turtle conservation project before moving on to Nicaragua. I then went on to pursue Latin American Studies, which included a particularly memorable year at the University of Costa Rica.

My life would change for ever in March 1999, when I noticed an advert in the *Guardian* newspaper. The BBC was looking for thirty volunteers to create a new society on a remote uninhabited island, for a television series to be called *Castaway*. The volunteers were expected to be entirely self-sufficient and cut off from the rest of the world except for the half-dozen video cameras that would record our lives for a year. (Little did I realize that those images would be beamed to the farthest corners of the globe, even flickering on to the screens of those mysterious Teatime Islanders.)

While those islands remained as elusive and seductive as ever, Taransay, our island home, served as a catalyst, introducing me to the benefits of communal living, fuelling my wanderlust and reigniting my fascination with islands.

A fascination with islands was part of my childhood duty – along with dragons, castles and mountains, islands represent all that is exciting for a child: escapism, freedom, safety and adventure. My early reading consisted of *Robinson Crusoe*, *Swallows and Amazons*, the Famous Five books and *Treasure Island*, so it seemed only natural that when I was twenty-six I should follow my literary heroes and go to live on an island for a year.

Robinson Crusoe of course was the fictional character created by Daniel Defoe, but he was based on Alexander Selkirk, a mariner who spent over four years marooned on the uninhabited island of Juan Fernández. Selkirk, however, was not the first sailor to be castaway on a tropical island. The 1700s were an age of great maritime exploration, and the seas were dotted with ocean-going traffic, so it is not surprising that many sailors ended up shipwrecked on the reefs of uncharted islands, often for years at a time. The populations of many islands today are the descendants of ship-wrecked sailors.

Not all castaways are involuntary. I had read of one who made the headlines in 1957. A passenger on a passing ship thought they had seen someone on the beach of the uninhabited Henderson Island, part of the Pitcairn archipelago. The Pitcairn islanders confirmed that it wasn't one of their people and sent a search party to investigate. They found Robert Tomarchin – an American – and his chimpanzee Moko. At first Tomarchin claimed he had been accidentally stranded on the island but it later turned out that he had asked to be dropped off there. He stayed on the island for six weeks before spending a short period on Pitcairn and then returning to the USA.

Tomarchin, like me, had chosen his island. Shipwrecked castaways in modern times are extremely rare. Maritime sophistication and technology have reduced the risks in going to sea, and society has evolved to find a new way of becoming marooned – by answering an advert. I had done just that. I am often asked what inspired me to answer such an ambitious call, but I was not the first. One of the world's most famous castaways, Lucy Irvine, answered an advert in *Time Out* magazine: 'Writer seeks "wife" for a year on a tropical island.' Lucy went on to spend a year living with a strange man on Tuin Island in the Arafura Sea.

There's something about the castaway lifestyle that appeals to people. I was intrigued by the public's fascination and decided to conduct my own experiment. Short of a travelling partner for some of the more remote islands I hoped to visit, I placed a small advert in *Time Out*: 'CASTAWAY WANTED for remote tropical island adventure'. I had anticipated a flood of replies from aspiring castaways and adventurers, but was staggered not to receive a single one.

Where were all of these romanticists that had deluged the BBC with tens of thousands of applications for *Castaway*, or the thousands that had applied for *Shipwrecked* and *Survivor*? It made no difference; for me, discovering new islands had become a necessity.

I had found it difficult to integrate back into the 'real' world after my year on Taransay. I had been bewitched by the island. It seemed to have an invisible hold on me, and I struggled with daily life back in London. I found fumes too intoxicating, noises too loud, artificial lighting too bright, food too rich; but above all, without the omnipresent island wind I felt like I was suffocating in the stale, still London air. I used to hide in my room dreaming and wishing

I was back on that island, and reverted to my childhood passion of poring over maps.

Alain de Botton once wrote that the best part of travel is anticipation and memory, and maybe that is why maps are so perfect: none of the reality of travel, just the mental pleasure. I spent hours staring at maps, wondering what all those little places look like, and who lives there. They offer a one-way ticket away from the real world. Even on Taransay, on cold, wet days I would sit by the driftwood fire in the schoolhouse and disappear into the children's atlas for hours at a time, sailing across the oceans and visiting the islands of my dreams.

I've always been envious of the early explorers, able to sail the oceans in search of new lands and islands – then name them after themselves. Some early explorers and cartographers went so far as to make up entirely fictitious islands complete with first-hand accounts and lavish illustrations. Today these islands are more commonly known as phantom islands.

Among these phantom islands, the Isle of Demons was reported to be inhabited by monsters and demons whose sole purpose was to torment and attack passing ships and anyone foolish enough to stray ashore. The tale of Frisland was even immortalized in print and is the story of a nobleman who travelled to the island to help its king defeat neighbouring islands. Buss Island was one of the most persistent in mariners' minds and wasn't taken off some maps until the twentieth century. Some clever sailors even managed to sell it to the Hudson Navigation Company. To this day some believe that the island really does exist. Antilla Island was reported to be two thirds the size of Portugal and inhabited by seven Spanish bishops fleeing the mainland. Hy-Brazil comes from Irish folklore and is the mythical land of gods which was sometimes seen off the Irish Coast. It appeared on maps for many centuries but no one could ever find it. The legend of Ursula and her eleven thousand virgin companions has her visiting islands in the far reaches of the Atlantic before her untimely martyrdom back in Europe.

Icebergs, clouds and even mirages have all been misidentified as new islands. As late as the 1920s, Bartholomew's *Great Survey*

Atlas, the bible of the British cartographer, still showed the Anson archipelago, a non-existent island chain between Hawaii and Japan named after Lord Anson, who had seen it only on charts of a Spanish galleon he had seized off the Philippines in the 1800s. Until the 1980s, the globes (by the historic globe manufacturer, J. R. O. Globus of Munich) that were featured on Lufthansa tickets around the world placed the non-existent Matador islands – inhabited by a colony of shy albino lepers according to their British discoverer – just north of the equator, and even the National Geographic Society's 1982 world map depicted these imaginary islands as a cluster of unnamed dots.

It was during one of the many rainy days on Taransay that I discovered Dr Roger Stephenson, a fellow castaway, had a secret. He was a closet isleophile. Roger had spent time as a doctor on two of my Teatime Islands, Pitcairn and St Helena.

His experience fuelled my own enthusiasm. I had waited until 1982 to catch a glimpse of a real-life Teatime Island. It was the outbreak of the Falklands War, and I watched with fascination as my first images of these remote UK islands came on to the screen. I was certainly surprised: they looked like Wales with fewer trees and more rain, and the people looked like Dorset farmers. A little disappointing really, although I was still intrigued that these little pockets of England could retain their British culture in such faraway places. And my questions about Pitcairn, St Helena and Tristan da Cunha were still unanswered.

When I first applied for *Castaway*, my friends all thought I was totally bonkers. Why would anyone volunteer themselves to spend a year on a windy, wet, cold island in the North Atlantic. 'Are you mad?' they spluttered into their pints when I first told them about the project. Their fears were confirmed when, after my return to reality, *Hello!* magazine offered to send me anywhere in the world. It seemed only natural for me to choose another isolated windy island, this time in the South Atlantic: the Falklands.

As a child I had been thrilled to discover a map of the Falkland Islands in one of my old *National Geographic* magazines. I had been particularly delighted to discover that the archipelago included

Bob's Island and Puzzle Island, not to mention Fanny Island, Knob Island and Shag island. I used to snigger into the map at this dazzlingly smutty array of names.

The Hebrides were my first childhood experience of island life. My Scottish nanny, Katrine, took my sister and me for a holiday on the island of Eigg, in the Inner Hebrides. I had been particularly thrilled to visit one of my daydream expedition favourites, partly because I felt sure it was the home of Cadbury's Creme Eggs.

We had spent an idyllic week fishing and walking on the beautiful island, where we had been staying with the laird, Keith Schellenberg. As a child I had been totally unaware of and oblivious to the bitter feud between Schellenberg and the islanders, which would finally become unique among island stories of recent years.

The islanders and the laird were locked in dispute over the running of the island. Affairs soon deteriorated and after Schellenberg's Rolls-Royce mysteriously caught fire the two camps had been reduced to playground tactics. The islanders dismissed Schellenberg as a 'landlord in the worst tradition of nineteenth-century feudalism', while Schellenberg retorted by accusing the islanders of being 'rotten, dangerous and totally barmy revolutionaries'.

Eventually Schellenberg sold the island, and according to records the islanders cheered his final departure. As the boat pulled away from the jetty he shouted at them: 'You never understood me. I always wanted to be one of you.'

This 'us' and 'them' mentality spread to us on Taransay, in the form of 'islandism'. The BBC castaways managed to assimilate to island life because we were creating our own society, rather than integrating into one. We had arrived as mainlanders, but we left as islanders. The transformation was startling and rapid. It took just a few weeks for us to become territorial, possessive, shy, suspicious of outsiders and very snobby about our island. I don't know how or why it happened, but it affected all of us. By the end of our year we were like fallow deer, dipping behind rocks at the first sign of a stranger on 'our' island.

Eigg hit the headlines again in 1997 after the islanders managed to buy the island from the last of its nine lairds. The money raised by the Eigg Trust, a partnership made up of the island's eighty-six residents, the Highland Council and the Scottish Wildlife Trust, was augmented by donations from island-lovers all over the world. One donor contributed £750,000 towards the buy-out on the understanding that they remain anonymous.

While Eigg had managed to weather the mental storm, another island hadn't been so lucky. I visited Eigg's neighbouring island of Rum to write a story for one of the broadsheets. The islanders had been embroiled in a scandal that had headlined the Scottish press for months and they were naturally fed up with the press. I, the paper had decided, would be a perfect envoy.

'RUMPY PUMPY ISLAND', screamed the headlines of the Scottish tabloids. The country had been gripped by the real-life castaways, after it emerged that a young mother had run off with her husband's best friend. Adding insult to injury, the police had been called on to Rum to confiscate the jilted husband's gun after fears that he was a danger to himself and to the other seventeen inhabitants of the island.

The final indignity came when Scottish National Heritage, who owned the island, informed the deserted husband that he would have to leave his house and the island, as it was his wife that had been the employee and therefore entitled to accommodation. Tensions rose, the Scottish press flooded the island and matters reached such a pitch that nearly 95 per cent of the islanders sought medical treatment for stress.

'It's all your fault,' explained an islander as I sat in silence in the late-summer sunshine. 'Taransay put the spotlight on remote islands,' she continued. 'If it hadn't been for *Castaway*, the press wouldn't have been so interested, and we would have been left to sort out our problems in private, rather than the public airing that made our lives miserable.' My experience on Rum alarmed me. What would the Teatime Islanders make of me, and more importantly was I an 'us' or a 'them'? On Taransay we had received letters from remote island communities all over the world confiding in us and commending us. I'd felt I was an 'us' but now I wasn't so sure.

The effect of the pen on islands is an interesting one. I wondered how I would be received by the remote island communities that I intended to visit. Certainly on Taransay we had been wary and suspicious of our resident writer, Mark McCrum, whom we nicknamed the 'detective'. I knew that a string of travel-writers before me had left a trail of destruction in their wake.

The problem with small islands is that everyone is easily identifiable, and a writer or journalist can often open a Pandora's box of debilitating gossip, which is endemic on small islands. The *Castaway* book very nearly tore our small island community apart when it was finally published. What I had discovered on Taransay is that islands have extremely fragile equilibriums that can be easily upset by the presence of an outsider.

Mark McCrum, the author of the book about our year on the remote Hebridean island, wrote that he could never have written his book by staying all year on that 'mad and magical' island. 'Even in two days you find yourself getting sucked into the latest drama,' he wrote, 'it's too easy to take sides and get far too involved in the ever lively local politics, which the castaways always tell you they wish would go away, but somehow can't help feeding.'

At university I joined the university Royal Naval Unit, where I became a midshipman assigned to HMS *Blazer*, a P2000 Fast Patrol Boat on which I would spend weekends training in the Solent, and holiday time away on deployment as far afield as Norway and Gibraltar.

During a number of these deployments we sailed throughout the Channel Islands. I had been charmed by these Britannic islands with their Gallic twist, but it had been one island in particular that had intrigued me.

Brecqhou Island is a 160-acre, treeless island off Sark. It was bought by the reclusive Barclay twins, David and Frederick, in 1993 for £2.3 million. They had spent more than £25 million building a turreted Gothic castle. The brothers filed for independence from Sark and even designed their own flag, which depicted the two twins in the corner. They had declared the island 'closed', guarding it with dogs and security guards and even a patrol vessel to chase away any unwanted visitors.

What intrigued me was the juxtaposition that islands represent, on the one hand offering a safe haven for their residents, while on the other acting as a catalyst for conflict and even war. The very fact that Britain was willing to go to war with Argentina in 1982 for the Falkland Islands illustrates their significance, but on what grounds? They have no obvious assets or resources and yet we continue to send governors and fly the Union Flag. Indeed, the British government has agreed to carry out a study into the feasibility of building airports on St Helena and Pitcairn, a seemingly vast expense for the islands' tiny populations.

Islands have had a rich recent history of warfare, from the Falklands War to the most recent stand-off between Spain and Morocco over an island no larger than a football pitch. The Spanish-owned Parsley Island, just 200 yards off the coast of the Moroccan mainland, was the scene of a Moroccan occupation in mid-2002 when a dozen troops landed on the uninhabited island and planted their flag.

The incident led to a full-blown diplomatic row in which ambassadors were expelled and warships sent for. Spain reinforced its garrison in Ceuta, a Spanish enclave in northern Morocco. Hadn't the world learnt from the Falklands? Was a minuscule island called Parsley with nothing more than a few goats really worth fighting for? The confrontation was eventually resolved. The Moroccans vacated the island, and the Spanish replaced the flag and stationed some Spanish soldiers on the small outcrop.

Islands, it seems, no matter what their size, location or strategic value, will always be worth fighting for. And islands are also excellent platforms for fighting from: one of the largest military establishments in the world is hidden away in a remote corner of the Indian Ocean.

While researching the Teatime Islands, I met Alan Huckle,

head of the Overseas Territories Department at the Foreign and Commonwealth Office. He had been wonderfully helpful and encouraging about plans for my island odyssey, until I mentioned Diego Garcia in the Indian Ocean. 'You can't go there,' he snapped. 'Cancel it from your list, Garcia is totally off limits,' he barked. I noticed his skin had gone a soft shade of rouge. 'Not even the Prime Minister is allowed to visit,' he added by way of closure. Cagey Foreign Office ministers and mysterious islands in the Indian Ocean that are out of bounds to all, including heads of government, sounded like a John le Carré novel.

I volunteered to live on Taransay for a number of reasons, but primarily because I wanted to experience island life first hand. I wanted to know what it was like to be self-sufficient and to live independently from the mainland. I wanted to know what it was like to live in isolation. I had visited islands before but always was an outsider looking in, never an insider looking out.

The more I learned about these remote outcrops of the British Empire the more I needed to visit them. I wanted to know how they regarded themselves and their place in the world. While giving an interview on Radio Scotland I was asked whether I now consider myself an islander. 'No,' I replied without thinking.

'But you are,' said the interviewer rather triumphantly. 'Great Britain is an island, therefore we are all islanders.'

And so we are, but being an islander is a state of mind. A resident of the Isle of Man, or Jersey, and a Londoner will regard themselves very differently, as will a native of Rathlin Island, or Bardsay, and someone from Jersey.

On Taransay we considered ourselves a unique island with our own self-sufficient community, independent from Harris and Lewis. Harris and Lewis also see themselves as independent from the Scottish mainland. It seems that the smaller and more isolated the island, the more fiercely that sense of independence is felt.

There was little serious concern in Britain about how the construction of the Channel Tunnel might affect our island status. But compare this to the huge vocal outcry on Skye when they built the

Skye bridge to replace the old ferry service. Islanders were up in arms at this challenge to their island status.

I spent the year after *Castaway* visiting a number of small islands off the coast of Great Britain and Northern Ireland. I was mesmerized by the similarities between the communities I met and our temporary community on Taransay. I was startled by the familiarity of their resourcefulness and of their unremitting suspicion of outsiders.

There is a very definite island mentality, and I wanted to compare my own experience of it to some of the most remote island communities in the world, to find out why the Teatime Islanders choose to live in such abject isolation, many miles from the services of a modern society. I wanted to find out whether an islander must always live on an island. And to discover whether or not a Londoner like me could ever consider myself a real islander or whether I'm just a wannabe.

There is an old verse that was sent to me by an island-lover:

> If once you have slept on an island
> You'll never be quite the same;
> You may look as you looked the day before
> And go by the same old name,
>
> You may bustle about in street and shop
> You may sit at home and sew,
> But you'll see blue water and wheeling gulls
> Wherever your feet may go.
>
> You may chat with the neighbors of this and that
> And close to your fire keep,
> But you'll hear ship whistle and lighthouse bell
> And tides beat through your sleep.
>
> Oh! you won't know why, and you can't say how
> Such a change upon you came,
> But once you have slept on an island,
> You'll never be quite the same.

Rachel Field, 1926

I am often asked how the year on Taransay affected the BBC castaways, and it is perhaps tribute to the power of islands that nearly a third of them have moved permanently to island homes. And as for me, I embarked on my own adventure. An island odyssey in search of the remaining islands of empire. A journey to Tristan da Cunha, Ascension, Pitcairn, the British Indian Ocean Territories, St Helena and the Falkland Islands.

It was a search that would take me to the faraway corners of the earth in search of some of the most extraordinary islands in the world, the Teatime Islands.

1. Tristan da Cunha

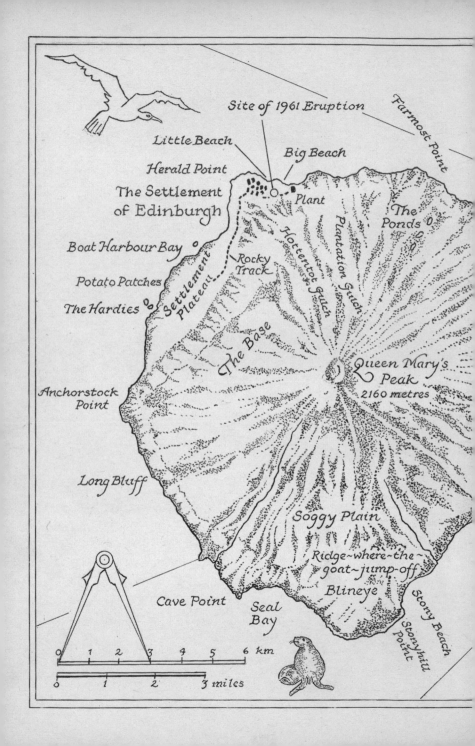

Site of 1961 Eruption

Little Beach

Herald Point

The Settlement
of Edinburgh

Boat Harbour Bay

Potato Patches

The Hardies

Farmost Point

Big Beach

Plant

The Ponds

Hottentot Gulch

Plantation Gulch

Rocky
Track

Settlement Plateau

The Base

Queen Mary's
Peak
2160 metres

Anchorstock
Point

Long Bluff

Soggy Plain

Ridge~where~the~
goat~jump-off

Blineye

Cave Point

Seal
Bay

Stony Beach

Stonyhill
Point

0   1   2   3   4   5   6 km

0   1   2   3 miles

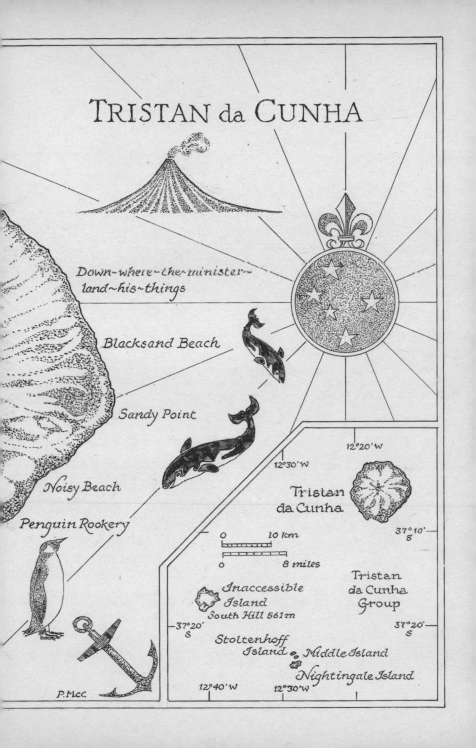

TRISTAN da CUNHA

Down~where~the~minister~
land~his~things

Blacksand Beach

Sandy Point

Noisy Beach

Penguin Rookery

P. McC

12°20'W

12°30'W

Tristan
da Cunha

37°10'
S

0   10 km

0   8 miles

Tristan
da Cunha
Group

Inaccessible
Island
South Hill 561m

37°20'
S

Stoltenhoff
Island

37°20'
S

Middle Island

Nightingale Island

12°40'W

12°30'W

'Goin' anywhere nice?' asked the taxi driver, his eyes framed in the rearview mirror.

'Tristan da Cunha,' I replied, as we sped through the deserted streets of London on our way to Heathrow on a frosty January morning.

'Near Magaluf, innit? Fink the missus and me 'ad fish and chips there once.'

'It's a little further south actually,' I ventured warily, conscious of how much black-cab drivers hate being told where a place is.

'Oh yeah, Portugal innit? Me mate Trev went last year,' he said triumphantly.

The 'knowledge', it was clear, did not extend beyond the boundaries of the M25.

'Actually, it's in the middle of the South Atlantic somewhere between South Africa and South America,' I corrected.

'Blimey,' he gasped, ''oo'd live there?'

Who indeed? The answer had eluded me since I was a child, and, I had concluded, the only way to find out was to visit.

I still knew very little about this tiny outpost, so little in fact that I had called on the advice of an expert to help me with my packing.

'Sorry to bother you,' I had apologized, 'but is Tristan da Cunha hot or cold?'

I was talking to Michael Swales, whose phone number I'd found in a Falkland Islands newsletter. His details had appeared next to an article about the hurricane that had recently devastated Tristan da Cunha. I had hoped he would be able to help me decide between my Marks & Spencer shorts and my Helly Hansen thermals.

I knew that Tristan da Cunha was around the same latitude as Cape Town, but it was also in the South Atlantic ocean, just two thousand miles from South Georgia, and I was still none the wiser as to whether it was temperate or arctic. That it had penguins and elephant seals was a clue, but I wasn't sure that was enough to assume it would be chilly.

'I think you'll find it a little like a Scottish summer,' replied Swales with staggering ambiguity. That could mean rain, wind, sun, snow, heat or even hurricane force winds, which, as the article had explained, had devastated the island in May 2001. It was the worst storm to hit the island in over a hundred years, churning the sea into a heavy mass, tearing roofs from buildings, bringing power cables down and killing many cattle and sheep. Communications were severed and the island had been left totally isolated from the rest of the world.

The disaster barely made the news in the UK, with the *Sun* newspaper confining the report to a paragraph on page 18 which stated little more than the fact that the remote island had lost the roof of its pub to the storm. I had been even more surprised to read in the newsletter that the Falkland Islands government had pledged more money to the island's disaster appeal than the UK government.

Michael Swales, I soon discovered, was something of a Tristan da Cunha guru, having been involved with the island for nearly fifty years. He had first visited it in 1955, as a Cambridge undergraduate, on an expedition led by Robert Chambers. A biology student, Swales had joined the expedition to visit and chart the hitherto unexplored and uninhabited island of Gough deep in the South Atlantic, 250 nautical miles south of Tristan da Cunha.

The team set off aboard HMS *Magpie*, bound for Tristan da Cunha, whence they would continue to Gough aboard a local fishing-boat. The team and their ten tons of provisions finally arrived on Gough in November 1955, where they built the first base there. They named it Goncalo Alvarez after the first Portuguese navigator to sight the island.

During this landing, however, the expedition leader, Chambers, slipped and lost the use of the lower part of his body. The weather deteriorated, and without adequate shelter his condition grew worse and he soon developed pneumonia. Fortunately for the expedition, the fishing-vessel was still in the vicinity and he was evacuated back to South Africa.

Despite this early setback, the expedition was a resounding success, and the team of zoologists, meteorologists and botanists spent six months studying and mapping the island. It was during this survey that the young Swales was able to leave his mark on the island in the form of Michael's Col and Swales Peak.

Getting to the island had been one thing, getting off it would be quite another. The South Atlantic is a watery desert with little to no shipping. The Foreign Office, who had sponsored part of the expedition, struck a deal with the South African government. The team of meteorologists had concluded that the island was vital to South Africa for predicting South Atlantic weather patterns, and an agreement was negotiated between the two governments that in return for a 2.5 acre allotment on Gough on which they could build a weather station, the South Africans would collect the team. The SAS *Transvaal* arrived in late 1956 to collect Swales and his colleagues.

Gough had been the expeditionary home, but it was the people of Tristan da Cunha who had captured Swales's imagination. A close relationship had been forged over the ensuing fifty years, during which time Swales had made a number of return visits to the isolated island.

World communications may have improved since then, but Tristan da Cunha remains as remote and inaccessible as it was in 1955. With no airport, the only way of reaching the island is aboard the Royal Mail Ship *St Helena*, which visits the island just once a year, sailing from Cape Town in South Africa.

I had booked a berth on this annual voyage and had organized to board the ship in Cape Town for the five-day journey to the most remote inhabited island in the world.

'It's rather a coincidence that you should call,' Swales had continued, 'as I'll also be on the voyage to Tristan da Cunha.' I thanked him for his help and we agreed to chat more over a cup of beef tea somewhere in the southern hemisphere.

That wasn't the last stroke of chance, as the next day a middle-aged couple introduced themselves at the British Airways check-in as Anne and Frank Dakin. They explained that they were the parents of Helen Dakin, a television director I had worked with while filming BBC 1's *Animal Park*.

We swapped pleasantries and they asked where I was going. I recalled the awkward conversation in the taxi and thought it best to keep my answer simple. 'Cape Town,' I replied. 'And yourselves?' I reciprocated.

'Oh we're going somewhere you probably won't have heard of. It's called Tristan da Cunha, an island in the middle of the South Atlantic.' That will teach you to be so smug, I thought to myself.

Anne and Frank Dakin were farmers from the Midlands who had become involved with Tristan da Cunha through their late son Jo, who in a strange twist of fate had been part of one of Michael Swales's later expeditions to the island.

In 1982 Swales had organized a return expedition to the island that had so enchanted him as a young student. Swales, by now a teacher, surprised the scientific world by announcing his plans to map nearby Inaccessible Island with a team of sixteen- to eighteen-year-old students from his school, Denstone College.

The science world had frowned on his plans and been critical of his intentions, which it thought foolhardy. But the Royal Geographical Society gave the project its blessing and eventually, with the help of the Foreign Office, Michael Swales and a team of fourteen young men set off from Cape Town laden with twelve tons of stores on an island adventure.

The young team spent eight months mapping and surveying Inaccessible, just as Swales had done on Gough almost thirty years earlier. It was during the expedition, on a rare visit to nearby Tristan, that the group had found themselves stormbound for several months. The Tristanians looked after the young men, who became part of the family.

One of those young men was Jo Dakin. During those months marooned, Jo had been 'adopted' by an island mother, Margaret Repetto. Margaret treated him like her own son, feeding him and even dressing him in her own son's best clothes for the island dances. She knitted him socks and jumpers, and when they finally returned to Inaccessible, she would send over cakes and fresh pastries whenever the islanders went to check up on them.

The expedition had been a triumph and the team had returned to the UK to a tumultuous reception. The Dakins wrote to the Repettos to thank them for being so kind to their son, and a friendship began between the two families separated by five thousand miles of ocean.

Several years later it was the Dakins' chance to repay the Repettos for their kindness, when Margaret and her husband Lindsey's daughter, Elaine, came to study in the UK. Just as the Repettos had treated Jo like a son, the Dakins treated Elaine as a daughter.

Tragically, their son Jo died shortly after Elaine arrived in the UK. Somehow the Dakins got through the tragedy and their relationship with Elaine Repetto strengthened as she stayed on in the UK to train as a nurse. She eventually fell in love with a Glaswegian officer on the RMS, and they married and moved to the Mull of Kintyre, where she still lives with her husband and two children.

For the Dakins, this would be the first visit to the island that had become so much a part of their lives.

Tristan da Cunha was first sighted in 1506 by a Portuguese admiral named Tristão da Cunha. Tristan and the nearby islands were then forgotten for around three hundred years, until in 1810 a whaler named Jonathan Lambert from Salem, Massachusetts, landed on the island together with two other sailors, an American named Williams and a half-Italian called Tomaso Curri.

Lambert was responsible for some of the islands' more colourful history. He declared himself king and renamed the islands the 'islands of refreshment'. He even made his own flag of blue and red diamonds on a white canvas, which flew proudly from a driftwood mast.

King Lambert's reign was short as he and one of his subjects, Williams, were both drowned in a boating accident just two years later. According to historians, Lambert accumulated a vast wealth in his short tenure, from the sale of penguin and elephant seal oil. Curri, the remaining castaway, allegedly confided to British soldiers some years later that a treasure of gold sovereigns lay buried on the island. A treasure that has never been found.

Tristan da Cunha is, however, one of the few islands in the world from which treasure-seekers have returned with a profit. In 1864, when the American Civil War was raging, the southern states sent a brig named the *Lark*, with Howard Summers as its captain, from the east coast of America to buy supplies in South Africa. She had on board a sea chest full of gold bars and over $70,000 in cash. The money had been plundered in the Union, and since the war appeared to be finishing in a victory for the North, the captain decided to run the *Lark* aground and bury the treasure.

Summers, with the aid of a crew member, Henderson, managed to get the chest from the wreck and they successfully buried their valuable treasure. Unfortunately for them, another ship bound for the United States soon arrived, and to avoid suspicion the two returned to the US. Summers died shortly afterwards, and Henderson was the only one who knew about the buried treasure.

Henderson decided to embark on a recovery mission, but he had no money with which to finance such a journey. For several years he attempted to procure a ship to reunite him with his buried wealth, until eventually he was able to return aboard the *Rover*. He sailed to the remote island, dug up his booty and returned to the US a wealthy man, but rumour spread and one day Captain Summers's son appeared and successfully demanded that he receive his father's share, half the treasure. Henderson, however, had spent so much on the expedition that he ended up without profit.

The flight to Cape Town was relatively uneventful until, half-way across Africa, somewhere above central Zaïre, we hit a storm. Lightning flashes illuminated the thick black clouds that clung over the African savannah far below. I scrunched my eyes tightly closed in the hope that if I ignored the worsening weather, then it would disappear. The plane was buffeted around like an empty tin can. I clenched the arm rest with my thoroughly gnawed finger nails as a bead of sweat made a bid to escape from my forehead.

The plane was jostled and buffeted like a paper aeroplane. I had never heard screaming on a plane. It felt like we were in a giant washing-machine as we tumbled through the air. I scrunched my eyes still tighter, and just when I didn't think things could get any worse, we dropped like a penny from the sky. We had hit an air pocket. My body strained against the seat belt, my neighbour kissed the ceiling. Like on a horrible roller coaster gone wrong, we stopped tumbling, only to hit another pocket of air a few minutes later. Within five minutes the whole experience was over and we continued to our destination.

I was shocked in the taxi from the airport to pass mile upon mile of slum towns. Huge fences had been erected along their boundaries. Whether this was to keep people in or out, or was simply an attempt to conceal this embarrassment from tourists on their way to the increasingly popular city, I couldn't be sure.

It was a warm Cape summer's day by the time I reached Duncan Dock next to Cape Town's recently restored Victoria and Alfred Dock. The docks were a forbidding place with their towering cranes and humungous ships. Like the slums on the road from the airport, they had been cut off from the city by an enormous perimeter fence.

Table Mountain towered behind. She was shrouded in her regular blanket of cloud. The Cape sky was crystal clear but for the white cloth that clung to her summit as if she were being prepared for some giant's banquet.

Cape Town is often described as one of the most beautiful cities in the world. I would argue that while the setting is spectacular, the city is actually rather ugly with its high-rise buildings and ever-encroaching slums.

The RMS *St Helena* was dwarfed between two huge fruit ships when I finally found her. She was much smaller than I had imagined. Her blue hull dipped into the murky waters. Her upper half had been painted a dazzling white, while her single funnel was a sun-bleached yellow, on which was mounted the ship's crest, a lion with a fish-tail holding a crown.

The present RMS *St Helena* was built in 1989 to serve the island of St Helena in the South Atlantic, some two thousand miles north of Tristan da Cunha. Until 1977 the *Union Castle* mail service between Southampton and the Cape had provided the islands of St Helena and Tristan da Cunha with a vital link to the UK. Neither island had nor indeed has an airport, and the ship provided the outposts with important supplies and communications.

The end of the *Union Castle* service spelled disaster for Tristan and St Helena, and the British government sought to replace the service. The vessel chosen was the *Northland Prince*, which had been built in Vancouver for the British Columbia–Alaska coastal trade. She was refitted and renamed the RMS *St Helena*. She served her island namesake for twelve years, providing her transport, cargo and mail requirements. In 1982 she was appropriated to serve as a supply ship in the Falklands War that was raging several thousand miles away.

A new ship was commissioned as part of a British government aid package to the Overseas Territories and the new RMS was launched in 1989. She was twice as big as her predecessor with berths for up to 128 passengers and space for 2,000 tonnes of cargo. 'Just how must post does Tristan receive?' I thought as I imagined her hold brimming with thousands of tons of mail.

The front of the 344-foot ship was dominated by a huge white crane that was busy lifting containers into her deep hold. The stern of the ship appeared to be the passengers' quarters. A huge red ensign on her stern stood to attention in the brisk Cape breeze.

Although principally a cargo ship, the RMS was very much a passenger liner, and every effort had been made to ensure a comfortable journey. The poop deck had been fitted with tables and chairs and even a small seawater swimming-pool, the onboard library provided passengers with an array of literature that seemed to be dominated by Jackie Collins novels, and the sun lounge offered endless cups of tea and coffee. There was even a gym for those looking to shed a few pounds from the punishing amount of eating and drinking that was to follow during our five-day ocean voyage.

The word that best describes my cabin was cosy. I had chosen one of the slightly cheaper cabins deep within the bowels of the ship. These cabins were normally reserved for St Helenians who use the RMS as a ferry service between the UK and their island, but for this voyage, in the absence of any commuters, I had the two bunks, sink, table and cupboard to myself. The little porthole provided a watery view of the ocean next door, while an antiquated radio allowed me to listen in to the BBC's World Service.

I stood on her deck and watched the quayside below. Ships raced to complete their loading. I stood spellbound as an army of forklift trucks danced around the jetty, loading thousands of boxes of grapes into one of the ships. Another was laden with huge mahogany tree-trunks weighing many tons each, and representing hundreds of years of growth. All the while the RMS was busy filling her hold with teabags, Marmite and bags of post. How thoroughly British, I thought.

Across the harbour, workmen were busy repairing a floating oil rig that had been towed in from Angola. Sparks flew as angle-grinders and welding-torches illuminated her ugly frame that grated against the bright-blue sky behind.

The crew of the RMS were largely Saints from the ship's namesake, but I did meet one young woman who turned out to be my first real-life Tristanian. With her mousy blonde hair and her fair complexion, she looked more South London than South Atlantic.

The origin of the present population goes back to 1816, when a British garrison was stationed on the island, at the time of Napoleon's imprisonment on St Helena. Upon Napoleon's death, one Corporal Glass of the Royal Artillery, and from Kelso in Scotland (the same place as Selkirk, and as Bligh of the *Bounty*), obtained permission to settle on Tristan with his family. He changed his title from Corporal to Governor Glass. He became the patriarch of all the Tristanians. He was the Adam of Tristan's Eden.

In the years to come, the dangerous shores of Tristan da Cunha were responsible for many shipwrecks, but Governor Glass thrived, and he was soon joined by a number of other 'castaways'. One of these was a sailor named Thomas Swain. He had served with honour under Nelson – indeed, it was Swain that caught Nelson as he collapsed, mortally wounded, on the deck of the *Victory*. A valley on the island named Tommie's Eyeloose still bears phonetic testament to Swain: it was here on the island that Thomas kept his oilhouse stored with seal oil, which he would sell to passing ships.

Another ancestor was a Dutch sailor named Peter Green (Pieter Groen). He was shipwrecked when his schooner, *Emily*, foundered off Tristan's shores in 1835. He liked the island and decided to make it his home. On the death of Glass, Green became the island's chief. For the next fifty years he was to be the driving force behind the island, over a period of time in which the islanders rescued more than 250 shipwrecked people. He is remembered by Big Green Hill.

Before long there were a handful of men living on Tristan da Cunha, but it wasn't until an English whaler named Captain Amm sought refuge on the island that they set about searching for some slightly less hirsute castaways with whom to pass those long and lonely nights.

Bearing in mind the location of Tristan, this wasn't a simple case of popping along to the local pub on a Friday night, and in the absence of a number 11 bus and a curry house, the Tristanian bachelors sought to remedy their deficiency by applying to Captain Amm, from the sloop the *Duke of Gloucester*. Amm was sent on an important mission: to find some 'good looking women' with whom they could share their lives.

Amm undertook his job with diligence and professionalism, and upon reaching St Helena several months later he drew up a notice and pinned it to the barracks wall. The notice ran: 'The good and honest seamen on Tristan da Cunha, an island south in the Atlantic, on the edge of the world's oceans, seek life mates who will all be guaranteed marriage a few days after a successful landing.' What sort of response would a similar note provoke today?

The lucky ladies were to present themselves at the quayside, whence they would be transported free of charge to the island, and to their eager new husbands. Five women took on the challenge of the world's most unusual blind date. It appears that Captain Amm was so embarrassed by his matchmaking role as the Cilla Black of the South Atlantic that he 'threw' the women on to the beach and immediately set sail.

The castaways waited excitedly for their beauties to arrive. So eager were they that one named Repetto boasted that he would marry the first woman to set foot on the island, regardless of her age or beauty. How disappointed he must have been when the first off the boat was a very fat and rather old woman accompanied by her four children, with a mangle under her arm.

And thus it was that the seven surnames of Tristan were born:

GLASS
GREEN
HAGAN
LAVARELLO
REPETTO
ROGERS
SWAIN

In 1943 the Royal Navy set up a shore base, HMS *Atlantic Isle*, and Tristan became a communications and meteorological centre. People were offered work, and money was introduced for the first time, putting an end to the bartering of penguins. The islanders were introduced to the commercial world. It wasn't until 1950 that the Colonial Office set up a venture to exploit the crayfish industry. A canning factory was built next to Edinburgh, the island's capital, and a regular sea route was established to South Africa.

It was dusk when we finally got under way. A pilot boat helped us navigate through the busy Cape waters and out into the open ocean beyond. A South African film crew hovered above in a news helicopter, ready to broadcast the rare visit for the evening news.

I stood at the railing as Table Mountain turned pink with the setting sun. A smile spread across my face as 'Rule Britannia' played on the ship's Tannoy system. I sipped on a glass of Pimm's and watched as dusk fell, transforming Cape Town into a haze of blinking lights.

My first dinner aboard was a rather solitary affair. Overcome by seasickness, the majority of the passengers were still getting to know their loos, and I had been left stranded alone at my table with only the menu for company. Someone must have spotted my discomfort and I was invited to join the captain's table.

Captain Roberts introduced me to Mr Hollamby, the governor of St Helena, and his wife, and to Colin, the ship's purser, and his wife. I later learned that Colin's wife had been the former governor of St Helena's spouse. During the endless passages aboard the RMS, Colin and she had had an affair. She had ended up leaving her husband for Colin, to whom she was now happily married.

The difficulty with this was that Colin was the purser of the only ship on which the then governor could travel. Former husband and lover would be forced to spend five days together each time the governor was called away on business. He must have dreaded a summons from Whitehall.

The story was well known and I could have sworn I caught the current governor, Hollamby, eyeing Colin with suspicion, and couldn't help but notice how Mrs H had been sat as far from Colin as was possible at a circular table.

The captain was a classic 'Captain Bird's-Eye' skipper, straight from central casting. He had a big white beard to keep his face warm during long winter nights at sea. I later learned that his ship's-nickname was Captain Tickety-boo, which in naval parlance means a perfectionist.

The governor was a friendly fellow. He and Mrs Hollamby, his El Salvadorian wife, had been on St Helena for two years, and this was his second visit to Tristan da Cunha, of which, as it was a dependency of St Helena, he was also governor.

For the Hollambys this annual three-day visit to Tristan da Cunha would take nearly four weeks, as St Helena, also without an airport, was a further six-day sail from Cape Town. The governor lamented the fact that half his year was spent aboard the RMS on his way to 'wretched' meetings in Whitehall. 'While most governors can hop on a plane and be in the UK the next day,' he explained, 'it can take me more than a week to get to a meeting, and another week to return.'

The following day I was joined at breakfast by my three seasick dinner companions: Brian, a career diplomat from the United States, Bob, an entrepreneur from Anguilla, and Lars, a Swede living in Saudi Arabia.

Brian Penn worked at the American consulate in Cape Town. He had a white mop of hair and wore glasses that magnified his eyes. He had worked in South Africa for two years, before which he had worked in South America, spending time in Guatemala, Colombia and Ecuador, where he had met and married his wife. His job had variously involved looking after American interests and engineering coups.

Brian told me that he had been working in Quito at the time of 'el Loco', the self-proclaimed madman of Ecuadorian politics who had somehow become president. He had eventually been declared clinically insane by his own party, and with the aid of Brian and his sponsors had been deposed from power. I hoped Brian wasn't planning the same plot for Tristan da Cunha.

In fact Brian was visiting on what he termed a 'courtesy call'. He had been sifting through various State Department documents when he discovered that he, as the American consul for Cape Town, was also responsible for the 'welfare and safety of any Americans on Tristan da Cunha'.

'That means any Americans who get shipwrecked are my responsibility,' he beamed. As far as I knew, the late King Lambert had been the last American on Tristan, and he had drowned. I decided to keep this little thought to myself.

Bob Conrich lived on the Caribbean island of Anguilla (also an overseas territory of the UK, and favourite playground of Britain's rockocracy). With his spectacles and his Father Christmas beard, he gave the overall impression of a genial garden gnome. Bob was travelling to Tristan by chance. His actual destination was St Helena, but he had heard about January's detour to Tristan da Cunha and had decided it was worth a visit.

Bob was an entrepreneur and he was on his way to St Helena with a rather unusual and lucrative business venture for the islanders. He had concluded that as an overseas territory of the UK, St Helena was technically a member of the EU. He had therefore established that the island could be used as a market gateway for products entering Europe. He worked out that ships from Korea and Japan could bypass the Suez or Panama canals, and use St Helena as their European entry point. I asked Bob why captains would be prepared to make such a lengthy detour to an island with neither a harbour nor a single nightclub or brothel.

'It's simple,' he replied, rubbing his forefinger and thumb together, 'we pay them to use St Helena.' Hang on. I thought the island was supposed to make money not lose it in this venture?

'Say a ship carries 6,000 cars with a manufacturing value of $10 million,' he explained. 'We pay the captain $100,000 to come here instead of Southampton. Importation duty on the cars is then paid to the St Helena government, who according to EU law get to keep it.'

Bob estimated that the small island two thousand miles to the north could earn up to a million dollars for every ship using the island's non-existent harbour.

I wasn't convinced, even if his name, Conrich, did imply Robin Hood principles.

And then there was Lars the grumpy Swede. All I ever discovered about Lars over more than a dozen dinners can be reduced to the fact that he worked for a communications company in Saudi Arabia, which he didn't particularly like, and that he had ended up on the RMS by accident because he had missed his intended Caribbean cruise. The shipping company had suggested he might enjoy this trip instead; which, unsurprisingly, he didn't.

There were fifty-one passengers aboard the RMS. I was younger than most of them by several decades. Most were past retirement age and were heavily in their 'cruising' years. I have never been attracted to cruises. The idea of living aboard some ship resembling a floating council block seems utterly hideous.

Ocean travel is about getting close to the natural world. It is about the smell of the sea air and the salty spray. It is the movement of the ship and how uncomplicated life is on board. It is about indulging the senses, and the excitement of man against the sea. Cruise liners cheat passengers of these maritime treats. With their restaurants, shopping malls, cabarets and even, in some cases, ice rinks, passengers could be in some particularly horrible metropolis rather than on a beautiful ocean.

I was impressed with the simplicity of life aboard the RMS. The fact that she was half cargo, half passenger ship gave her an endearing quality. Instead of games arcades, we had a scrabble tournament; instead of cinemas, we were given lively lectures about the history of the islands; and in the absence of casinos, we were taught 'frog-racing'.

Frog-racing was a tradition born on the old *Union Castle* service between the UK and South Africa, and kept alive by some of her old crew who now worked aboard the RMS. They gave passengers a wooden frog each; by jerking on the string threaded through each frog, the passengers bounced their frogs along the deck towards a finishing-line drawn in chalk.

Until recently the ship had included clay pigeon shooting in the entertainments programme. Clays would be launched off the ship's stern while passengers attempted to shoot them from the sky at the same time as trying to keep their balance despite the ship's movement. This had been one of the most popular activities until one elderly woman lost her balance and swung the gun towards a passenger. The shipping company had decided to quit this little hobby while they were ahead.

Over the next few days, lubricated by endless cups of tea, faces became names.

There was the retired naval commander from Scotland who could always be found on the ship's bridge with his binoculars glued to his face in search of some invisible enemy.

There was a rather solitary expat school teacher from Papua New Guinea whose favourite place was a stool next to the ship's bar, where he would invariably be found with a pint of draught beer in his hand.

A Frenchman named Pierre, from Paris, was on his way to the island to repair a meteorological antenna that had been brought down in the storm. He was always playing on his Game Boy in the sun lounge.

Helen Morrison, a Scotswoman, was visiting the island to return a scrapbook she had been given as a young girl scout. The book had been made by the children of Tristan da Cunha for the Queen's coronation in 1953. Helen had struck up a writing friendship with the island, and fifty years on she and her husband had decided to visit it and return the book.

Marigold Mann was the ship's grandmother. She reminded me of Miss Marple as she sat in the corner of the sun lounge working on her embroidery. She had first come up to me during tea. 'Do you live on Ladbroke Street?' she had asked. 'Umm, yes,' I replied, convinced that I was being followed to the ends of the earth by an eighty-year-old stalker. 'I thought so,' she said. 'I live at the same number on Ladbroke Way. I get all your post, you know, illiterate postal workers, you know.'

Eddy was a regular on the Tristan voyage, and this was his tenth trip to the island. A hotelier from St Ives, Eddy had a penchant for the accordion and the piano, and each January he would close his little hotel and join the RMS as the entertainments officer, allowing passengers to digest their food to the accompaniment of 'Alouette' on the accordion.

And then there was Harvey, a cross between Harry Enfield's drunk and a military commander with his booming, slightly slurred speech that had a habit of tailing off into some indecipherable mumble. Apart from being one of the oldest passengers on the ship, Harvey also sported one of the youngest wives.

He came up to me one day as I watched a school of dolphins that were escorting us, dipping in and out of our bow wave. 'Look at those ruddy great fish,' he gasped, before turning to me. 'You're that chappy from the telly island,' he slurred. 'Super gal that Joanna Lumley,' he smiled. 'Very envious of you, she's a super looker. What I wouldn't do to be castaway with her.' He returned to his binoculars, which he held to his face back to front. 'Bloody fish have disappeared now,' he exclaimed as Flipper leapt into the air.

The rest of the passengers were twitchers, identifiable by their incredibly practical anoraks. They could always be found treading a well-worn path along the ship's decks, binoculars in hand, scanning the horizon for the 'pink-nippled niknak' or the 'purple-bottomed warbler'.

'A YELLOW-TOED BOG-SLAPPER,' would come the war cry, followed by a stampede of Gore-Tex. The twitchers would train their binoculars into the blank sky, before one would make a correction. 'No it isn't, it's a greater yellow-toed bog-slapper.'

While the twitchers twitched and the stitchers stitched, I, the loafer, loafed. My days aboard the RMS could be broadly reduced to eating and sleeping, with an occasional break in between for tea and a wee.

For five long days we sailed across the vast empty ocean, until finally, as dawn broke on the sixth day, Tristan da Cunha's dark silhouette appeared on the horizon. She must have been an awesome sight to early sailors, a mountain in the ocean, her sheer black slopes reaching high into the clouds that mask her features.

The island had been visible for many miles before we began our approach to her seemingly impenetrable cliffs. Albatross and gulls swooped overhead and a school of dolphins danced around the keel as we edged ever nearer to the corners of civilization. The vast blanket of cloud spilled over, and wisps of mist streamed down the mountainside, licking the green vegetation that clung to the gullies.

Slowly we edged our way around the island. First we approached Sandy Point, where the islanders spend their summers and also the location of the apple orchards. The ship rounded the Ridge-where-goat-jump-off (the site where the island's last goat was driven over the cliff as the islanders rid Tristan of the 'eat everything' pests) and then continued south-west past Deadman's Bay and round

Anchorstock Point until finally we caught a glimpse of the Hardies and the island's famous potato patches.

Tristan da Cunha has some of the greatest place names in the world, each one a historical document of some event in the island's past. Where-Times-fall-off marks the place where a dog named Times tumbled over the cliff. Blineye is named after a one-eyed bull that liked to graze there. Deadman's Bay is where a drowned man was washed ashore. At Runaway Beach deserting soldiers sought refuge and Snell's Beach is where a Mr Snell was washed overboard from a dinghy and only just escaped a shark attack.

Jew's Point got its name after the *Joseph Somes* was wrecked in 1856. She had been on her way from England to Australia with a load of gunpowder, when fire broke out on board. The captain gave the order to abandon ship. The lifeboats were lowered and they set out for shore. There was a heavy swell, and the crew and passengers struggled with the heavy oars. One of the passengers aboard the fleeing lifeboats was an elderly Jew who found it particularly difficult to handle the oar in the heavy seas. Therefore he was given responsibility for bailing out the boat, in danger of foundering in the ever-encroaching surf. Shortly before they reached the shore, where the islanders were waiting for them, the captain shouted out to the Jew: 'Bail, Moses, bail, lest we sink!' And from that day the place where they landed has been known as Jew's Point.

Directly south of Jew's Point is a narrow opening in the cliff with the name Down-where-the-minister-land-his-things. This is from another incident, when the British East India Company's ship *Blenden Hall* ran aground on the island of Inaccessible in thick fog and heavy seas. It was almost impossible to land, but the majority of the crew and passengers were lucky to reach the safety of her shores. There they spent three months before the Tristanites could rescue them in longboats from the main island of Tristan da Cunha.

However, before the rescue expedition arrived, the passengers had been forced to endure the drunken lawlessness of the ship-wrecked crew. They plundered the passengers and were both violent and aggressive. There is a story that they buried much of their stolen booty on the island, and that it remains hidden somewhere on Inaccessible to this day.

The passengers were saved just in time as the sailors had planned to murder all of the male passengers, so that they could share the women on their new island home. The passengers' joy at their 'liberation' was intense. One young woman swore she would never forget the islanders' hospitality and kindness, and some years later, after she related the story to her son, he decided to devote his life to 'christianizing' the island. J. G. Barrows took holy orders and became a missionary. Forty-eight years after his mother had been shipwrecked, he journeyed to Tristan. The weather was too bad to attempt a landing, and the captain insisted that they continue on for South America. But Barrows persuaded the captain to land him and his belongings on the east coast of the island, hence the name.

On Taransay we had also done a little bit of renaming. Pig Bay was named after Molly the pig and her piglets that had been landed there. Black Pipe Beach was named after a huge section of oil piping, big enough to crawl through, that had been washed ashore. Loch na Budget was named after we spent our entire budget on water-piping to supply our settlement with water from the loch. Buoyland was our favourite place to go beach-combing for fishing floats and buoys. And my personal favourite, Inca Raah, was named after my dog Inca, as a rather suitable accompaniment to the already rather well-named Ben Raah.

Angry clouds hissed like a snake's tongue down the bluffs. It was as if the island had been caught naked and was trying to hide its modesty. The island blushed as the towel of cloud slipped revealing the peak of her nipple illuminated by a ray of bright sunshine. The cloud soon closed in and the peak was once again shrouded.

At 8 a.m., and in dead-calm water, we arrived at Edinburgh on the Seven Seas, the most remote island capital in the world.

The VHF radio crackled to life for the first time since we had left Cape Town nearly a week earlier. 'Good morning, RMS *St Helena*, welcome to Tristan da Cunha,' announced a bright voice. 'This may seem like a strange question,' it continued, 'but do you have a dry-cleaning service on board?'

It was the island administrator, Bill Dickson, and he wanted to launder his entire collection of Thomas Pink shirts.

While most of the UK's overseas territories are administered by a governor, those that are too small to necessitate the permanent presence of such an important 'minister' are assigned an 'administrator'. As it is a dependency of St Helena, Governor Hollamby is also the governor of Tristan da Cunha, while Bill Dickson acts as his man on the ground.

Bill was a typical Foreign Office employee. He and his girlfriend Trish were two of just half a dozen 'expats' living on the island. Bill was recognizable by his overlarge suits and his sunburnt skin, while Trish favoured pink miniskirts and high heels.

Edinburgh was neatly nestled on a small green plateau. She looked like a picture postcard village as the early-morning sun illuminated her brightly coloured roofs. With her neatly laid out roads and her pretty gardens, she looked more like a Lego village than a storm-lashed settlement in the middle of the South Atlantic.

Behind her were the 2,000-foot cliffs that soared up to what islanders called the 'base'. Just to the east of the settlement was the big black reminder of Tristan's greatest disaster.

It was on a fine spring day, 10 October 1961, then the islanders' world was turned upside down. Just 200 yards from the tiny settlement of Edinburgh, a 150-foot-high column of lava spewed into the air. The ground began to shake, and for the islanders it appeared that the end of the world was nigh. Their island was about to explode and sink back into the inky black ocean whence it had been born.

An SOS was sent to South Africa and the 270 islanders abandoned Tristan aboard their longboats, bound for nearby Nightingale. The Dutch ship *Tjisadane* of the Royal Inter-Ocean Line was on its way from South America to South Africa when it received the mayday. She altered course and rescued the castaway castaways.

The journey from Nightingale to Cape Town took less than five days, but for the islanders who had never left their shores it was a journey through time, and in less than a week they were transported from the Middle Ages to the present day. The ordeal was traumatic.

In South Africa they were discriminated against as 'bourbon-whites', before they moved on to the UK, where the press trumpeted them as 'the forgotten people of the loneliest island in the world'. It was a miserable time for the Tristanites, who were housed in former army barracks at Calshot camp near Southampton. They had been torn from their island home and thrown into a world they couldn't understand, and in which they were viewed as circus freaks.

They remained in the UK for nearly two years, until the island was declared safe, and they were allowed to return home and rebuild their lives. While the physical damage could be rebuilt, the emotional scars would be harder to heal. Memories are still tender among the older generation of islanders, many of whom refused ever to leave the island again.

I can't imagine how hard those two years must have been for these 'simple' islanders. It took me nearly a year to reintegrate fully back into society after just a year living on an island that wasn't even particularly remote. Lights had seemed far too bright, smells too numerous. I had a permanent headache from the fumes and food was too rich for my tummy, which had become accustomed to simple, wholesome foods. Noises were too loud. The sky was small, the buildings large and intimidating. The pace of life was hectic and people cold. I felt lonely living among so many strangers.

'What's it like being back in civilization?' people would ask. This isn't civilized, I would think to myself as I listened to another argument on a bus and watched a cab driver hurling abuse at some cyclist.

What must it have been like for these islanders that had never seen a car or a building higher than a bungalow? They knew nothing of television or cinema, and had certainly never seen an aeroplane. And now they found themselves living in this strange society where people conformed to a regulated 'normality'.

Before disembarking on to the island, we had to clear Customs, which consisted of a man in a British police uniform who collected a £10 landing fee from each passenger and issued them with a visiting permit valid for three days. 'I bet you don't have to change the ink pad much,' I smiled as he stamped my passport. His scowl told me that this was not the first time he had heard that remark.

Once we had been processed, landing-barges arrived to ferry passengers ashore. The design of these rather crude-looking boats is purely functional, giving them the overall appearance of reinforced baths. Even in calm seas, the swell makes boarding these floating tubs a particularly hazardous affair, so split-second timing is required.

The gangway clung to the side of the ship, just a few feet above the water, while the barge rose several feet in the swell, bashed against the side of the gangway and fell away fast as the swell receded. Passengers had to estimate when the side of the barge reached the optimum height, then make a careful leap, usually aided by a guiding hand, before the barge dropped away again. The side of the barge was about a foot wide, with another drop of about four more feet down to the flat bottom of the tub. One miscalculation could result in a crushed foot or, worse still, a tumble into the waters below.

Anne and Frank gazed at the island ahead of them. I watched as they drew a line with their eyes across the landscape, following every cliff and bluff, matching them with the images they had formed in their minds. They had never set foot on Tristan da Cunha and yet it was an island with which their lives had become entwined. As if reading a novel, they had drawn their own pictures of the people, the buildings and the setting. They had walked the island many times in their dreams, but was it as they had imagined?

'Exactly,' answered Frank. 'But much bigger,' added Anne, her eyes brimming with tears. Their eyes returned to Tristan. 'There's the Repettos' house,' announced Frank proudly pointing to the tiny settlement, 'the one with the green roof and the pink flowers in the garden. Margaret's a very good gardener, you know.'

The barge lumbered on through the swell, riding up on to the crest. Every now and then Anne and Frank would catch a glimpse of another familiar building. They would just have time to point before the boat was dragged back to the watery dip of the swell, and the horizon was replaced by a mountain of waves. The Dakins' eyes remained fixed on the shoreline.

As we approached the shore, the skipper let the barge ride to the top of the crest before cutting the engines. He then waited for the boat to settle into a trough before opening the engines up at full throttle. We surged through the narrow entrance of the sea defences before making a sharp right turn into the tiny harbour and pulling alongside the harbour wall, where a steel ladder led us to the wharf and dry land.

The Repettos were waiting on the wharf. 'Aunty Anne,' cried Margaret, as Anne struggled up the steep ladder. The two couples clung together in an emotional embrace.

Margaret was wearing a white floral blouse. She had thick black hair and wore tortoiseshell glasses. She looked Italian.

The small landing bustled with life, as men in identical blue overalls dashed about gathering lobster pots and lowering the island's famous longboats into the waters using a huge crane mounted on the quay. It could have been a Cornish fishing-village.

I had been surprised that, except for the Repettos, the islanders had largely stayed away from our arrival. On Taransay we had always regarded the arrival of the delivery boat as a time of celebration. School would be postponed and tools downed to give everyone the chance to savour the experience. For the Taransay castaways, boats had represented the outside world and confirmed to us that life did indeed exist beyond our television community. It had scared us and comforted us at the same time.

I followed the steep path that led from the jetty to the picturesque settlement above. Nestled at the foot of the mountain, Edinburgh on the Seven Seas was a small village of around a hundred houses. 'WELCOME TO THE REMOTEST ISLAND', announced a sign.

There is very little flat ground on Tristan. In fact, the small plateau on which the settlement stood was about it, the rest of the island being the steep slopes of the volcano. Interestingly, the peak of the volcano at 5,000 feet can be seen only from the water, as it is obscured by the 'base', which rises to 2,000 feet. It is this sheer cliff to the base that dominates the backdrop of the island's settlement, with its lush green gullies and its cascading waterfalls tumbling on to the plateau below. I was reminded of the scenery from the film *Jurassic Park*.

Edinburgh is neatly laid out with carefully manicured lawns and picture postcard gardens of bright flowers. The white-walled homes were decorated with buoys, ropes and old fishing-nets. The houses were shielded from the wind by tall hedges of flax that grow throughout the settlement as an organic barrier against the elements. I walked past one house that appeared to be nothing more than a roof. On closer inspection I discovered that it had in fact been built into a bluff, affording it maximum protection from the winds.

I was still surprised at the absence of locals, as I wandered through the deserted streets. The first place I came to was the Government Building, a low, white structure which houses the administrator's office, the treasury, the police station, the prison and, of course, the video library.

The Government Building was also home to the council chamber. Although the governor of St Helena has executive power over the island, the island also has its own government, comprising eleven different departments. The administrator is advised by the island council, led by the chief islander and made up of eight elected members (including at least one woman) and three appointed members. The councillor who receives the most votes in the election is appointed chief islander. Elections are held every three years.

It seemed incredible that Tristan da Cunha was effectively run by five systems of government, starting with the UK government, then the Foreign and Commonwealth Office, followed by the governor of St Helena, then the administrator of Tristan, then the Tristan government accountable to the island council, which is headed by the chief islander. This chain of bureaucratic shenanigans I later discovered was cause for the greatest concern among islanders.

The current chief islander is James 'Jimmy' Glass, the great-great-grandson of Corporal William Glass. Jimmy, in his thirties, is the youngest chief islander in the history of Tristan, and what's more, this is his second term.

The romantic in me had imagined the chief islander walking the isle with red robes flowing in the breeze, aided by a stick topped with a sheep's skull, not this bright, softly spoken young man in jeans and T-shirt with a tendency to giggle a lot. His skin was tanned, his mullet and goatee a little eighties. His gentle demeanour masked an impressive background. As well as being chief islander, he was the head of the island's Natural Resources Department and its conservation officer. He had acquired experience as a fisheries officer in the Falklands and the Shetlands.

Tristan is largely self-sufficient, relying on the revenue from crayfishing and the return on investments. Tristan's lobsters are renowned for their quality and fetch huge prices, particularly in the Far East, where they are favourite wedding delicacies. A factory on the island prepares them for export, which in the case of the Far East involves removing the claws (the delicacy) and discarding the bodies, which are pulverized into an excellent potato fertilizer.

Jimmy was responsible for setting strict quotas in an attempt to avoid over-fishing and the risk of losing their most important industry. It is estimated that the island earns £250,000 a year from the sale of lobsters, enough money to finance the island's health care and education. In a bizarre twist to small-island life, the islanders set the quotas, fish for them, act as fishery patrol and, most surprisingly, fine themselves for any over-fishing.

The main employer on the island is the government, which employs a staggering 146 people, while the next biggest is the crayfishing industry, with twenty-three staff working in the factory. The average wage is £1,500 a month.

Health care on the island is rather good, with a resident doctor and two nurses, and a reasonably well-equipped hospital, which also doubles as a dentist's clinic and optician's. The hospital had been partly destroyed in the hurricane, although repairs were well under way.

While Tristanians are some of the healthiest people in the world, the island is suffering two worrying trends. The first is the prevalence of asthma, which is estimated to affect more than half the islanders, and the second is the rising rate of obesity. The asthma has been traced as inherent in the islanders' genes, but obesity is a new phenomenon on an island that has traditionally thrived on hard physical labour. Researchers have pointed to the increase in the use of cars and a rise in the import of canned foods and sweets to explain this trend.

I was surprised to see so many cars parked along the streets. There are more than sixty cars on Tristan and just three miles of road. I was amused to hear that the island's lone policeman sometimes goes out with his speed trap, in an effort to uphold the island's 15 m.p.h. speed limit. The island had recently suffered its most serious traffic accident, when a young man came off his moped after hitting some loose volcanic rock on his way to the patches. He had been medevac-ed to Cape Town with a spinal injury. I read on the island's notice board an announcement from the administrator informing islanders that with immediate effect MOTs were increased to £1.50 and road tax to £3.

While the hospital provides excellent health care (and plenty of inhalers), the greatest dangers for islanders are accidents and illnesses that can't be treated on the island. These are known as 'medevacs', and on an island that is a five-day voyage to the nearest big hospital, 'ambulances' can take weeks or even months to arrive, and the problem doesn't end there. Medevacs, once recovered or treated, often find themselves 'castaway' and marooned on the shores of South Africa until a ship is ready to return to their remote island. In an effort to improve this situation, the island's government have bought a property in Cape Town called Tristan House, in which visiting islanders can live for a minimal sum.

I continued on my walking tour of Edinburgh, visiting the Catholic church of St Joseph and the Anglican church of St Mary the Virgin. Next door to St Joseph's was Jane's Café.

I was amused that most of the ship's passengers had converged on the island's tea shop. Hadn't they had enough tea aboard the RMS? I was positively fed up with the stuff. I felt like a bloated teapot.

Jane's is the only café on the island and is a popular place for locals to unwind at the weekend. Fish cakes and crab stick sandwiches were on sale for 50p each. Behind the small counter was a box of KitKats and a box of Walker's salt and vinegar crisps.

The hub of the island's social life is Prince Philip Hall, which apart from doubling up as the dance hall and indoor sports centre is also home to the pub. The roof of Prince Philip Hall had been destroyed in the 2001 hurricane, and a lack of funds had meant that they had been unable to replace it.

There is just one bus service on Tristan da Cunha, a minibus running the three miles from the settlement to the potato patches that operates just once a week. It is here that the families cultivate their annual supply of potatoes on small allotments.

The island has developed a distinct way of life that relies on small-scale subsistence farming, and each weekend, having completed their weekly job, every islander descends on the 'tater patches' to tend to their crop. Some families have even built little cottages next to their allotments in which to spend their weekends. Here in the most remote corner of the earth, people still felt the need to get away for the weekend. I imagined the congestion as Tristan's sixty vehicles raced to get out of town and down to the country a mile away.

As well as the potato patches each family is permitted seven sheep, one milking cow and one dog. The islanders thrive on collective community action, and each year a number of days are set aside for various tasks.

Apart from livestock and domestic animals, there is one other species that looms large on Tristan, the rat. Rats first came ashore aboard ships that foundered on the island's hungry shores, and they have since threatened to overrun the island on a number of occasions. Islanders have sought expert advice, but unable to call on the services of Rentokil they have come up with their own unique alternative, Ratting Day, a particularly jolly occasion when Tristanians compete against one another for the title of king rat-catcher.

Rats have posed a threat to small islands for many hundreds of years, so Tristan da Cunha is not the only island to be harassed by these rodents. Hidden away in a remote corner of the South Atlantic, 250 miles south-east of Tristan da Cunha, is one of the rainiest places on earth, which also happens to be one of the United Kingdom's last outposts, and a dependency of Tristan da Cunha, Gough Island, the island of Michael Swales's 1955 expedition.

Directly in the path of the Roaring Forties and receiving in excess of 100 inches of rain per annum, Gough must have one of the most miserable climates in the world, which is probably why it is uninhabited except for half a dozen dedicated meteorologists who live there, cut off from the rest of the world, free to wallow in the excessive rainfall and meteorologize to their hearts' content – an island of castaway John Kettlys and Michael Fishes, ruminating about cumulonimbus cloud formations and weather patterns.

Apart from the migratory meteorologists, Gough is also home to two native birds, the Gough bunting and the Gough flightless moorhen. And because of its unique flora and fauna, and the fact that it is still relatively untouched by man, the island has been classified by UNESCO as a World Heritage Site.

Which explains the chaos in Whitehall some years later when the FCO received an urgent memo in which it was reported that an 'alien' had been spotted on the remote island. This was not some intergalactic extraterrestrial or even an ambitious Argentinian, but something far more threatening to the island's fragile ecosystem – a rat.

An international emergency team was scrambled from across the world and dispatched to the island to avert an ecological disaster. Rats have decimated the bird populations on a number of the South Atlantic islands. Tristan da Cunha has been particularly affected by the pests. The Tristanians had recently approached a company for a quotation for eradicating the rodents from their island. They resolved to stick to Ratting Day after they were quoted $1 million. A similar situation on Gough would seriously compromise a unique and irreplaceable environment.

The team spent several months on the island searching for the lone rat. It must have been like searching for a needle in a haystack to look for such a small rodent on an island of 7 miles by 3.5 miles. They left the island ratless, concluding that there was no rat there and that the witness must have been mistaken.

Gough may be isolated, but it is also the location of one of the region's most recent shipwrecks. On 17 November 2000, the MFV *Edinburgh* reported that one of her small fishing boats containing two crew members had capsized and sunk in Battle Bay on the north-west side of Gough Island. One man managed to get ashore while the other man drowned.

Several attempts were made by boat to reach the marooned man, but the swell and the strong winds prevented a rescue. The *Edinburgh*'s RIB (rigid inflatable boat) had been overturned in the storm, leaving another man dead and two more stranded on Gough. The three beached men managed to retrieve the dead seaman.

Within hours of the tragedy a rescue team was scrambled from Tristan da Cunha. The team included Lewis Glass, Conrad Glass – the island's chief of police – and James Glass, the chief islander. The team of six set off aboard the MFV *Kelso* and headed for Gough, some 250 miles away.

In the meantime, the leader of the South African meteorological team had organized two members of his group to set off overland to try and get supplies to the injured survivors, but the appalling weather conditions and difficult topography soon forced them to retreat to their base.

The weather continued to deteriorate, and the rescue team was unable to get closer than 500 yards offshore. Radio contact was established and the men were granted permission to kill penguins and shearwater petrels and take their eggs in order to survive. According to the report on the tragedy, the men refused to kill a single bird. 'This is a bird sanctuary,' they replied, 'we can't kill the birds.'

Nearly a week later the weather began to improve. A rocket line was rigged and fired to the shipwrecked survivors. The line reached the island and supplies were tied to the end using marker buoys, but it was still too dangerous to attempt a rescue. Three days later, nearly ten days after the tragedy, the SAS *Potea* with a helicopter aboard completed the rescue of the men, and the Tristan team returned to their island. Saved by the Glasses.

Alongside the administrator's house half a dozen Tristan longboats were lashed down along the path. Lighter than the Pitcairn long-boats, the Tristan craft have been adapted for launching and landing through the surf on exposed beaches. Each boat consists of one thickness of canvas over a light wooden frame. The average length is twenty-six feet with a beam of about six feet. As a reminder of their long days in the UK in the early sixties, one of the longboats still bears the name of the camp at which many of the islanders lived for nearly two years, Calshot.

Traditionally, Tristan's fishing-boats were made from a wooden frame stretched with mail sacks. So great was the demand for these sacks that islanders were encouraged to write more and therefore increase the number of sacks arriving on the island. Although the boats are still made to the same design, sacks are no longer used.

To avoid storm damage, all the fishing-boats must be kept ashore. A crane is used to lift the boats to and from the water and one of the island rules strictly stipulates that all boats be ashore by sunset.

Fishing is a communal task undertaken by every islander. Fishing days are called when conditions are right and are signalled by the beating of an iron cylinder that hangs in the middle of the settlement (rather confusingly, the same cylinder is used as a fire alarm).

Above the harbour were several large warehouses made from corrugated iron that had been painted white. A rather crude hand-painted sign above the pink stable door of one announced that this was the island 'supermarket'.

Boxes of Tesco's own-brand rice crispies competed with second-hand clothes. Marmite was sold alongside Neutrogena moisturizer and Heinz spaghetti hoops vied for space next to Barbie dolls. This whole retail experience was topped off with Radio 1, which was playing through the Tannoy system. I decided Chris Moyles didn't suit Tristan.

As I lingered next to the selection of South African colas, I overheard a conversation between the check-out girl and her customer. 'The man with the white beard and the shorts,' whispered a young girl with a surprisingly plummy voice. 'I saw him sneezing,' she continued, scrunching her face in disgust. This had been followed by much head-shaking by the two of them, before the customer wished the check-out girl good day and left with a polka dot hanky held close to her face.

This was one of the reasons the islanders had stayed away from our arrival: germs. Islanders by the very nature of their isolation have very weak immune systems, leaving them prone to catching any new lurgies arriving on the island.

On Taransay, each visit by the film crew and production company was invariably followed by some cold, flu or other bug that would sweep through our community like a forest fire. The islanders on Tristan were equally vulnerable, and this explained the absence of the elderly, who would shut themselves up until the ship left.

The younger population, however, overcame their health fears when, to celebrate his newly laundered shirts and our safe arrival on the island, the administrator decided to throw a garden party, with his girlfriend Trish, at the Residency, their modest island home.

The Residency, like most of the homes on the island, was a single-storey building made from breeze-blocks, painted white and covered with a corrugated-iron roof, which in their case was green. A wooden gate led to a coral path that led past the neatly manicured garden to the front door. In fact there was very little to distinguish this house from all the others on the island apart from the shiny new Land-Rover parked outside with the licence number TDC 1.

And so it was that the Gore-Tex gaggle found themselves sipping glasses of champagne on the lawn of the Residency. The Union Flag fluttered in the early-afternoon breeze.

I found it difficult to distinguish between crew, passengers and Tristanites. I couldn't recognize half the passengers without their binoculars on, and there was such a jumble of hair and skin colours that at one stage I found myself asking a woman where her home was on the island, only to discover that she was an accountant from Surrey and a passenger on board.

Eventually I spotted a man I felt sure was a genuine Tristanite. I had seen him somewhere before, but was certain he was a 'native'. I grabbed a glass of Pimm's and went over to introduce myself.

'Hello,' I said, holding out my hand, 'I'm Ben.'

'Conrad,' he barked, squeezing my hand to within an inch of its life.

Conrad Glass was in his mid-thirties with a thick black goatee and the ubiquitous weathered skin.

'You were on *Castaway*, weren't you,' he continued with perfect diction. I was beginning to wonder whether I had muddled him up with another unsuspecting passenger when he explained that he was the island policeman. He had also been the man to stamp my passport.

A native of Tristan, and distant relative to William Glass, Conrad had recently completed his police training at Hendon police academy in North London. After graduating, he had returned to Tristan da Cunha, where he was now the lone officer responsible for maintaining island law and order (and upholding the speed limit).

'Where h'are you staying?' he asked.

One of the curiosities of Tristanian English is the inclusion of an 'h' at the start of words that begin with a vowel. Thus 'arm' becomes 'h'arm', 'evening' becomes 'h'evening' and 'egg' becomes 'h'egg', h'etcetera. To add to the complication of pronunciation, 'ing' becomes a simple 'an' and sometimes they forget about the past or future tense.

The question 'Are you going to the potato patches this evening?' becomes 'Is you goan down tater patches this h'evenan?' Now, if you say that with a plum in your mouth, you will sound like a true Tristanian.

In my erratic planning and organizing I had overlooked the little matter of accommodation. The island has a strict law that requires any visitor wishing to visit for any length of time or who wishes to stay ashore to first obtain written permission from the island council, who convene several times a year to discuss applications. I had overlooked this little bureaucratic formality and had been warned by Colin, the purser, that it would be impossible to sleep ashore without permission.

Tristan da Cunha has a stiff vetting process. It receives several sackloads of letters each delivery from people wanting to move to the island. But it is not so much the romances of these urban idealists in search of the castaway experience that require scrutiny as the poisoned ink of journalists and travel writers.

Simon Winchester visited the island in the eighties and included a chapter about the visit in his book *Outposts*. The islanders were horrified to read his account, and some years later, when he returned to the island as a tour guide aboard the *QE2*, he was refused permission to come ashore.

Winchester opened the islanders' eyes to the effect a writer or journalist can have on the often fragile equilibrium of small island communities. Travel writers can normally disguise their characters as unique unidentifiable individuals within a large community or even continent. Islanders are stripped of that anonymity by the nature of their isolation. Ben from Taransay can be identified far more easily than Ben from England, or even Ben from London.

Mark McCrum, a former travel writer, had been commissioned to write a book about our year on Taransay. We had been suspicious of him and his delving questions from the start, but as the year wore on familiarity made us warm to 'detective McCrum'. It was only after the book had been published, and a copy smuggled on to the island, that the damage became apparent. Feuds and factions that had remained strictly taboo had been laid bare and recorded permanently in black and white, complete with candid comments and quotations.

In hindsight, I can see that Mark had done a brilliant job at annotating our unusual year, but at the time, when sensitivities and egos were delicate, it had opened a can of worms and led to a total breakdown in relations.

I explained my lack of planning to Conrad.

'I think something could be arranged,' he smiled. 'Leave it with me,' he said, before disappearing.

I spotted Lars sulking in the corner of the garden and asked him what he thought of the island. 'A Scottish willage full of Italian-looking people speaking a funny English,' was his rather accurate verdict.

One of the island's visiting rituals I discovered was to tee off with golf club and ball from the administrator's lawn. The target was not some volcanic bunker but a bull in the next field. The idea was to hit the thoroughly pissed-off-looking beast on the flank. It was just lucky visitors were so awful at golf.

Governor Hollamby was first up. He lifted the club high into the air, and then dropped it hard with a satisfying clunk. The ball sailed through the overcast sky and straight into the administrator's new Land-Rover. The crowd roared their approval.

By 6.30 everyone was thoroughly pissed, and it was at this opportune moment that Brian from the US consulate in Cape Town decided to introduce himself to 'his' people.

'Ahuum.' He cleared his throat loudly for attention. He was wearing a safari suit that was perhaps better suited to the wilds of Africa than Tristan.

He addressed the assembled gathering like the president himself. 'I would like to take this opportunity on behalf of the United States government to inform you lucky people from Tristan da Cunha that after extensive research we have discovered that your island falls within the remittance of the US Consulate-General in Cape Town. I am therefore responsible for all US matters concerning the island, and for any American sailors that may be shipwrecked here. I have therefore travelled the five days from South Africa to present you with a gift from the United States government.'

The giggling stopped at the prospect of a gift from the wealthiest country in the world. What could it be? Maybe it would be an open cheque to repair the school, or better still a new pub!

'I would like to present Tristan da Cunha' – necks strained forward in anticipation – 'with this wonderful book about the Hubble space telescope.' The garden filled with a mixture of sighing disappointment and suppressed giggles.

Brian, sensing this disappointment, attempted to win back his pissed audience. 'It's actually a very good book, with some great pictures . . . it's, err, very informative, and of course if anyone has any questions regarding the United States, just pick up the phone. Remember, we are only a call away.'

There was more suppressed giggling from the islanders, who had been busy campaigning against the government's recent price increase to $15 a minute for internet and phone use.

Next it was the administrator's turn. 'I would like to announce', slurred the administrator, lubricated by the Pimm's and lemonade, 'that the last longboat will be leaving in just five minutes' time. Anyone who misses it will be placed in the stocks and splattered with guano.'

As the assembled crowd began to disperse, Conrad returned. 'Good news,' he said. 'h'I convened the h'island council, h'and they have agreed to let you stay with Lewis and Yvonne Glass h'as h'it's their turn.' In an astonishing act of utopian democracy, the islanders take it in turns to convert their homes into instant £20 a night B&Bs.

The RMS was scheduled to sail onwards to Inaccessible and Nightingale, where it would spend two days, before returning to Tristan for the governor, the Dakins and Pierre the Frenchman who was busy repairing the antenna. I would finally get the opportunity to experience real life on Tristan.

I watched anxiously as the RMS disappeared towards the horizon, thankful that I had packed my toothbrush and a spare pair of pants for such an eventuality and hopeful that she would return. I wasn't ready for another year as a castaway just yet. I was comforted by the fact that the governor and his wife were also marooned. They would have to return for the governor, wouldn't they?

Conrad offered to drive me to the Glasses' house in the police Land-Rover. I asked him whether there was much crime in this close-knit community.

'No.' He shrugged his shoulders.

'So is there anyone in prison now?'

He shook his head with a smile. 'We don't have much crime here,' he explained with a sigh. I got the impression that Conrad longed for a bit of action, in which he could put all that North London riot training to good use. Instead, the most he ever had to deal with was a 20 m.p.h. speeding Lada, which would invariably turn out to be a relative anyway.

Lewis and Yvonne lived in the far north-west of Edinburgh, in the house nearest to the 1961 lava flow. I recognized their house from a photograph in *Back to Tristan* by Arne Falk-Ronne, a Dane who had returned with the islanders after they had been allowed home. Their home had been badly damaged in the eruption. Lewis worked in the crayfish factory and Yvonne was a schoolteacher, and together they had one son, who was off boarding at Denstone College in the UK.

Since Michael Swales's expedition to Inaccessible Island in 1982–3 a close relationship had been forged between his school, Denstone College, and the islanders of Tristan da Cunha, and a scholarship had been started to allow islanders the chance to complete their secondary education in the UK.

The Tristan government finances islanders wishing to continue their education in the UK. This commitment is undertaken on the strict understanding that the islander return to Tristan for a minimum of two years once their training is completed, repaying the island with their new skills, whether it be nurse-training or fisheries management.

Ann had told me how the chief islander had come to visit Elaine at their home in England shortly after she first arrived. He had taken her aside, out of earshot, where he had given her a firm reminder of where her loyalties lay and of her future commitments to the island.

Lewis came out to greet me. 'You travel light,' he smiled at the sight of my toothbrush wrapped up in a pair of pants. He was wearing the by now familiar blue boiler suit. 'Welcome,' said Yvonne as she placed a steaming cup of tea into my hand and ushered me like an invalid to a chair. 'Our home is your home now,' she smiled.

I couldn't believe how much 'stuff' they had. I saw two deep-freezes, a huge fridge, a microwave, an oven, toaster, bread maker and Moulinex blender, a deep-fat fryer, two televisions, a video and a stereo with more lights than Blackpool beach. A very young-looking Queen Elizabeth II overlooked this electrical store from above the fireplace.

'You must be starving,' insisted Yvonne, and before I'd even had a chance to finish my cup of tea, I found myself being escorted to the kitchen table and presented with a steaming plate of Tristan's finest, potato and lobster. I could get to like this place, I thought as I tucked in.

Lewis had been chief islander in the early nineties. He had been succeeded by Jimmy Glass, but he remained on the island council. He had a warm face and thick head of curly black hair.

'You are the *Castaway* boy, aren't you?' he asked. I nodded. My cheeks bulged with succulent lobster, his with aitches. 'We watched you on the *Kumars at No. 42*,' he smiled. 'Very funny. And what do you think of our island?'

'Amazing,' I replied, conscious that they were both staring at me. I noticed how large his hands were.

'And why are you here?' he continued more suspiciously. I explained that I had myself lived on a remote island and that I had become interested in islands as a consequence. 'So you're writing a book,' he continued.

'Sort of,' I said, embarrassed that it had been so obvious.

'As long as you don't write anything bad about us,' he continued with a warm smile and refilling my glass of water.

The island was holding a party for the governor and his wife and Conrad had invited me along. As I wandered down the street to the pub where the party was being held, I noticed people streaming past me with assorted plates of food. A young boy dashed past with a dish of sausage rolls, then an elderly woman with a plate of cheese and pineapple sticks. I soon discovered that in this ever-resourceful society, preparation of party food was divided fairly among the community.

The pub was a simple affair: a plain room with an even plainer bar stocking cans of South African beer and spirits. The tables had been pushed to the side to create a dance floor for those wishing to get down and boogie to the country and western music that was playing.

Mr and Mrs Hollamby arrived with Bill and Trisha. The islanders looked uncomfortable in their skirts and ties, and even less at ease with the governor and his wife in attendance.

The governor read a speech to the islanders in which he warned the Tristanians about the hazards of dependency, economic and otherwise. He highlighted the growing problems of drug abuse and alcoholism that were afflicting St Helena. 'Don't let it happen here,' he said.

Jimmy Glass had prepared his own speech on behalf of the islanders. He criticized the governor and the administrator for failing to communicate with one another, and for their lack of planning and foresight.

He was referring in part to the bungled planning to improve their harbour. The islanders were concerned by the number of cruise ships passing the island that were unable to allow their passengers ashore owing to bad weather. These tourists had been cited as a future parallel income for the island, but fewer than 50 per cent were ever able to come ashore in the rough seas.

This could only be assured by strengthening and increasing the size of the harbour to allow ships to land their passengers safely. Unable to finance the project itself, the island government had sought aid from the UK and the EU. In the meantime, the islanders had been assured by the previous administrator that the money would be granted. The Tristanian government invested a significant amount of its own capital in the purchase of heavy moving equipment, but by the time of my visit, several years on, the funding had still not been granted and the digging equipment was sitting on the wharf rusting in the salty air.

'Jimmy' explained that Tristan was left 'purposeless' every three years by the changeover of governor and administrator. 'We are on a directionless path,' he slammed. He continued to explain that Tristan was a resourceful community with the potential of a strong future, whereas other overseas territories had been struggling. 'The only thing stopping that', he explained, was 'the lack of communication and planning.' In short, the Foreign Office were messing things up.

I felt uncomfortable as I watched the administrator, his face already beetroot from a day on the water, and the governor squirm, unsure of whether to smile or frown. Bill, I noticed, was attempting to do both at the same time. It was most unflattering, I thought.

The next morning I was woken by a voice from the living-room: 'Long delays between junctions 3 and 4 and heavy congestion in both directions of the A3.' The recently installed satellite dish allows islanders to pick up the British Forces Broadcasting Service, a TV channel for overseas troops that provides homesick soldiers around the world with a compilation of British programmes.

The fact that Tristan da Cunha is on GMT means that islanders can watch some programmes in real time, and so it was that I shared my breakfast with GMTV, listening to the silky tones of Eamonn Holmes while Yvonne and Lewis sat shaking their heads and tutting 'not again' to the announcement that junction 18 on the M25 was closed for roadworks.

I asked Yvonne whether she had ever been to the UK. 'Once,' she replied, barely able to tear her eyes from the weather report that predicted snow across much of England.

'Did you like it?' I pressed.

'Too many people,' she returned. 'I prefer it here, we have everything we need, Tristan is a good place to live.'

'But don't you ever get bored with the island or claustrophobic?' I asked.

'Bored? There are still parts of the island I have never visited,' she explained. 'I have never been to the summit nor to the ponds,' she continued.

I was surprised that a woman in her mid-forties had still not entirely explored her homeland. Admittedly there are many places in the UK that I am yet to visit, but Great Britain is considerably larger than the 38 square miles that is Tristan da Cunha.

'Is there nothing you miss?' I puzzled.

'How can I miss something if I never had it in the first place?'

she replied, tired of the same questions asked by visitors time and time again. I was embarrassed at the stupidity of my questions. I had always assumed I had some sort of affinity with small island communities and that we had a mutual understanding, but I now realized that I was no islander. I never had been and never would be in the true sense of the word. For the Tristanians, the only time they had ever missed anything had been during their 'exile' in the UK, when they had missed their island.

At 8 o'clock sharp, Lewis kissed Yvonne goodbye and headed off to the factory in his blue boiler suit with his lunch box under his arm. It was a sight of domestic bliss as Yvonne stood in the doorway watching her husband disappear down the narrow street.

Yvonne was due at St Mary's school, where she was a teacher, at 8.30. She had invited me to visit the children and tell them about my own island experience. St Mary's is the only school on Tristan da Cunha. There are currently thirty-six pupils, but it has had more than a hundred. The small school is centred around a little courtyard, off which there are six simple classrooms and the assembly room, which also doubles as the island's library.

One of the classrooms had been destroyed by the hurricane that swept through the island the year before. The room was still covered in a film of filthy rainwater and soggy tarpaulins, unrepaired owing to a lack of funds.

The school was surprisingly well equipped, I thought as I sat in the assembly room waiting for the little castaways to gather. In the corner of the room on one of the piles of books, I noticed Brian's 'gift' to the island, the Hubble book.

I was troubled at the prospect of addressing these young Crusoes. It was like asking a child to talk to a classroom full of teachers. Where on earth was I going to begin? I had given this chat hundreds of times before, but usually to people who had never even seen a sheep let alone slaughtered one. Here I was sitting in front of some of the most resourceful ten- and eleven-year-olds in the world.

The young blond, brunette and ginger castaways filed into the small assembly room, staring intently at this stranger in their midst.

They had a mixture of suspicion and curiosity written across their sun-kissed cheeks. Despite our location I was struck by the normality of it all.

Nervously I began to explain a little about Taransay and the *Castaway* project. I was terrified. What would they think of this mad Englishman? The children sat attentively as I told them about my year as a BBC castaway. I told them about our beautiful island and about the wooden pods in which we lived. I showed them photographs of the little schoolhouse above the beach and of the Taransay children. I told them about Scraggy the pet sheep and Molly the pig. I told them about my long walks in the hills with Inca, and of our cold swims in the North Atlantic. I explained how we would collect driftwood and cut peat for our little fires, and how we had caught a wild deer with a fishing net. I nearly drowned in my own tales as I reminisced.

'Are there any questions?' I asked at the end of my talk.

'Did you have any penguins?' asked a young girl.

'No.' I shook my head. 'But we did have chickens,' I added, hoping to impress her.

'Did you have whales?'

'No,' I repeated.

'Donkeys?'

I shook my head again.

'How often did a boat come?' asked a young boy suspiciously.

'Every couple of weeks,' I blushed, embarrassed by how 'uncastaway' we had actually been. I wanted to impress them, I was desperate for these young Tristanians to like me. I wanted to join their gang and become their friends. Instead they had sussed me out, and revealed me for the pseudo-islander I really was.

'Do you want to come fishing?' asked one of the boys as I sat in the corner sulking. At last I had made a friend. We arranged to meet down at the harbour after school. That gave me a chance to explore some more of the area around Edinburgh, beginning with the unusually named Pigbite.

Pigbite is just to the east of the settlement and gets its name from an incident over a hundred years ago when one of the inhabitants was chased and bitten by a pig. Pigs have been extinct on the island since 1984, and with this reassurance I followed the path that had been cut through the lava flow until I reached the nearest the island gets to a beach, a beach strewn with large boulders and pounded by the heavy surf.

Pigbite, I had been assured, was the best place to see the island's penguins and seals, as they liked to sunbathe on the sheltered beach. To my disappointment, the place was deserted. It was as I turned to return to the settlement that I noticed a plume of smoke streaming from the lava. 'VOLCANO,' I was about to scream when I noticed a Dennis rubbish truck rumble past towards the 'eruption', which turned out to be the island's rubbish dump, where most of the island's refuse was burned.

I was due to meet the boys at 3.30 p.m. down at the wharf. They were already there when I arrived. 'What are you fishing for?' I asked.

'Dinner,' they replied in chorus. As with so much on Tristan, a trip to the supermarket is substituted by dipping a hook into the rich waters and catching dinner.

The boys were after the tasty five-fingers and the tiger fish. 'What's the biggest fish you can catch from here?' I asked.

'Well, Willy caught h'a shark yesterday,' announced Dominic without a glimmer of emotion, for this was apparently quite a normal happening.

'Was it large?' I pressed.

''Bout the size h'of you,' he answered, sipping on his can of Coca-Cola.

Tristan da Cunha is a vast volcano that shoots up from the seabed. Just a small ledge was all that existed between us and the sea wall dropping down thousands of feet below. Whales were a common sight in front of Edinburgh and locals had even given them names. Although I never saw one myself, Lewis had told me that the islanders could often hear them at night, puffing and blowing and sending their strange cries reverberating around the steep cliffs above Edinburgh.

'Look,' cried one of the boys pointing to the empty horizon, 'the *Agullas*.' I was wondering whether they had spotted some strange seagull or even one of the pet whales when one of the boys explained that it was one of the island's fishing-boats, returning from South Africa.

The RMS is far too expensive for most Tristanians, and except for emergencies islanders use their fishing-trawlers, the *Agullas* and the *Kelso*, to commute. The ships spend many weeks at sea, fishing for crayfish. The trawlers then drop their haul at Cape Town several times a year, giving the islanders a rare opportunity to do some shopping.

I had been surprised at how well dressed the islanders were. Admittedly they favoured practicality over aesthetics because it takes the best part of a year for a clothes order to be delivered, and while the introduction of the Next directory had revolutionized the island's shopping, it was still a fashionista's worst nightmare.

Catalogue shopping is popular on Tristan, with islanders ordering from Argos and even Boden. I had been particularly surprised to catch Lewis flicking through a copy of *Exchange and Mart*. He was looking to buy a car and had spotted a Land-Rover for sale. The problem was that it was in Nottingham, 5,000 miles away. Test drives and engine checks are not an option on Tristan.

I stretched my eyes to the horizon, and even with the aid of binoculars, I couldn't see a thing. 'H'over there,' repeated the boys, pointing to nothingness. It was nearly ten minutes before I could see the pin prick on the horizon.

Unlike the arrival of the RMS, that of the *Agullas* was a big event. Where the RMS was nothing more than a boatload of ogling voyeurs, the *Agullas* brought friends and family. It seemed that most of the island had turned out for her arrival, as hundreds of Tristanians descended the steep path to the wharf below.

The *Agullas* weighed anchor just off the settlement and the barges once again set off to ferry passengers ashore. The boys told me that about a dozen islanders were returning, including a young Tristanian girl with her new Scottish husband, who would be visiting the island and his new 'in-laws' for the very first time.

There was something terribly Scottish, I thought, about marrying someone from a cold, wet, windy island rather than a tropical one. I tried to imagine what might be going through this young Scot's mind at the prospect of what I had been told would be two years on a remote island with a family he did not yet know.

With just three hundred people, and only seven families, Tristan da Cunha has a very limited gene pool. I had almost imagined this to manifest itself physically, and part of me had expected the worst, but instead I found a society where the only distinguishing characteristic appeared to be the inhabitants' weathered faces.

I watched as the Scotsman was embraced by a bevy of big-busted in-laws. He looked gangly and pale next to the Tristanians as his new family marched him up to the settlement. I caught his eye as he went past, and watched his terrified expression turn to confusion as he recognized me sitting on the little wall.

I slept fitfully that night, only to be woken early the next morning by a ship's blast. The RMS had returned from her cruise round the outlying islands, and that had been our signal to return to the ship for the return voyage to Cape Town.

Lewis and Yvonne had left a gift for me. I had been struck by the islanders' generosity during my short visit. I unwrapped the old South African newspaper dated 1995 to find a pair of hand-knitted socks and a mug. A broad smile enveloped my face as I examined the mug more closely. A penguin was printed beneath the words

TRISTAN DA CUHNA

I imagined the islanders' horror at receiving their order from the UK, only to discover the island's name misspelt.

As I wandered back down to the little jetty, past the factory and Jane's Café, I caught up with Aunty Anne and Uncle Frank. I hadn't seen them since we arrived a few days earlier. 'What did you think?' I asked.

Frank shook his head, lost for words. 'A dream come true,' he said. 'A very very special place,' added Anne emotionally as we boarded the barge and returned to the RMS *St Helena* for our voyage to Cape Town.

Anne, Frank and I stood at the ship's rail as the RMS weighed her anchor and began to pull away from the little settlement. 'Do you think they've found it yet?' asked Anne of Frank. A small smile appeared on his face as he hugged his wife. Frank explained that before they departed they had left an envelope with the islanders. Inside was a cheque to repair the school and a plaque with their son's name for the wall. 'We didn't want to make a fuss, so we asked them not to open it until we had left,' explained Anne. 'Jo would have been thrilled,' she added, her eyes fixed on the island.

A tear welled in my eye as the island disappeared over the horizon.

I had been told the story of one young American who had spent a year on the island. So sad had he been when he left that he had remained at the stern of the ship for the entire five-day journey to Cape Town, tears streaming down his cheeks all the way, his eyes fixed on the ocean behind.

I thought back to my conversation with the black-cab driver in London all those weeks earlier. ''Oo'd live there?' he had asked, and as I watched Tristan disappear over the watery horizon, I answered knowingly, 'I would,' out loud, hoping someone, somewhere, would hear me.

2. British Indian Ocean Territories

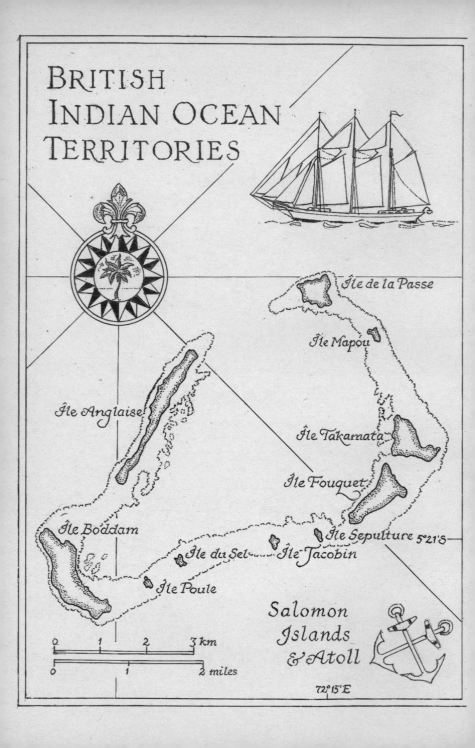

BRITISH INDIAN OCEAN TERRITORIES

Île de la Passe

Île Mapou

Île Anglaise

Île Takamata

Île Fouquet

Île Boddam

Île Sepulture 5°21'S

Île du Sel · Île Jacobin

Île Poule

Salomon Islands & Atoll

0   1   2   3 km

0   1   2 miles

72°15'E

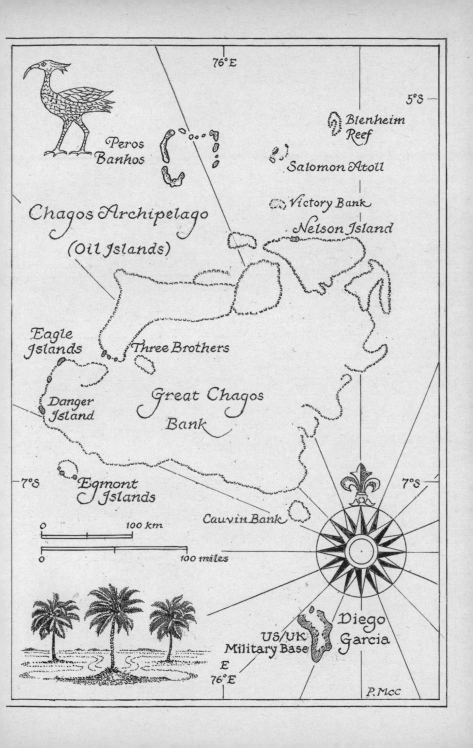

76°E

5°S

Blenheim Reef

Peros Banhos

Salomon Atoll

Chagos Archipelago

(Oil Islands)

Victory Bank

Nelson Island

Eagle Islands

Three Brothers

Great Chagos Bank

Danger Island

7°S

Egmont Islands

7°S

Cauvin Bank

0   100 km

0   100 miles

Diego Garcia

US/UK Military Base

E

76°E

P. McC

'See you in Mali,' I tapped into my computer. I was e-mailing Charles Veley, an American millionaire. I'd arranged to meet him two weeks later.

I had met Charles once before, in the slightly chillier climes of the South Atlantic. He had been aboard the RMS *St Helena* bound for Tristan da Cunha. He stood out from the crowd, not only since he was several decades younger than the rest of the passengers, but also because of the rather glamorous blonde with whom he was travelling.

Charles Veley was a thirty-something American who belonged to a club called the Travellers' Century Club. The TCC is based in Los Angeles and was created in 1954 for those who have visited more than 100 countries. Members are provided with the TCC's definitive guide to the world: 'the list', consisting of 317 countries and their dependencies. The challenge is then to complete the remainder of 'the list', and conquer the world.

Charles was in a hurry. A dotcom millionaire with both youth and money on his side, Charles had visited more than two hundred countries in almost as many days. While Europe, the Americas, Africa and the Middle and Far East had been relatively simple 'conquests', it was the more remote and obscure lands and islands that demanded time and patience. We had chatted briefly about the British Indian Ocean Territories over a cup of Earl Grey tea, exchanged e-mails, and the expedition had been planned in cyberspace.

Later that afternoon I received an e-mail from Charles: 'I sincerely hope you mean Male with an "e" and not Mali with an "i". It may be difficult to sail to the Indian Ocean from a land-locked country in West Africa,' came his wry reply. 'Of course I meant

Male,' I typed gingerly as I tore up my plane ticket and searched for my travel agent's number. Hardly an auspicious start.

The British Indian Ocean Territories or Chagos Archipelago are in the middle of the Indian Ocean centred at about 6 degrees south, 72 degrees east. They are roughly 2,000 miles east of Africa and 2,000 miles west of Singapore, and about 500 miles from Gan in the south of the Maldives. The group consists of fifty-five islands and they form the southern end of the Laccadives—Maldives—Chagos atoll chain. The British had taken the islands along with Mauritius from France as a colony in 1814. The islands of the archipelago, also known as the Chagos, were known locally as the Oil Islands because their coconut oil lit the streetlamps of Mauritius and the Seychelles.

Mauritius and her dependencies had been part of the British Empire until 1964, when a rather complicated deal was struck. It was agreed that Mauritius would be granted independence from the UK, on the understanding that for a one-off payment of £3 million the Chagos islands would be excluded from the deal. The islands were deemed of 'significant' geographical interest and would remain British. And so the British Indian Ocean Territories were formed.

This new British colony was given a flag, a commissioner, a customs office and a police station. A handful of Royal Marines were stationed on the islands and even stamps were produced. The population of the islands, when they became the British Indian Ocean Territory in 1964, was around 1,500, most of whom lived on Diego Garcia. They were called the Ilios and were descended from slaves introduced to work on the small copra plantations. Most were fifth-generation islanders.

The British Indian Ocean Territories are split into three distinct island groups or atolls, and my intended destination was the Salomon Islands, the most northerly atoll in the territory. But they are a notoriously difficult destination, isolated both politically and geographically. I was on my way to one of the most secretive places in the world, a place 'not even the Prime Minister can visit'. A journey that would begin in 'Male with an "e"', the capital of the Maldives.

I left London in the pouring rain aboard Sri Lanka Airways flight 502 bound for Colombo via Male. The majority of the passengers were Sri Lankans returning home. The exceptions were a handful of love-struck honeymooners (who were practically queuing up to join the mile-high club) and me, all bound for the tropical paradise of the Maldives.

Robinson Crusoe wouldn't have liked the Maldives. They may have the obligatory heat, sunshine and palm-fringed white-sand beaches, but they are distinctly lacking in rivers, lakes, mountains, wildlife, agriculture and, in fact, anything conducive to life, unless all you need for survival is a jolly good tan. Maldivians must import everything from eggs to fruit. The only exception appears to be the local Coca-Cola plant, given special dispensation by head office to produce the soft drink using sea water – still not much good if you're trying to cut it as a self-sufficient castaway like old Robbo.

Eight hours after leaving London, we began our descent to the turquoise waters below. Cameras on the belly and nose of the plane allowed passengers to become back seat (should that be seat back) pilots. I sat mesmerized as I flicked between belly and nose and watched small fishing-boats flick across my screen at several hundred miles an hour.

Less than 0.4 per cent of the Maldives is dry land, which consists of about 1,192 small, low-lying coral islands. According to the *Guinness Book of Records*, the Maldives are the flattest country in the world: none of it rises more than 10 feet above sea level. The capital of this watery republic is Male, a small island measuring just over a mile by half a mile, with a population of 65,000. Taransay was nearly four times as large as Male with a population of just thirty-six.

I had read somewhere that the Maldives were sinking. In fact, it is the ocean that is rising, and according to the United Nations-sponsored Intergovernmental Panel on Climate Change the sea level is forecast to rise between 20 and 86 centimetres by 2030. A rise that would leave much of the Maldives another Atlantis.

During our descent, Male did not look like a city doomed to be submerged. Not an inch of the capital had been left idle, and the result was a top-heavy city that looked as if it could topple over at any moment. From the air it looked like a cartoon town, the sort drawn on maps to represent cities, with a collection of skyscrapers and mosques jutting disproportionately from the map.

We came to a halt outside the small terminal, and a rickety pair of steps was wheeled to the aircraft. It seemed strange walking along the tarmac in the salty sea air, to the sound of crashing waves. With a skip in my step I collected my bag and bounded over to customs.

Once through Customs, I was met by a man with incredibly hairy eyebrows. It was difficult to say where his brow finished and his hair line began. He was holding a sign that read 'Mr Bean'. I gambled that he meant me. 'Welcome, Mr Bean, Mr Charles is expecting you,' he beamed as we made our way to the water taxis for the twenty-minute boat trip to Male.

Rainy London already seemed a distant memory as we glided across the tepid waters of the Indian Ocean to the capital, where Mr Charles was waiting.

Charles was sat at the pool bar when I arrived. Neatly dressed in chinos, a Ralph Lauren polo shirt and aviator sunglasses, he sipped on a bottle of Bud. The look was *Top Gun* meets Harvard freshman.

'There's good news and bad news,' he said after giving me a hearty slap on the back. 'The good news is that Jeff flew in from Singapore this morning, and Ted's flight from Cairo arrives in an hour.' He was referring to our travelling companions on this quest to visit the British Indian Ocean Territories. 'The bad news', he continued, 'is that our plane is broken, we can't get to Gan until tomorrow, we have to stay in Male.'

Charles had organized our onward travel to Gan, an island in the Addu Atoll, several hundred miles to the south of Male. There we had arranged to meet a yacht called the *Dream Voyager*, which would take us south to the BIOT.

Apart from boasting the longest stretch of driveable road in the Maldives, at a whopping ten miles, Addu Atoll has a rather colourful history. The Maldives had been part of the British Empire until

1964, and while Britain did not overtly interfere in the running of the archipelago, it did establish a significant Royal Air Force base on Gan.

In 1957, the newly elected president of the Maldives, Ibrahim Nasir, challenged the British presence on Gan and demanded a review of the situation. An insurrection by the people of Addu and Suvadiva followed; they objected to Nasir's demand that Britain cease employing local labour. The islands cut ties with the north, and Abdulla Afif Didi became president-elect of the 'United Suvadiva Islands'. This short-lived rebellion was soon quashed when an armed fleet was sent by President Ibrahim Nasir. Afif fled the country to the Seychelles, where he still lives, and the islands were restored to Maldivian authority.

Male looked like a giant Christmas tree: the town had, quite literally, been painted red – and green, the national colours. And a creeping jungle of fairy lights had suffocated the entire island: buildings, cars, trees, even the guns on the decks of the warships at anchor in the harbour had been dressed in twinkly red and green fairy lights. A battalion of flags filled any gaps that had been left.

I was particularly impressed by the military procession through the narrow streets. The red and green tinsel that decorated the soldiers' semi-automatic weapons was made even more surreal by the music of the kilted bagpipers to which they were marching. I dreamed in red and green that night, interrupted only by the 24-hour drilling. A team of Japanese engineers were busy reinforcing the island wall, a concrete barrier that stops the Indian Ocean from spilling over and creating a tropical Venice.

The next morning it was a relief to catch the water taxi back to the airport, where our newly repaired plane was waiting to whisk Ted, Charles, Jeff and me off to the real Maldives. I was not sad to say adieu to Male.

Ted, it turned out, was not an Egyptian, but another American, living in Cairo, where he ran a travel agency. He was also a member of the TCC, having joined after falling in love with Barbara, another member. They had met at a cruise liner convention, and their relationship was now founded on their meeting up six times a year on various cruises around the world. In a rare union of convenience they were able to indulge their list and their lust at the same time.

I had never met Jeff before, although I had lived with him for nearly a month. He had also been on the RMS to Tristan da Cunha with Charles and myself, but I had never had a chance to speak to him. He had been travelling with his young Indonesian wife and their child.

His likeness to Ron Howard, the *Happy Days* actor and now Oscar-winning director, was uncanny. It wasn't even a likeness – it was an exactness. He even had the same mannerisms. From time to time I found myself calling him Ron.

Jeff owned a successful company supplying computer parts around the world. For Jeff business was travel and travel was business. He journeyed the globe with his satellite phone glued to his ear and his laptop firmly in his lap. Jeff had been following 'the list' for several years. 'I like to spend time in each place,' he explained in between satellite conference calls to Singapore and Indonesia.

Jeff had been travelling in Indonesia when he spotted his future wife. She was just sixteen and he forty-six, but it was mutual love at first sight. He converted to Islam (giving him the enviable advantage over other TCC members of a visit to Mecca) and they married within six months.

His wife, who had never previously set foot outside her small village, now found herself trailing Jeff around the world. 'She's been to 120 countries so far,' stated Jeff proudly as he recounted with a chuckle how his young wife, once content with economy train travel, would now travel only first class on planes, and refused to travel on ships altogether after the Tristan da Cunha trip. She had been so seasick that she had emerged from her cabin only once during the entire voyage.

The flight to Gan was spectacular. The Maldives are most impressive from the air. At sea level, they are just one low, flat piece of land after another, but from the air each is as distinctive as a snowflake, each island a unique shape surrounded by a rainbow of blues and turquoises. In places clusters of islands produce their own distinct shapes and patterns.

Gan was stiflingly hot when we arrived. The terminal of the former RAF airport was now little more than a single room with a desk and a fan. It hadn't been difficult for the crew of the *Dream Voyager* to find us as we were the only ones on the flight and they were the only ones in the airless terminal.

The taxi stirred up a thick cloud of dust that settled on the coral stone houses as we sped through the empty streets. The town's population of 16,000 were hiding from the mid-morning heat, giving the island the feel of a Wild West ghost town.

Gan, like an undeveloped Male, had no bars or cafés, a couple of shops called Hey Mister selling tourist tat, and lots and lots of dust. This wasn't the island paradise I had read about in magazines – Gan was more like a cat litter tray.

The contrast between dusty grey street and shimmering ocean couldn't have been greater as we reached the water's edge. A crumbling concrete wall marked the boundary between sea and land. A fleet of wooden fishing-boats bobbed up and down on the dazzling waters.

The *Dream Voyager* looked splendid anchored alone in the bay, where she towered over the green palms that had been turned a shade of grey by the clouds of dust spewed up by the cars. Only a handful of yachts pass through Gan, and she had caused quite a stir among the locals.

She was a 95-foot, 100-ton, two-masted wooden schooner. She had been built just two years before, with the primary objective of sailing honeymoon couples around the island paradise. Two years in the unremitting tropical sun had bleached her beyond her age. We had chartered her to take us as near to the British Indian Ocean Territories and as close to Diego Garcia as we dared. Five hundred miles of open ocean lay ahead of us and I could only hope that the ship's hull was as sturdy as the newly-weds' beds.

She was a comfortable yacht. A huge canopy stretched from the mast to the back stay, providing shelter for the helmsman. A large table on the deck allowed for al fresco dining. Each of us had the comfort of our own wooden cabin complete with en suite bathroom, something that was going to be particularly useful in the days of seasickness that followed.

A crew of seven would accompany us on our southern adventure. Giyas and Gardir were our two captains (a Maldivian law states that vessels must have two captains, one for national and one for international waters), Gamini was our chef, Said the engineer, Mohammed our general looker-afterer, and I was never really sure what Coco and Suriya did. Except for Gamini, who was from Sri Lanka, the rest were Maldivian.

While the journey is difficult enough to organize, permissions are even harder – that is to say, impossible. BIOT enjoys a unique status.

I have always been intrigued by the Foreign Office, seduced by the apparently glamorous 'Ferrero Rocher' lifestyle of the suave diplomat. I had applied to become a civil servant in the FCO but had failed to meet the strict entry requirements. While planning my journey to BIOT, the prospect of dealing with the FCO still held some appeal. I wasn't prepared for the moment that urbane pleasantries became a brick wall.

I first met Alan Huckle, head of the Overseas Territories Department, at the Royal Geographical Society in Kensington, London, at a function for Falkland Islands conservation. He had been accommodating and helpful, until I mentioned the BIOT and specifically Diego Garcia in the Indian Ocean. 'You can't go there,' he insisted. 'Cancel it from your list, Garcia is totally off limits.' I knew the island contained a sensitive American military base, but I was surprised at his hasty dismissal. What I soon came to learn was that it also told a tale of government betrayal and international duplicity.

In 1964 a secret British–American conference was held in London to discuss the West's concerns with China. It was at this conference that officials discovered the significance of this obscure archipelago in the middle of the Indian Ocean that allowed access to Asia, and more significantly the Middle East. The presence of an emergency airstrip on the island, which had been built by the RAF during the Second World War, sealed its fate.

In 1966 Britain signed a 'defence' agreement with the United States, leasing the British Indian Ocean Territories to the USA for fifty years, with an option for a twenty-year extension. It wasn't the copra oil or the unspoilt beaches that attracted America, but the strategic location on which they would establish a mid-ocean station. They particularly wanted Diego Garcia, with its huge lagoon, as an intelligence, military and naval base and later as a nuclear weapons depot and refuelling point for US bombers. As the British had discovered in the nineteenth century, whoever controlled the Chagos Archipelago controlled the Indian Ocean.

A deal was struck that, in return for Diego Garcia, Britain was allowed a £5 million discount against the retail price of a single US-manufactured Polaris submarine. It was agreed that for security reasons the islands should be handed over, in the official jargon, 'fully sanitized' and 'swept' – in other words, empty.

There was one problem. British officials had somehow over-looked the existence of the Ilios and assumed the islands to be uninhabited. What were they to do with 1,500 natives?

The family portraits were already being hung in the submarine and there was no going back. Whitehall decided to rewrite history and a law was passed in London making it illegal for anyone to come to the islands ever again, or, indeed, to be there in the first place, without a permit. The existence of the Ilios was erased, and they were now illegal tenants on their own island home.

In the summer of 1971 a group of officials arrived from Whitehall informing the islanders of the new law, and of the fact that they were consequently now 'squatters'. They were ordered to pack up, and that evening were already sealed below the deck of a ship bound for Mauritius.

By 1972, the US Defense Department told Congress that 'the islands are virtually uninhabited, and erection of the base would thus cause no indigenous political problems'. By December 1974, a joint UK–US memorandum stated that there was 'no native population on the islands'.

The bewildered inhabitants were dumped at Port Louis in Mauritius, without housing or work. The minuscule amount of money with which they had been 'paid off' (on the understanding that they renounced their rights ever to return to the islands) left them in abject poverty.

A cruel irony is that the Mauritian government was reportedly paid £3 million to take these forced refugees. Nearly the same as the discount the US gave Britain for a Polaris submarine in return for the islands.

I knew of just one other 'civilian' to have visited Diego Garcia, and that was author Simon Winchester, who visited the islands illegally in 1985. Winchester had been to Diego Garcia aboard an Australian yacht. His skipper had demanded they use the harbour as a 'port of refuge'. Winchester was able to spend a day or two there alongside an 'armada that made Pearl Harbor look puny'.

Since Winchester's trip in 1985, security had been stepped up in the British Indian Ocean Territories. Diego Garcia was crucial to the American war effort in both Afghanistan and Iraq and it was rumoured that for a time the island was holding some of the most notorious al-Qaida suspects.

'This isn't going to be nearly as bad as I thought,' smiled Ted. 'I was worried it was going to be a rough journey,' he sighed in relief. Thoughts of the war were far from our minds as we boarded the *Dream Voyager*. It was mid-afternoon, the wind was shifting and captain 1, Giyas, was keen to make haste. With favourable winds, the captain estimated, it would take us three days to reach Perros Banhos, the most northerly atoll and location of Boddam Island, the former home of the Ilios.

For the *Dream Voyager* and her crew this would be their first voyage outside Maldivian waters, and there was an air of anticipation. The sun beat down on the teak decks as we cut through the calm azure waters of the Addu Attol. I didn't have the heart to point out the huge waves breaking on the outer edges of the giant lagoon in which we were still safely sheltered. I didn't want to dampen anyone's enthusiasm.

Ted began to lose colour shortly after we left the shelter of the lagoon, when the first wave broke over our bow. Huge rollers crashed against us as we edged through the coral harbour. The air filled with spray, and Ted disappeared to get acquainted with the loo. A bond that grew stronger throughout the passage.

Jeff was not a light traveller. Apart from the ever-present satellite phone and laptop, there was the spare satellite phone and spare computer. There was also the video camcorder, the 35mm camera, and the digital camera as well as a studio camera complete with glass slides and a tripod. Somewhere into the recesses of his 'Mary Poppins' bag, Jeff had also packed a full set of diving-gear and, most importantly, ten bags of Animal Cookies.

'I can't believe you've never tasted an Animal Cookie,' gasped Jeff in genuine surprise at my unworldliness. 'Oh, man, you haven't lived,' continued Charles. 'Don't get me started on those little guys, I'll never stop,' shouted Ted from his sickbed. Animal Cookies, explained Jeff, were biscuits coated in a thick layer of pink or white icing sugar and then smothered in hundreds and thousands. 'And, man, are they good.'

What astonished me was that each bag weighed 500g, and Jeff had travelled all the way from the US via Singapore with TEN bags. That's 5 kilos of biscuits, half the weight of all that I was travelling with. Jeff, it appeared, wouldn't leave home without the company of these sugary beasts, and his wife had taken to filling every spare corner of his bags with them. These edible friends had travelled to more places than me.

But their shared love of pink biscuits was incidental – Charles, Ted and Jeff had all been brought together by the Travellers' Century Club. The chairman of the club was an entrepreneurial German named Klaus Billep. As well as running the TCC, Klaus also owned a rather lucrative travel company dealing in 'exotic' and 'inaccessible' travel. Funnily enough, Klaus's travel company specialized in organizing trips and expeditions to the very same countries that appeared on 'the list'. His 'list'.

The '-stans', for example, could be yours for a mere $15,000 (to include all the -stans of the former Soviet Union as well as Afghanistan). Jeff told me of one trip to North Africa he had taken with Klaus. He had been promised that for $5,000 Libya would be included in this exciting trip. The group, however, had been denied entry into Libya, and so, upon their return, Jeff complained. Klaus apologized for the misunderstanding, and joked that he might 'add it to his list anyway' for trying! Needless to say, neither man ever seriously entertained the idea of such an unsatisfactory fudge.

If only all record-breaking were so simple. For just a few thousand dollars, Norris McWhirter might then recognize me as the sexiest man on earth. Why didn't Charles just pay Klaus two million dollars and be done with it?

For those successful enough to complete the TCC list, their achievement is recognized with a lapel pin. I must admit that a lapel pin for the millions of dollars spent visiting some of the most hostile and remote places on earth seemed a little disappointing, but TCC champions wear the lapel pin with pride. They need also to remain alert to an ever-changing world. A single bloody coup, war or assassination can change the political map and necessitate a return trip to a newly formed or breakaway republic. The club's members must have found 1991 a busy year. 'Bollocks,' they must have spluttered over their morning paper as they read news of the break-up of the USSR.

Of my three 'country collecting' companions, Ted held the group record, with 297, but it was Charles that was attempting to break records. He had hit on the idea of becoming both the youngest and the fastest member to complete the TCC list. He soon tired of this challenge and asked the *Guinness Book of Records* whether they had a category for country-collecting.

Charles had been ecstatic to hear that no one had yet completed their official list, and, what's more, the Guinness list of the world consisted of just 263 places, 51 fewer than the TCC list. It was only on closer inspection that Charles noticed thirteen extra places:

1. Bouvet Island
2. Ashmore Island & Cartier Island
3. Clipperton Island
4. Coral Sea Islands Territory

5. Golan Heights
6. Heard Island and McDonald Islands
7. Howland Island, Baker Island, Jarvis Island
8. Kingman Reef
9. Paracel Islands
10. Peter Island
11. Queen Maud Land
12. South Georgia and the South Sandwich Islands
13. Spratly Islands

Charles also learnt that the current record holder as the most-travelled man was an American called John Clouse, living in Indiana. It appeared that Mr Clouse had visited all but Bouvet and the Paracels – extremely remote islands. Bouvet, an uninhabited isle belonging to Norway, is arguably one of the most remote in the world, roughly on the same latitude as the Falklands, but a thousand miles further east.

The race was on. Charles had decided to complete the entire TCC list as well as the 'Guinness 13', to ensure him a place in the *Guinness Book of Records*. It struck me as being as inadequate as the lapel pin, to recognize such an achievement in a single line in a book, but Charles had his own philosophy. 'I'll publish a book, get on to the US talk circuit, enter politics and eventually run for president.' As a thirty-year-old self-made millionaire estimated to be worth more than $300 million, he stood a better chance than most, I reckon.

The guys were nervous. They had been warned about the last attempt by a group of TCC members to visit BIOT. They had apparently strayed too close to Diego Garcia and had been 'chased' away by gunships. Charles, though, appeared to have done some clever diplomatic navigation – after all, who could refuse a man attempting a world record?

For three long days, stricken by seasickness, we crashed through the turbulent waters of the Indian Ocean. I spent my time variously lounging on the deck, re-reading *Anna Karenina*, spying on the crew at prayer time and watching Bollywoods with Mohammed.

Any spare time was spent listening to Jeff clinching another multi-million dollar deal on his hand-held satellite phone.

Early on the fourth day, palm trees were spotted on the horizon. 'Land ahoy,' I hollered: the British Indian Ocean Territories. Strips of virgin white sand appeared from the ocean as we neared the most northerly atoll. Rows of palms stood to attention in the gentle breeze. At times the sand seemed to disappear back into the ocean, giving the impression that the trees were growing from the water itself.

This was more like the paradise I had been expecting in the Maldives. Sun-drenched islands, with mile upon mile of unsullied beaches with talcum powder sand.

Slowly we edged our way into the huge lagoon of the Salomon Islands. An atoll is basically an underwater volcano, the peaks of which become islands and the crater of which is submerged, creating a vast salty lagoon. To the eye there is little difference between the lagoon and the rest of the ocean as the boundary is under water, in the shape of a huge coral reef. In places, the reef kisses the surface, allowing waves to crash along an invisible coastline, but generally, the reef remains hidden, and a dangerous hazard to sailors.

Mohammed stood at the front of the *Dream Voyager* shouting out estimated depths, and keeping watch for 'bobbies'. I had been fooled into thinking that he had spotted a police boat the first time I heard him cry 'bobby', but soon learned that these were the hazardous coral mountains that soar to the surface.

We were heading for Boddam, one of the sites of the expelled Ilios. From the water there was little to distinguish it from the other islands in the atoll: a gaggle of islands with sandy white beaches with thick forests of palms. The island had once been inhabited by a thriving community who worked the copra factory down by the water's edge. Several hundred had once lived on this tiny island, most employed by the Chagos Agalego Oil Company. It had been a long-settled and prosperous community with a church and school. Livestock had once been reared and the fragile land tended. One of the islanders' last plans before their eviction had been a scheme to turn Boddam into a free port where trans-Indian Ocean liners could call and their passengers be tempted by duty-free cigarettes and perfume, while swimming in the azure waters of the bay. Sadly the plan never had a chance to get off the ground, but I could see the temptation of the place.

As we neared the island, signs of its rich legacy began to appear. A huge white cross appeared next to a crumbling concrete pontoon that had collapsed into the tepid waters. As we approached the beach, a wild-looking man appeared between the palms, clutching a machete. His hair was matted, and his face crazed. My heart started pounding. He stared at us before disappearing again into the forest. I felt uncomfortable and unwelcome. Who was this scary-looking man?

I was surprised to see other people here at all. Dotted across the bay were dozens of yachts with their sun-bleached, tattered sails and barnacle-encrusted hulls. What was all this talk of closed islands? I was confused. Who were all these people and what were they doing here, making my epic adventure seem like a trip to Brighton marina?

The boat pulled up to the beach and I jumped into the shallow, warm water. I sighed with contentment. This might not have been Diego Garcia, but I had made it to the British Indian Ocean Territories. Next off the boat was Jeff, his video camera already recording as he provided a running commentary. He leapt on to the beach. Ted and Charles clapped. Then Ted jumped. Charles was the last to jump. He held his arms aloft, swung them theatrically and counted down: 3, 2, 1. He leapt into the air, landing on the white sand with his arms aloft. 'Two hundred and sixty-five,' he announced to the sky. There followed much back-slapping and congratulating, before the important process of 'documentation' began.

Photographic evidence was essential to prove that we had arrived in the British Indian Ocean Territories. To help with this Ted had brought a banner he'd had specifically painted in Egypt.

TRAVELLERS' CENTURY CLUB

BIOT – JULY 2002

While the banner was a triumph, the *Times* newspaper I was asked to hold up made me feel more like a hostage. Worst of all though, I couldn't help but wonder what had stopped them doing this back in the Maldives, where there were literally thousands of deserted beaches identical to this one. I kept my thoughts to myself and went along with the rituals.

Once finished I was free to explore the rest of the abandoned island. Next to the beach was a sign, 'WELCOME TO THE BRITISH INDIAN OCEAN TERRITORIES', below which were listed a number of local environmental laws, including the illegality of eating crabs or molluscs. It also asked visitors to 'respect the islands'. It was signed by order of the British Representative and seemed a touch hypocritical given the islands' recent history.

The sign was nailed to a crumbling old building, that looked out on to the turquoise waters. Above the door were two plastic spoons and a small sign, 'BY ORDER OF THE FORK'. Inside was a clutter of plastic chairs, a distress signal, a rubbish bin with the words 'KEEP DIEGO GARCIA CLEAN', and a number of newspapers and magazines, including an eighties copy of the *Sunday Times* and a slightly more contemporary *Express* magazine dated 1992. Also in this basket of papers were several books: the Koran and three Mills and Boons. They looked awkward huddled together so I slipped my old copy of the *Times* between them.

Railway tracks led from this dilapidated building. They had once been used for taking oil drums down to the now crumbling pier. Old lighters were still drawn up on the beach, as were harnesses for mules, which had once helped drag the trucks down to the loading-stage. Where St Helena had relied on flax for her economy, Tristan da Cunha on her lobsters, and Pitcairn on her stamps, BIOT had survived on the coconuts that blanketed the islands. They were exploited not for their sweet milk or even for Bounty bars, but for their rich oil that lit the street lamps of Mauritius and the Seychelles.

The copra-crushing mill, with its rusting cog wheels and its pock-marked boilers and hardwood pestle and mortars where the coconuts had been pressed, was in surprisingly good condition considering it had been abandoned and derelict for more than thirty years.

Shortly after the US–UK agreement in 1966, the British government bought the Chagos Agalego Oil Company for £1 million. They then closed it down in an attempt to cut off the islanders' employment so as to drive them from the island, before they tried the more direct route eventually taken.

'Hi,' came a cheery voice from behind the furnace. I was beginning to wonder whether I had contracted some tropical hallucinogenic illness, when a woman with a broad hat, unfeasibly large Jackie O sunglasses and a pizza appeared. 'I'm Carolyn, we saw you arrive this morning,' she continued with a soft Scots accent. She must have caught me staring at her hands. 'Tuesday is pizza day,' she explained holding it up proudly, 'the furnace makes an excellent oven.'

Carolyn was from St Andrews in Scotland. She had been living aboard her yacht in the atoll for eight months with her American companion, Glen.

Glen, I discovered, had his own Tuesday duties. While his partner was busy whipping up an unlikely pizza, Glen was busy with the weekly washing. The resourceful Robinsons had transformed a contaminated water well in the disused copra factory into a launderette. A washing-line marked the location with its patchwork of underwear and G-strings fluttering incongruously in the wind.

Glen and Carolyn had been to BIOT three times, but had been at sea for seventeen years, twelve of which had been spent with Arthur the cat, whom they dressed, rather strangely, in a cravat. I was intrigued to see pets here. One of the stories about the islands that had only just been made public, and had created more of a stir in the press than the forced expulsion of their inhabitants, was the way in which the pet dogs the islanders left behind were dealt with.

Before the islands could be handed over to the Americans, the British army had one last task to complete. Marcel Moulinie, the former UK-appointed official who managed the islands, had been ordered by BIOT commissioner Sir Bruce Greatbatch to complete the 'cleansing' of the islands by destroying more than 800 pet dogs that had been left behind by the islanders in their hasty departure.

Mr Moulinie claimed that he 'found the idea repugnant', but that he 'had to follow orders'. US sharpshooters were called in, but there were simply too many dogs. Poisoned meat was used, but this too was deemed to be too arduous and time-consuming, and thus it was decided to convert a copra-drying-room into a dog gas chamber.

'I first made the building secure, and then introduced into it pipes attached to the exhaust pipes of US military vehicles,' admitted Mr Moulinie in a writ. The dogs were then herded into the makeshift chamber and slowly asphyxiated.

The government of the United States was informed of the fact by diplomatic telegram, and before the day was finished a detachment of Seabees that had been hovering offshore, awaiting orders, landed with dozens of heavy earth-moving vehicles. The Ilios had become un-people, their dogs were dead, and the transformation of Diego Garcia could begin.

I asked Glen and Carolyn why they weren't on the other side of the lagoon with the other yachts. 'We prefer a little more privacy,' they giggled. Did they know anything about the history of the island? 'We've heard stories,' replied Carolyn. 'Did you know the islands are supposed to be haunted?' she continued. I asked her if she had ever seen anything. She hadn't. According to Gamini, our chef, the Chagos Islands are notorious for their ghosts. I changed tact and asked about Diego Garcia. 'Occasionally we hear B52s overhead on their way to Afghanistan.' Apart from that it was advisable to stay away, they warned.

Although the deserted settlement had long been suffocated by the vegetation which had all but choked the buildings, I had been surprised that the paths remained so clear. 'That's us,' they volunteered in proud unison, 'it's nice to put something back into the island rather than just taking from it.' I wasn't sure whether they were referring to the yachts on the other side of the lagoon or the British government.

I had always understood that Britain considered visitors to BIOT

Tristan da Cunha

Five days after setting out from Cape Town, Edinburgh, Tristan da Cunha's settlement appears off the ship's beam

Police Constable Conrad Glass heads out to act as immigration officer with some fellow Tristan da Cunhans

*A boatload of islanders aboard the 'Sandypoint Express'
head out to unload cargo from the RMS St Helena*

WELCOME
TO THE

TRISTAN DA CUNHA
SOUTH ATLANTIC

REMOTEST
ISLAND

*The sign used to read
'Welcome to the loneliest
Island', until the
islanders were advised
this made them sound a
little too 'sad'*

The house of Lewis and Yvonne Glass, my island home during my short visit. The 1961 lava flow stopped just short of their home

Welcome to
Nom... that
...pe t
...Rega...
...1
...ou
xx

The potato patches with the islanders, weekend 'huts/homes'

The settlement of Edinburgh, from atop the lava
flow from the 1961 eruption

Teeing off from the lawn of the residency building
during the drinks party

The 'Residency', the base soaring high above

*Administrator Bill Dickson and Governor David Hollamby
addressing the party assembled at the 'Residency'*

The island's only supermarket

Queen Victoria presides in one of the island's churches. Royal portraits are common on the islands

'Shark' fishing with the lads off Tristan da Cunha

Administrator Dickson prepares for our departure at the island's small harbour (notice his cleanly laundered Thomas Pink shirt!). Conrad Glass in background. Bill's girlfriend in matching pink trousers.

Gough Island. The meteorological station with the six South African scientists can be made out through the gloom

British Indian Ocean Territories

Île du Sel, Salomon Islands

KEEP
DIEGO GARCIA
CLEAN

TRASH CONTAINER

The old graveyard Île Boddam

Île Boddam
Salomon Islands
BIOT

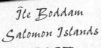

THIS WATER IS CONTAMINATED VISITORS DRINK THIS WATER AT THEIR OWN RISK. BOILING THE WATER FOR 30 MINUTES BEFORE DRINKING IS RECOMMENDED IN ANY CIRCUMSTANCES

BY ORDER OF THE BRIT REP

Sign on Île Fouquet

The French Oliver Twist asking for eggs

Wreck of the Lasquiti from Port Alberni British Columbia

Pierre, one of the BIOT 'travellers'

Andy from the Fisheries Patrol with

Filipino crew aboard their rig

British Indian
Ocean Territory

Zephyranthes rosea

60p

Île Fouquet

24P

Junonia villida

BRITISH INDIAN
OCEAN TERRITORY

the Traveler's Century Club (left to right)

Jeff Shea, Ted Cookson, Charles Veley

The Mauritius 2-pence coin found by Mohammed, dated 1963

Hidden paradise, Île Takamaka

Returning to the HMS Pacific Marlin

Remains of the Ilios Settlement on Île Boddam

A yacht in front of Île Fouquet

The Old Church in the settlement on Île Boddam

The Salomon atoll

St Helena

The RMS air taxi for
elderly passengers unable
to walk

The RMS St Helena anchored
off her island namesake

2P
25th Wedding Anniversary
St HELENA

Captain D.N.R. Roberts
requests the pleasure of the company of
MR B. FOGLE
in the Main Lounge

'Saintly' welcome for the RMS St Helena
with her royal cargo

HH Governor Hollamby with
HRH Princess Anne

Police parade in honour of Princess Anne
in front of the island's public library

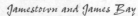
Jamestown and James Bay

Left to right – The Hon. Mr Justice Woodward QC;
The Hon. Mr Justice Appleby QC;
The Hon. Mr Justice Benson QC;
(aka: Bill, Dick and Brian). Jacob's ladder behind.

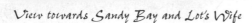

View towards Sandy Bay and Lot's Wife

Downtown Jamestown at rush hour

Jacob's ladder descending
to Jamestown

Colin Corker and his charabanc,
a 1929 Chevrolet

St Helena's Agriculture Fair at
Francis Plain

Radio St Helena's roving
reporters, covering the first
Royal visit in 20 years

Plantation House
(Governor's residence) and
Jonathon the Giant Tortoise

Napoleon's final resting place on St Helena,
Sare Valley. The body was removed from the tomb in
1840 and taken back to France, where it
remains at Les Invalides in Paris

STHE

The island's mist enveloped the interior. This is the road from Scotland to Longwood

The tricolour flies above Longwood House, Napoleon's home for most of his period of exile on St Helena. The house is now governed by the French

as a boil on their backside to be got rid of as quickly as possible, but Carolyn explained that their approach was less determined. 'They keep a close eye on us,' said Carolyn. 'And charge us $80,' added Glen. A week? 'For three months,' he said.

I was surprised to find such a relaxed policy, given America's stringent insistence on a 'fully sanitized' archipelago. Surely, international yachts free to come and go from all corners of the globe were more of a security risk than a community of islanders and their pets?

I left Carolyn and Glen to their chores and followed the sandy track past dozens of tumble-down buildings. I passed what appeared to be the old prison block, the roof long since collapsed.

In a clearing were the remains of the church. Although it was roofless, several of the stained-glass windows remained, as did a plaque with the date 1933. Opposite was another building with a wooden veranda on which still stood a dilapidated rocking-chair and an old bell. It felt strange walking around this deserted place. It now belonged to the ghosts of the Ilios, and I felt sure that, if I closed my eyes and listened, I would hear them.

Next to the church was a building in remarkably good condition, built in what looked like the French Colonial style. The shutters were closed. I lifted a catch and raised it up. A shaft of dusty light danced across the room and illuminated a graffiti scrawl: 'MAY YOUR HEART BE IN PARADISE'.

I walked around, wondering what it must have been like to live here. Someone had scribbled 'Chagos is the only true tropical paradise' on another wall.

Boddam was three quarters of a mile or so long. A sandy path meanders across the island, clearing a way through the thick forest of palms. I followed the path across the island until I came to the north shore. Waves crashed along a bed of coral that protected this exposed beach from the brunt of the open Indian Ocean. Flotsam and jetsam littered the beach.

A speckled light illuminated the island's interior, as the sun's rays bounced off the rich greenery, creating a mosaic of vibrant greens as rich as the ocean had been blue. It was only when my eyes had adjusted to the dim light that I noticed a man in the clearing. The same wild man who had emerged from the undergrowth earlier in the morning.

He was slashing a tree with his machete when I greeted him. 'Hi,' he replied sternly, with a barely discernible flick of the eyes. He continued chopping.

'I'm Ben,' I announced. He continued hacking at the fallen tree. Rivers of sweat cascaded down his bare back, soaking into the top of his oil-stained shorts.

At last he stopped, wiped his forehead with his grubby arm and offered me his sticky palm. 'Steve,' he said bluntly in a vaguely familiar accent.

'Where are you from?' I continued.

'The *Wanderer*,' he replied.

'I mean, where do you live?' I pried.

'The Ocean,' he smiled.

Steve no longer considered Hackney as home. He had lived on the seas for seventeen years, and now considered the ocean his watery home. I asked him why he had come to BIOT, to which he shrugged, 'Why not?'

Steve, it seemed, was in no mood for chatty chats. I left him to his chopping.

The path came to an abrupt finish in an area of dense vegetation. I was about to turn and return to the others when I noticed something man-made in the corner of my eye. I fought my way through the foliage and realized that I was in the island's cemetery. Thick moss and creepers clung to the tombs and headstones like a scene from a B-list horror film. Most of the inscriptions had been weathered beyond recognition, while others stood as a testament to the island's abandoned history. I wandered from stone to stone taking notes:

'ICI REPOSE HENRY CLARK le 13/7/31' read one headstone.

'RAOUL GABODHE Deceased 25 March 1952' read another.

It was pitiful to see the cemetery in such a decayed state. A garland of plastic flowers still clung to one headstone, and empty jars lay broken next to some of the graves as a reminder that mothers, fathers, grandfathers and even children had once been immortalized with fresh floral tributes.

Not normally spooked, I was unnerved by the utter silence here. No bird made a sound, and the surf of the ocean had been muffled by the thick forest of palms. I could hear my heart pounding. I apologized to each grave as I wandered around the cheerless place.

I bid my farewells, and set off back for the boat, saddened by the probability that this was as close as I was likely to get to the Ilios of Boddam.

In the absence of any postcard shops, I hoped to find a keepsake. I scoured the island, but was unable to find anything suitable until I noticed an old brick, half buried in the sand. I was thrilled to discover it was inscribed with the words 'COWEN – ENGLAND', and decided it would make a perfect if weighty memento.

Coco, Mohammed and Giyas were all waiting for me. Mohammed beamed. 'Mr Bean, look what I find.' He held out his clenched fist. I noticed how clean his nails were.

He unfurled his hand triumphantly to reveal a treasure of his own, a shiny bronze coin, nestled neatly in his coffee palm. The Queen's head glinted in the tropical sun. I took the coin from his hand and wiped away the sand. 'Queen Elizabeth II', read the back. I turned it over. It was a two-cent coin, clearly marked 'Mauritius' with the year '1963'. Now I am not normally prone to the green-eyed monster, but my eyes bulged, and my brain fizzed. I had walked through the dilapidated buildings and explored the overgrown graveyard, I had even found a brick, but a coin . . . The coin oozed history. I could practically hear it singing and giggling.

Mohammed was thrilled with his find. 'Where did you find it?' I asked, in the hope that I might find one.

'Over there,' he gestured messily. 'Coco has one too,' he said as an afterthought. Chef's teeth sparkled, as he waved the coin victoriously. My brick sitting heavily in my shorts was beginning to chaff.

Mohammed woke me early the next morning. 'Come quick, Mr Bean, we are being invaded.' On the deck Suriya and our international captain had their binoculars trained on the horizon. I could just make out the outline of a very large ship. So large in fact that she was unable to enter the bay.

We watched her for about half an hour, speculating about her 'mission', until a small orange speck appeared from her grey hulk and sped towards us. None of us said much but it felt exciting. Something was up.

The RIB was soon alongside the *Dream Voyager*. There were five men aboard. Four were in orange jump suits. The fifth wore a starched white naval uniform.

'Pull it together, lads,' screamed the officer, as his crew bungled the simple manoeuvre of pulling alongside. He was not a happy chap. He leapt aboard, clutching a briefcase and a scowl. 'Can I speak to –' He broke off mid-sentence as I appeared. 'Bloody hell,' he said trying to suppress a smile, 'long way from Scotland.'

'Can you stamp my passport?' squealed Charles, barely able to control his excitement, and with this the smile was gone from the officer's sunburnt face. Here we go, I thought, the lecture about the high sensitivity of the area and the importance of national security. 'Don't you know there's a war going on?' I could hear him saying.

'"Please" would be nice,' he said. Charles nearly kissed him.

The mood had lifted and our international captain came out with his paperwork. It was only then that I spotted the bucket of vegetation on the deck.

I had noticed cook collecting buckets of plants from around the deserted village the previous day. He didn't recognize them from the Maldives and wanted to take them home to plant in his garden. I knew this wasn't right but I had to think of my stomach. He was the chef and I still had an indeterminable number of feeding days left. If I upset him by challenging this environmental smuggling I risked eating 'spiked' food for the rest of the journey. I wasn't the flora police.

The bucket of greenery had been left on the deck in full view of Andy. 'Shit,' I murmured as he introduced himself to the captain, asking if there was anything 'illegal' aboard.

Andy was the senior fisheries protection officer, and he was responsible for patrolling BIOT waters. As well as fishing-vessels, he was also responsible for all private boats entering UK waters. He was accountable to the British representative on Diego Garcia, Commander Adam Peters.

Although there are many star-spangled banners on Diego Garcia, it is the Union Flag that flies the highest. The British Indian Ocean Territories are still a Crown colony, or overseas territory. The most senior inhabitant on Diego is the royal naval commander. The 4,000 American servicemen who are currently based there obey Her Majesty's laws, which are upheld by the island commissioner. He is helped by several dozen Royal Marines, a handful of Scotland Yard policemen and Andy.

Andy was from Ullapool in Scotland, but he had spent the last four years on fisheries patrol in the South Atlantic, patrolling the waters around the Falklands and South Georgia. He had been in the Indian Ocean for only a month. His new role included patrolling the waters around BIOT aboard HMS *Pacific Marlin*, with his Filipino crew, looking for illegal long-line fishing-boats and keeping an eye on the yachts at Boddam.

Andy was suffering from the climatic change brought about by moving to the tropics, and his pale Scots skin was red raw. To add to his misery he had just given up cigarettes and caffeine. Andy was a time bomb waiting to explode, and I wasn't prepared to be locked up with terrorists on suspicion of smuggling garden grass. I decided to take action, and while Andy went through the paperwork, I crept out on to the deck and dumped the foliage overboard.

One of the Filipino crew caught me red-handed. He grinned, and blushing I hurried back inside hoping he wouldn't tell. Formalities completed, I asked Andy about the other yachts. 'Vagrants,' he hissed, 'most of them have no environmental conscience whatsoever.' I tried to hide my blushing as he explained how they were trying to discourage visitors to the islands. Apart from Diego's 'security level', Britain was still embarrassed about its handling of the Ilios. It certainly had good reason to be.

'We don't like to encourage visitors to BIOT,' said Andy

stepping back into the RIB. 'Be good,' he smiled. I caught his frown as they pulled away on a floating bed of grasses. I smiled innocently as they disappeared back to their ship.

With the excitement of the morning over, we decided to explore these 'itinerants' anchored across the bay at Île Fouquet. It struck me as strange that these yachts should choose to anchor so near to one another. Surely the idea was to get away from it all?

We glided across the calm waters that sparkled like a bed of diamonds. As we reached the far side of the lagoon, Mohammed spotted something close to the shore. 'Bobbies,' cried Mohammed to Giyas at the helm. The engines shuddered angrily as Giyas threw them in to reverse. The anchor chain roared from its housing as it plummeted to the seabed below.

We came to a halt. Just fifty feet in front, two masts protruded from the tropical blue waters. Halyards and ropes dipped into the calm waters, below which was the dark outline of a hull. Mohammed was beside himself. Apart from the fact that we had nearly joined the boat in her watery grave, his mind had turned to treasure. I had never seen a wreck either and jumped eagerly into the tender to take a closer look.

The hull was just a few feet under the surface. On the side of it were the words 'LASQUITI, PORT ALBERNI, B.C.' While I contemplated the inescapable sadness of a drowned ship, Mohammed was already diving through the submerged hatch.

I suckered a snorkel and mask to my face and followed him into the warm waters. It was quite extraordinary. She was wedged between two bobbies, her side scarred with a huge gash. Her windows were cluttered with packets of Kool Aid, postcards and books.

Mohammed returned from her belly with a screwdriver in his mouth. 'They leave everything,' he spluttered in astonishment, 'take a look, Mr Bean.' I took a breath and dived down towards the hatch. Hundreds of brightly coloured fish darted past my mask, as I peered into her cabin. The floor was scattered with playing cards and videos. A computer lay on its side.

★

Our arrival in the Chagos had caused quite a stir. New yachts meant fresh food and it wasn't long before the *Dream Voyager* was surrounded by grubby little dinghies.

'I don't suppose you have any spare vegetables,' pleaded a middle-aged Italian man.

'Can we buy some diesel from you,' asked a German.

A young boy with a shaven head and a scrawny body appeared at the ship's railings. 'Please, sir, can we 'ave some eggs.' It was a French Oliver Twist.

For the crew this was their first experience of 'Western beggars'. After all, they lived in a 'honeymoon' land, where most newly-weds threw away their financial inhibitions with their clothes.

I watched them confer and debate on this unpredicted scenario. Chef insisted that our food stores had been carefully planned, and that we had to retain a surplus in case we were storm-bound. After much deliberation, he was dispatched to the galley. He appeared several minutes later with several dozen eggs, which he begrudgingly presented to our little Oliver Twist.

'For the children,' insisted the big-hearted Mohammed, with tears in hs eyes.

The young boy's face lit up as he carefully packed the eggs into his wicker hamper, and set off home as if this were a normal run to the shops.

It was during this little impromptu shopping party that disaster struck. A French family diving near the wreck of the *Lasquiti* had disturbed a shark. The family were able to swim ashore, but their father was unable to escape its angry mood.

He tried to swim for their small dinghy but the shark was too quick for him. It circled him several times before lunging at him with its razor-sharp teeth, tearing at his right arm. He struggled to beat the shark off his weary body, one arm hugging the inflatable boat, the other flailing wildly at the furious fish. Bleeding, he managed to punch the shark away before dragging himself into the safety of his dinghy.

I had seen the reef sharks patrolling the shoreline as I explored the island, but had been reassured by Mohammed that they are docile creatures that rarely attack humans. Besides, I had thought at the time, how many humans do they come into contact with in this remote archipelago?

Word of the attack soon reached the *Dream Voyager*, and the little gathering quickly dispersed as a rescue party of dinghies was dispatched.

'I go to the *Daisy* for the stitcher's 'elp,' called Pierre, as he leapt over the railing into his boat.

The 'stitcher' turned out to be an Italian seamer, who doubled as a pseudo-doctor for the floating castaways.

Luckily the shark hadn't taken a memento from the Frenchman. It had bitten into his arm and quickly released him, leaving a relatively clean wound for the stitcher to stitch.

The drama had caused quite a stir within the floating community, and Pierre soon returned to announce the injured man was recovering nicely with the aid of a bottle of whisky. Pierre was a Frenchman who had appeared in search of tobacco. He looked like a Gallic Mick Jagger, with a mop of thick, brown, shoulder-length hair that tumbled across his face, and his humungoidle shades. His body was sinewy, his skin a leathery hide from the relentless tropical sunshine that had turned mine a ketchup red.

'I think 'e was fishing,' explained Pierre as he dragged on a cigarette.

'But he was in the water,' I interrupted.

'Exactly,' he smiled, ''e was probably 'arpoon fishing' – a technique strictly banned in BIOT.

I was desperate to find out about the wrecked *Lasquiti*, and Pierre told me the story of what happened over a steaming cup of Earl Grey and a roll-up. He told me that the *Lasquiti* had gone down just two days before. The wind had shifted and the yachts had swung, their anchors dragging across the sandy bottom. While most had been safely pacified, the *Lasquiti* had continued to drag. The coral mountain tore into her side. Water poured into the cabin, and within minutes she had disappeared beneath the moonlit waters. The 'nomads' had rallied together and her Canadian crew had been safely rescued. While they hadn't had time to salvage anything, it was the loss of one particular item that had particularly upset them. Their pet rat. The wreck had been searched without success, although there was speculation that Willy had made it ashore.

The family had set up a Robinson Crusoe camp on shore, where they intended to remain until a salvage ship could be brought from Sri Lanka. From their hammocks they had a clear view of the two masts protruding from the water like giant chopsticks, a marker of the *Lasquiti*'s shallow grave.

We had spotted their little makeshift camp earlier in the day while we were exploring the shoreline. I had noticed a trunk with the Canadian flag and several plastic deckchairs around a smouldering camp fire, but the 'Crusoes' had seemed timid and we had left them alone.

Pierre explained that most of the yachts had been coming to Boddam for years, and that many stayed for more than a year at a time. They were organic hedonists, or 'ocean' people, as Steve had called himself. They lived by the sun, moon and tides, and their existence in BIOT was burdened by little more than the need to swap sides of the lagoon according to the season and the prevailing winds. Although these 'ocean' people considered this their own secret paradise, Pierre told me that at times there had been more than a hundred yachts anchored in 'paradise'.

I asked about the other yachts. Were they escapists too? 'There is all sorts 'ere, French, Germany, Italian, Briteesh, American . . . we are international, but we 'ave the same principles.' I asked him what they were, and once again he gestured around him. 'Life,' he winked. I wasn't quite sure what he meant. I'm not even sure he did himself, although it sounded Gallic and enigmatic as intended.

Although Andy had dismissed them as vagrants, they appeared to be an enormously resourceful community. Their yachts may have looked like tramps' shopping-trolleys with their sun-bleached tarpaulins, and jerry cans of fresh water that lined the decks, but this was a simple case of practicality over aesthetics. While almost all the boats seemed to have their own vegetable and herb gardens, one yacht had gone a step further, converting the foredeck into a chicken run.

What impressed me most was the community spirit that existed among these floating misfits. A temporary school had been started for the fifteen children living among the yachts, two of whom had been conceived and born in the islands – their names, Diego and Garcia.

Pierre explained how they often held beach parties, and that they never missed sundowners on the beach. One couple had even married in the dilapidated church. A temporary roof of palm fronds had been constructed and the church had been filled with night lights. The congregation had worn their Sunday best – shorts and tie – while Pierre had been volunteered priest, with a dog collar painted on to his neck.

Pierre had lived in the floating village with his daughter and dog for six months. He explained that he had tired of life's 'conformity' and had set out to find paradise. Had he found it, I asked. 'Is a good life 'ere,' he said with his heavy French accent, 'no one telling you what to do. Look at it,' he gestured, 'is paradise, no?' He looked at me for confirmation.

It was indeed paradise. In fact they were every bit the model island utopia, but there was something missing: the Ilios. They haunted these islands, like restless ghosts. The sun was red with their anger, the sea salty with their tears. Sorrow seemed to emanate from every corner. The spirit of the Ilios was still too raw for me and paradise couldn't exist in such a state.

The Ilios people had been shocked that the government of the United Kingdom could turn on its own people and neglect them. They had been proud of their heritage. Indeed, early visitors to BIOT described the islanders 'with their Union Jacks', and explained how they had been welcomed with a rather ragged version of the British national anthem, sung in English with 'heavy French accents'.

The islanders believed that they had been abandoned because they were the black descendants of slaves from Africa. The majority of the Ilios families had been living on their home island since the early nineteenth century, having originally come from India,

Madagascar, Mauritius and Mozambique to become fishermen and farmers, and to work in the copra plantations.

The fate of the Ilios was largely overshadowed by events elsewhere in the world, but their cause was championed in the UK by the Labour MP Tam Dalyell. In Mauritius, one of the evictees, Mr Olivier Bancoult, made the claim that the ordinance statement, under article 4, that 'no person shall enter the territory or, being in the territory, shall be present or remain in the territory, unless he is in possession of a permit or his name is endorsed by a permit' effectively implied that a person could be expelled from their own country for no reason, and it proved to Mr Bancoult that the ordinance was both unfair and illegal.

He took the case to the High Court in 2000, where it was fought by a noted South African barrister and civil rights campaigner, Sir Sydney Kentridge. Few thought the case would get very far, and indeed the Foreign Office argued that the case should be heard by the Supreme Court rather than the High Court. However, the case went ahead, and on 3 November 2000 Lord Justice Laws and Mr Justice Gibbs reached an astonishing verdict. Citing the Magna Carta and its provisions about the illegality of deporting any man from his own home, the court was unanimous in its verdict, and it was decided that article 4 of the BIOT ordinance should be quashed and that, by law, Mr Bancoult and the other islanders should be allowed home.

Naturally this was an enormous embarrassment for the British government, and then the foreign secretary, Robin Cook, announced that the government would not appeal against the ruling. Later that same day, the Foreign Office published a new ordinance which confined the banning order to Diego Garcia alone. The islanders would finally be allowed home. Except for the small problem of that British–American agreement for a fully 'sanitized' archipelago.

A group of Ilios had visited the archipelago shortly after the 2000 court ruling, to assess the practicality and viability of their return. Andy had spent days dismantling volleyball nets and al fresco dining-room tables that had been built by visiting yachties over the years. Although BIOT law forbids people from sleeping ashore, it hadn't stopped them building their very own little driftwood village. These floating nomads had essentially filled the vacuum left by the forcibly exiled Ilios.

A team of scientists from the UK had also been dispatched to study the feasibility of the community's return. I had noticed the boreholes across the island that had been used to study water levels. According to the results, the water table was far too low to sustain so many people. Perhaps unsurprisingly, they concluded that their return was environmentally impossible. Lobbyists had pointed out the high number of palms that were 'drinking the island dry', and argued that to reduce the number of trees by half would raise the water table the same amount.

Tam Dalyell, who has spent the last thirty years campaigning for the islanders' liberties and rights as British nationals to live on the islands, has been rewarded for his commendable and relentless political battle on behalf of the 'landless' Ilios by having an island named after him. Île Tam Dalyell now shares the same archipelago as Île Pierre, Île des Rats and Danger Island. The heavy British–Gallic influence is happily enhanced.

The Ilios are still awaiting an opportunity to return to Boddam. An advanced party had been due to arrive the same week we were there, but their application to visit had been refused by the FCO at the eleventh hour 'for security reasons'. According to the most recent reports, the Ilios are now suing the USA for $12 billion. In the meantime, the islands remain both one of the largest US military airbases in the world and the hidden oasis for a floating community of nomads.

Diego Garcia was tantalizingly close, just a few hundred miles south. I could practically smell the McDonalds. The international captain had been unimpressed with my suggestion of a little detour. 'Are you mad?' he had replied, eyes bulging with incredulity. Andy, the fisheries patrol officer, had been equally dismissive, laughing out loud at my idea.

The others had also haw-hawed it. They had achieved their goal.

The British Indian Ocean Territories had been well and truly TICKED, and satellite phones were already buzzing with their new fixtures.

This was my last opportunity to get to Diego Garcia. If Winchester could do it then so could I. The problem was that Winchester had the cooperation and support of his skipper – I was on my own.

There was only one way of getting to Diego, I concluded, and that was as a casualty. I had seen it in the films. All I had to do was feign injury or illness and we would be granted permission to land. It seemed simple enough, but what happened when they discovered I wasn't really sick at all? I wasn't sure how that worked in the films, and while I was prepared for myself to be arrested, I was concerned about the rest of the crew.

I would have to injure myself for real, and after a full bodily appraisal I decided that the only part of my anatomy that didn't seem particularly useful was my little finger. This wasn't going to be an easy task for someone who once fainted from a gerbil bite. I couldn't even give myself a paper cut, let alone a wound that would necessitate a dangerous detour to Diego Garcia's ER unit.

'For the book,' I said as I swung my cabin door closed on to my little pinky. A dark hand shot out from the corridor, catching the door millimetres from impact. Images of Diego Garcia faded as Mohammed's head appeared around the corner. 'Careful, Mr Bean, you could cause yourself an injury,' he smiled.

As we sailed out of the lagoon, the young French boy appeared bouncing across our bow wave in his small dinghy. He was waving frantically. 'I 'ave a gift,' he hollered, holding up his small wicker basket.

Mohammed and Chef helped him aboard and he handed them the gift wrapped in old newspaper. 'For the eggs,' he smiled before disappearing down the rope ladder. Incredulity turned to disappointment as they unwrapped their reward – it was a bottle of whisky, forbidden under their religion.

The British Indian Ocean Territories are one of the most beautiful places I have ever visited. I had been mesmerized by the virginal beauty of her unspoilt beaches, rich lagoons bursting with sea life and her fresh air unpolluted by fumes or noise. There can be few such idyllic places in the world that have been left unharmed by man, but that is what made BIOT all the more poignant.

A thriving people once lived here, working the earth and enjoying *their* land. They worked in the little copra factory and played cards in their comfortable thatched houses, they drank in the little bars and the children were taught in the small school, they tended their gardens and their livestock and made plans for the future. I had been impressed by the initiative and resourcefulness of the floating community that had filled the void and horrified at the prospect of B52 bombers setting off from this peaceful island chain on their way to drop another payload on to another shell-shocked population. 'You know they've got nuclear bombs there,' explained Tam Dalyell on the phone when I called to ask him about the present situation with BIOT.

The British Indian Ocean Territories may look like paradise but for the Ilios they are a paradise lost.

3. St Helena

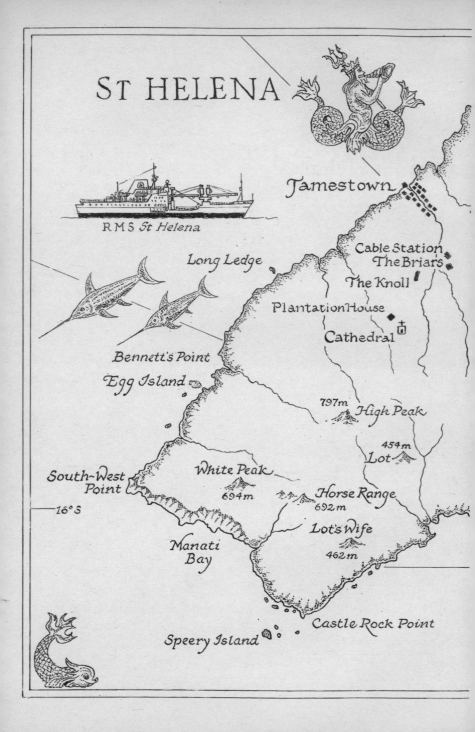

St Helena

Jamestown

RMS *St Helena*

Long Ledge

Cable Station
The Briars

The Knoll

Plantation House

Cathedral

Bennett's Point

Egg Island

797m   High Peak

454m
Lot

White Peak

South-West
Point

694m

16° S

Horse Range
692m

Lot's Wife

Manati
Bay

462m

Castle Rock Point

Speery Island

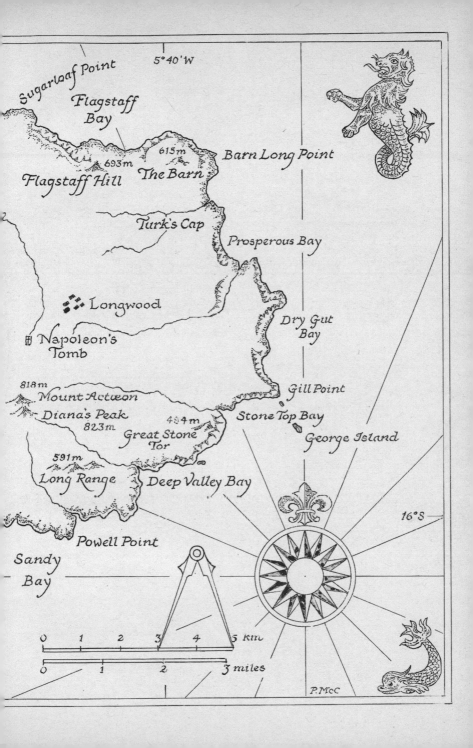

A flotilla of boats joined us in the bay, as thousands of people lined the quay, waving and cheering. The jetty was swathed in bunting and a troop of flags stood to attention in the stiff afternoon breeze. In the distance I could hear the boom of a band. The excitement was contagious, and a grin draped itself across my sunburnt face.

A special VIP launch had been laid on, and I would be among the first to leave the ship. The governor arrived looking splendid in his starch-white uniform with his extravagant plume of feathers that gave him the look of a strutting peacock.

The launch *Wideawake* pulled alongside our ship, and within minutes we were weaving between boatloads of waving well-wishers. Fishing-vessels sounded their horns as we crashed across the Atlantic surf towards the shore and the various dignitaries that awaited us.

Camera bulbs flashed as I stepped ashore. I felt like royalty as I strode along the promenade to the accompaniment of a marching band.

'Excuse me, sir, would you mind staying there.' A burly British policeman pushed me to one side with his elbow, holding his other hand to his earpiece.

Soon a gaggle of giggling schoolgirls arrived, weaving between my legs and jabbing me with the sticks of their Union Flags as they fought for a better vantage point. A woman with a camcorder poked me in the side, and with one quick manoeuvre slipped in front of me, further obscuring my view and pushing me even further back. The crowd shifted like a running tide, and before I knew it I had been dislodged to the very periphery like the runt of the litter.

I caught a glimpse of a pick-up truck as it sped past. It was loaded with a number of cases, including a tatty old blue school trunk, on the side of which, embossed in peeling gold, were the words 'Her Royal Highness Princess Anne'.

I had arrived on the island of St Helena, a far-flung outpost of the United Kingdom in the South Atlantic, at the same time as the island's first royal visitor for nearly twenty years. Princess Anne was visiting as part of the island's quincentenary celebrations.

The island was first recorded five hundred years ago by a Portuguese admiral, João de Nova, who discovered the island on 21 May 1502 while returning from a victory in India. He named it in honour of St Helena, the mother of Emperor Constantine, and claimed it in the name of the King of Portugal.

The Portuguese realized the geographical significance of the island, between the Cape of Good Hope and the Cape Verde islands and it became a regular calling-point for ships to replenish and resupply. Somehow they managed to keep the existence of the island a secret for eighty years, until an English explorer named Captain Cavendish landed on the island in 1588.

The secret of the island was out and the Portuguese took the decision to abandon her for fear of piracy and looting from British and Dutch privateers. The East India Company took possession of the island under a charter from Richard Cromwell to occupy and colonize any Portuguese possessions, and in 1659 Captain Dutton, with his wife, was ordered to the island as St Helena's first governor. A castle was built and the settlement named Jamestown, after the Duke of York, who later became King James II.

The island struggled to maintain its non-indigenous population but a shortage of food in 1671 led to a mutiny, during which Governor Cony was imprisoned before being shipped back to England. The following year, the Dutch successfully captured St Helena in a bloodless victory. The new governor and his people escaped for Brazil.

The occupation was short-lived as the British sent a 'task force' and retook the island. Unrest continued with further mutinies in 1684 and 1693. Times continued to be turbulent. In 1694 a plot was sabotaged in which the island's black slaves had conspired to kill every white man on the island. In 1706 the French arrived and stole two ships from the harbour. The Christmas Mutiny of 1783 occurred after Governor Hutchinson banned alcohol from the island.

St Helena is not easily accessible as it has no airport and the nearest mainland is Angola, nearly 1,200 miles to the east. Brazil lies 1,800 miles to the west. Situated at 5°43' west and 15°56' south, St Helena's nearest land is Ascension Island, another British possession located 703 miles to the north-west. The only way of getting to the island is aboard her namesake, the RMS *St Helena*, which ploughs the Atlantic between Dorset and Cape Town six times a year, stopping at Ascension and St Helena.

I had sailed from Ascension Island on the same two-day voyage as the Princess. In fact I had travelled with her all the way from Brize Norton in Oxfordshire, whence we had both caught the RAF Tristar to Ascension, though I had spotted her just once aboard the ship, during bingo.

On the RAF flight she had been secreted in the front of the plane away from prying eyes and shielded by a camouflage blanket, behind which the captain warned us not to peek, in case we caught a glimpse of the Queen's daughter sleeping.

The royals had once travelled the world aboard the luxury of HMY *Britannia*. In fact, the Princess's father, the Duke of Edinburgh, had visited St Helena in 1957 during a round-the-world tour aboard *Britannia*. During my Royal Naval Reserve days I had been the officer of the watch aboard HMS *Blazer* for HMY *Britannia*'s final voyage into Portsmouth harbour. Thousands of well-wishers had lined the harbour front cheering us along. *Blazer* had been the lead ship and under my watch I was responsible for navigating her into the harbour.

Princess Anne had openly shed a tear that day as her family's floating pile had been decommissioned. I had to wonder now whether the tear was one of genuine sorrow or for the prospect that future travels would include bingo with the *hoi polloi*, and hiding behind camouflage blankets on air force transport planes.

She had been a 'good sport' during the bingo. She had appeared dressed in khaki, with a baseball cap pulled low over her head, her bun sticking through the hole at the back, and sat flanked by her two Met bodyguards in the small lounge while the numbers were called out. I couldn't imagine them playing at Buckingham Palace.

The Princess had of course been seated at the captain's table. Princess Anne's dinner companions had been issued with a strict code of social etiquette, one of which implored them not to ask her any 'direct questions'. Quite what that meant had been the subject of some debate, and it had been concluded that as long as you started every question with, 'My friend Harry was wondering . . .' then it would be 'indirect' and therefore perfectly acceptable – 'My friend Kevin wanted to know if it's true your dog is a killer?' So on and so forth.

One Scottish couple, the Bolloxes, wouldn't have to worry about royal protocol. They had been asked if they would like to join the princess at the captain's table. It transpired that the couple were staunch anti-monarchists – 'Would we f***,' they had cried in disgust.

I had spotted her bodyguards before I noticed the princess. Their chinos, ties and blue blazers at odds with the T-shirt-and-shorts-wearing passengers. Only towards the end of the voyage did they relax into chinos and polo shirts.

What had struck me as particularly strange were the bum bags they insisted on wearing. I had spotted one of them unzipping his out on the deck one evening. He had pulled out a very impressive James Bond-style satellite phone, not much larger than a mobile phone, but it was the other piece of 'hardware' that caught my attention: a shiny little gun.

Although the royals' bodyguards rarely travel armed, they had been particularly twitchy about the princess visiting a place that they had been unable to recce. They had therefore decided to take advantage of travelling with the RAF and within UK 'waters' and had chosen to travel armed. I made a mental note not to tease them about their stuffy appearance.

I had been amazed by the scale of St Helena when her silhouette first appeared on the horizon. She appeared vast, much bigger than I had expected. Her cliffs, sheer, soared into the low cloud cover. Her coastline was jagged, headlands ripping into the rough surf. Waves crashed against her rock face, sending plumes of spray hundreds of feet into the air. St Helena appeared impenetrable, a fortress in the South Atlantic, which of course is exactly what she had been to her most famous 'castaway', Napoleon Bonaparte.

The period of St Helena's history with which most people are familiar began on 15 October 1815. It was on this day that HMS *Northumberland* rolled into town with arguably the most famous prisoner of all time, Napoleon.

Islands, by the very nature of their geography, have consistently made secure prisons. From Alcatraz and Robben Island to Devil's Island, they all evoke powerful images. We sometimes called Taransay 'HMP Taransay'. St Helena's remoteness and isolation were deemed to make it a perfect place in which to incarcerate the scourge of Britain.

Napoleon brought with him a period of prosperity to St Helena. The population of the island rose from about 6,000 to more than 8,000. To limit the chances of Napoleon's escape, the island's governor implemented strict rules and regulations. Curfews were rigorously enforced, and even fishing-boats were subject to severe restrictions.

On the day of Napoleon's arrival, there was a huge crowd of people waiting at the wharf to meet this 'celebrity' visitor. To avoid this unwanted attention, it was decided to bring him ashore after dusk, when Jamestown would normally be deserted. However, the curious onlookers remained, and armed soldiers were required to force passage through the crowd with their torch-flames.

It must have been a miserable prospect to be marooned on this rocky outpost for a man who once had the world at his fingertips. I used to imagine him kneeling in front of his map of the world, wondering where next to conquer, moving his little metal soldiers around. I doubt he had ever noticed tiny St Helena.

Apparently Napoleon grabbed an eyeglass as he first approached the island. He peered at the bleak island and turned to the man standing next to him, remarking dryly, 'It is not a pretty place to live. I would have done better to stay in Egypt.'

I could have repeated his sentiments. St Helena certainly wasn't a looker from the ocean. What had happened to the lush green valleys and forests of pine that I had been promised? From the deck of the RMS she looked like a huge ugly blob of rock in a very cross sea.

It had been an impressive welcome by nearly half the islanders. The arrival of the RMS is always a big event on the island. Her return from Dorset had taken six weeks. I waded my way through the gathered throng. I wondered whether the islanders had waved Union Flags for Napoleon's arrival – or even for Jimmy Saville, for that matter, who was the last 'celebrity' to visit the island just a month ago aboard the *QE2*, much to the islanders' excitement.

St Helena's main town, Jamestown, is neatly nestled in a long barren valley that runs down to the water's edge at James Bay. The town is dominated by two severe cliffs; the town has periodically been the victim of rock falls starting from them. I was struck by how arid the valley appeared. There were no trees and the slopes were streaked with scars from previous falls.

Midway up the cliff was Jamestown's very own version of the Hollywood sign in Los Angeles; painted on the rock in huge white letters were the words 'WELCOME PRINCE ANDREW'. This giant piece of confused graffiti dominated the town. Had the islanders been misinformed? I later learned that it had been on the cliff for nearly twenty years, since the Prince's visit in 1984.

It was during Prince Andrew's visit to St Helena that the then governor provided one of the richest minor moments in British television. Dressed in his white uniform, with his sword and plumed hat, he went to clasp Prince Andrew's hand as the prince jumped ashore. Unfortunately, he descended a step too far. His foot kissed the slime and he slipped into the South Atlantic, in front of his royal guest and the world's media. The present governor, Hollamby, had made a conscious effort to avoid a repeat performance and I imagined a team of Saints busily sweeping and scrubbing the steps free of gunge before our arrival.

Governor Hollamby had tried to persuade the Saints to paint a new welcome sign for Princess Anne, but they had refused, as a statement of their frustration at the citizenship débâcle of the 1990s. She could visit their island and they would welcome her, but there would be no new graffiti.

The citizenship issue is a hot potato on St Helena. Margaret Thatcher's introduction of the British Nationality Act in January 1983 stripped the Saints of their rights to British citizenship. The islanders were asked to surrender the passports that had been rightfully theirs since the Royal Charter of 1673. The Act was passed to prevent an influx of immigrants before the handover of Hong Kong to China. When the RMS *St Helena* and her Saint crew had returned from service in the Falklands War, the islanders had been outraged to learn that the Falklands were exempt from this Act, but St Helena was not. Through the Act the St Helenians lost the right to live and work in the UK, effectively making them prisoners on their own island.

Families were forced to supplement their income from the island's weak economy, where GDP is just £2,500 per year, and island prices are high as a result of import and shipping costs. While the Falklands conflict filled a gap in the Saints' economy, providing work opportunities on both the Falklands and Ascension Island, Saints were unable to work in their 'mother' country, the UK, because of their 'non-British' status. It has been estimated that £1,500 per year flows into the island economy for every person employed offshore. Finally, after years of campaigning, British citizenship was returned to the islanders in July 2002, in the form of a spanking new burgundy passport.

St Helena's harbour consists of a sturdy sea wall built along the side of a steep cliff, though the incessant surf means that ships are unable to moor alongside but must anchor in James Bay, before unloading their cargo on to a special launch designed to ferry containers back and forth. Passengers embark and disembark the same way, on a special passenger ferry, the *Wideawake*, although there is an alternative, the 'air taxi'.

The air taxi, I hasten to add, is not the smart sea plane I had at first imagined. In fact, it is a specially designed crate for passengers with walking difficulties. Passengers sit in the DIY crate which is then lowered over the side of the ship and on to a special launch, from which it is then winched by crane directly on to the wharf, thereby avoiding the hazardous obstacle course of ladders and slippery steps endured by most. It was a truly comical sight, half a dozen purple-rinsed perms blowing in the breeze, walking-sticks propped against the side, as the box of geriatrics was hoisted over the side of the RMS. It reminded me of a box of Quality Street.

The islanders had been preparing for this royal visit for months. Back in 1815 they had just two days' notice to prepare for Boney's arrival, and while they made plans for more permanent accommodation, it was agreed that he should stay in the house of Henry Porteous, on Main Street in Jamestown.

Jamestown itself has hardly changed since Napoleon arrived here nearly two hundred years ago, with its sea wall, the old gates, the castle and the botanical gardens, although the smart turquoise Olympic-size swimming pool probably wasn't there.

Main Street in Jamestown is the island's hub. The Georgian-façaded houses with their wooden porches and peeling paint gave the town the overall look of a film set. It reminded me of an American frontier town. I half expected to see John Wayne ride into town and tie his horse to one of the porches. The Consulate Hotel, with its colonial livery, and the Wellington Hotel, with its startling blue paintwork, dominated the street, also home to the post office, Cable and Wireless office, Spar supermarket and DIY store, and to a small clothes shop. Further along were the White Horse pub, Standard pub, bakery and all-important video library.

St Helena was the South Atlantic's very own little Cuba, though its fleets of sixties and seventies cars – Ford Anglias, Capris and Consuls, Morris Minors, old Minis, Austin Healys – lacked the glamour of their US counterparts. It was like stepping into a time warp. I was disappointed that peoples' clothes weren't similarly and wonderfully anachronistic.

As I wandered down the busy street, a woman with white-blonde hair and distinctly un-Saintly features came rushing up. 'Ben, isn't it?' she asked, slightly breathless from running. I nodded. 'My friends and I were wondering whether you would like to join us for a drink in Donny's,' she smiled.

Donny's, I had been told, was the place to be and be seen. Donny's was the China White's of St Helena. It is situated conveniently close to Customs, and I had been surprised to see so many returning Saints heading straight for the bar rather than for home. It was a simple affair, constructed from two ship's containers with part of their sides removed to create a bar. Plastic tables and chairs allowed drinkers a view of the RMS in James Bay, so they could keep an eye on the proceedings. Donny's only opened when the RMS *St Helena* was in town, which didn't seem like a great marketing policy when the ship visits only six times a year; but the ship was in and Donny's was buzzing.

Sally turned out to be a single mother from Brixton who had decided to move to St Helena on a whim. With her ten-year-old daughter she had upped sticks and come to live on the island for two years, and was working in social care.

Sally had wanted to bring her young daughter up in a crime-free environment, where she was free to grow up naturally, free of the vices of South London. Unfortunately for Sally, their island home had been burgled just a week after they arrived, and all of her daughter's toys and clothes had been stolen. As if that weren't enough, her daughter had also been subjected to racist bullying at school. For Sally and her daughter, St Helena had been tougher than Brixton.

Sally introduced me to Vanessa, a pretty blonde from Tanzania. She had trained in veterinary medicine at Edinburgh University and had come to St Helena on a six-month placement to help train up locals in basic veterinary needs. I had in fact met her a year before while on a writing assignment in Zambia.

She had come with her boyfriend, who I gathered had spent the six months bored rigid. He explained that he had seen every single film from the video library, and had been on every walk on the island.

'Hello,' boomed a rather large Saint wearing a T-shirt and extended his hand, 'Stedson,' he said.

'Er, no, it's a panama,' I responded, my confusion exacerbated by the beer that now swilled around in my sun-baked head.

'My name's Stedson,' he repeated. My blush ran into my sunburn.

Stedson, I soon learned, had been the assistant-butler to the Earl and Countess of Bradford at Weston Park. He had also lived in France as the butler to Comtesse de la Veldene at the Saint-Georges château. Stedson had the accent to match his credentials. He sounded like a cross between Prince Charles and Brian Sewell.

I was told that his favourite trick was to stand down on the wharf as a cruise ship ferried its passengers ashore. He would stand there in a ragged pair of jeans and tattered T-shirt looking every bit the stereotypical native, before scaring the lights out of the curious passengers by shouting in his booming Queen's English, 'Welcome to St Helena.'

While Stedson had picked up his Queen's English abroad, the English dialect spoken on St Helena still has remnants of old English mixed with some South African influence. It has a slight musical lilt to it. The distortion of the letter 'i' is a characteristic of Saints' speech. 'Sick' becomes 'suck', and 'six', 'sux'. Word order is sometimes muddled too, for example: 'How is you be?' There is also the tendency to reduce words: 'except' becomes 'cept', 'that' becomes 'dat', 'think' becomes 'tink'. There is also confusion between 'w' and 'v'.

The St Helenians, like all island communities, had tired of being treated like circus curiosities by visitors. Sally told me that she had been in the hairdresser's next to the Consulate Hotel when a cruise ship arrived in James Bay. Offloading its two thousand passengers, it doubled the population of Jamestown for the entire day, swamping the town with a geriatric tidal wave of perms and zimmerframes.

Two elderly American women had peered around the door. 'Look, Marge, she's having her hair cut.'

'Isn't it quaint?'

'Take a picture, Marge.'

At this point Sally told the anoraked voyeurs where to go.

★

'Ben?' said a man as I swigged on my bottle of Victoria beer. 'It's Jo, Jo Terry, from Shelco,' he explained. 'We were expecting you in July,' he smiled. I explained that I had changed my plans owing to work commitments back in the UK. 'So what do you think?' he asked.

Jo Terry was a bit of an Essex lad, a bit of a geezer. He was on the island as the sole representative of a £100 million project to build an airport. He was a strange choice, I thought.

It was a subject that seemed to dominate all topics of conversation on the ship and on the island. Without an airport, the only means of travelling to or from the island has been the RMS *St Helena*, a ship that is 70 per cent subsidized by the FCO.

While the sale of fishing licences to Japanese tuna vessels raises nearly £1 million a year, the island still has to resort to aid from the UK. It receives budgetary aid, a shipping subsidy for the RMS (to cover the losses incurred), and development aid. More than 70 per cent of the islanders are employed by the UK government.

For many years the islanders had discussed the viability of building an airport, thereby improving access to the island and opening up the prospect of tourism to bolster the waning economy, but only recently had a serious proposal been submitted. A consortium called the St Helena Leisure Corporation (Shelco), a sub-group of Arup, had put together a proposal to build an airport and resort on the island.

Shelco proposed that St Helena Airways serve the island with direct flights from Dubai and Bermuda as well as fortnightly flights to Ascension and the Falklands and twice-weekly flights to Cape Town. The idea was to encourage high-value, low-volume tourism.

One of the problems facing Shelco's idea is that although Ascension is an overseas territory, the runway is leased to the American government, who do not allow civilian aircraft to land. Even the weekly RAF flight from Brize Norton to the Falklands must seek special permission before refuelling. A site has been proposed, in Prosperous Plain, on the east side of the island, which is the only flat part.

I had been summoned to Shelco's London office as soon as they heard that I was writing a book about the island. Sir Nigel Thompson, deputy chairman of Arup, was spearheading the campaign. The £102 million, ten-year construction project includes the airport, a five-star hotel, a golf course and luxury villas. The UK government has committed £26 million to the airport in lieu of the renewal costs of replacing the RMS *St Helena*. The remaining project costs were to be raised by Shelco.

I had been aboard the RMS *St Helena* on my way to Tristan da Cunha when the vote had taken place. Nearly 75 per cent of the Saint crew had voted in favour of the airport, thereby voting themselves out of a job.

Although 72 per cent of Saints voted in favour of air access, many were cautious about its effect on the fragile character of the remote island. The problem is that St Helena is caught between a rock and a . . . sea. The island currently receives £10 million annually in aid. Tied to the UK purse strings as they are, self-determination is extremely limited.

The environmental impact of the airport is a significant hurdle for Shelco, who anticipate substantial rock-blasting and earth-moving to create the runway, over three quarters of a mile long. But it has been estimated that the project would create 200 jobs, while there would be further incentives to St Helenians to start up their own enterprises that would offer such tourist services as fishing, riding and restaurants.

The Shelco consortium had waxed lyrical about the potential for tourism and the importance of the airport for the future of the island. Many people had predicted that with the return of British citizenship the island's population would continue to decline as Saints set off for better job opportunities within the EU. But the construction of the airport would take nearly ten years and would demand a substantial work force; even after completion, the need for airport staff, hotel workers and airplane crew would create numerous new jobs for the islanders.

Sir Nigel and team had been thrilled with the outcome of the January vote on St Helena, but the proposal had since been rejected by the Department of Foreign and International Development (DFID) and the St Helena government, on the grounds that another consortium might come up with a cheaper and more efficient option.

Shelco, who had already invested millions in the proposal, had decided to sit it out, and had sent Jo Terry and his wife to live on the island until the deal was done. Jo, I concluded, had been sent to squat. I doubted that he and his Asian wife would leave until the airport got the go-ahead, and I had the feeling that they might be there for some time.

Welcome ceremonies had been planned in front of the courthouse, where a temporary wooden stage had been constructed and decorated with the island's flora. Princess Anne sat next to the governor, who looked more like a toy soldier than a governor. The sun beat down on the gathered crowd, who watched with a mixture of awe and amusement as the island's thirty policemen marched up and down, their brass buttons polished to within an inch of their lives, their white gloves blinking as they caught the sun.

Princess Anne told the islanders 'how envious Mummy was' at her visiting St Helena. 'Mummy' had visited St Helena as a young girl in 1947 with her parents, King George VI and Queen Elizabeth. I imagined the royal family sitting around the dining-table before the Princess's trip. 'How delightful,' the Queen would say. 'Now you must visit Donny's,' she would smile, 'and give Jonathan the tortoise a pat from me.'

Speeches over, the princess went to meet some of the island's cubs and scouts, with the governor in tow. I caught his eye as they wandered past, and he gave me a quick wink. We had of course met nearly a year earlier on the voyage to Tristan da Cunha, of which he is also governor. His smile practically reached his ears. He looked like a child with a new toy.

The day of the RMS *St Helena*'s arrival had been declared a national holiday in celebration of the royal visitor. School was cancelled and shops were closed, and over the Tannoy came the announcement: 'This is Radio St Helena. Because today is a holiday, there is no news. Thank you.' At which point the station resumed its diet of country and western music.

Opposite the court was Jacob's Ladder, a laughably horrible set of 699 steps that lead from the town up 602 feet to Half Tree Hollow on the cliff above. The steps were completed in 1829, when there used to be a tramway up the side of them, operated using a system of pulleys and ropes, that transported manure fertilizer from the stables in Jamestown and was used by the military to carry ammunition and supplies above.

Each year the islanders hold a race up and down the 699 steps, and I was told that it has been ascended in less than three minutes, while the descent could take just a minute, using the locals' tradition of sliding. This involves lying face up on the railings which rise on either side of the giant staircase, extending the arms behind one rail while tucking the heels over the other, and sliding to the bottom. Apparently, little boys used to do this carrying hot plates of soup from the cookhouse at the top to the sentries below, balancing the plates on their tummies.

It took me nearly ten times the Saint record to climb the steps. I felt physically sick, and by the time I reached the top the world was a dizzy mess. My morale hadn't been helped by the six giggling girls who had yomped past me, leaping two steps at a go, as I wheezed up one step at a time.

I had seen Half Tree Hollow from the ship, when it had appeared as nothing more than a clutch of weathered bungalows nestled on a cliff top, but the spectacular view from the top has to be one of the best in the world. The plateau slopes gently towards the cliff edge, where it then drops away 1,000 feet to the sea below. The panorama of the South Atlantic extends to the end of the earth, all 180 degrees of it. You can see the curvature of the earth.

Half Tree Hollow itself was less than inspiring; in fact it was a total disgrace. There was no half tree, nor a hollow; what there was, was a landscape strewn with rubbish and building materials. It seems that planning permission is not an important issue on St Helena.

I was desperate to try out the world's longest slide, but I had been hoping to find a young local willing to train me. Alas, the girls had long disappeared by the time I reached the top, where I was alone except for a mangy dog.

Jacob's Ladder certainly looked steeper from this height; I climbed on to the rail and assumed the position I had read about. It felt very awkward and extremely precarious. What bothered me in particular were the little bumps that seemed to protrude from the railings and which kept catching my T-shirt. I decided to take the non-conventional way down, by walking.

I had chosen to stay in the rather intimate surroundings of Harris's guest house on Main Street. Irene Harris and her husband had converted their two-storey house into a bed and breakfast. 'How did you get off the ship so soon,' pouted Irene, her hands on her hips. 'We was told you wouldn't be off till midday,' she continued. I explained that I had been allowed to come ashore in the VIP launch. 'How did you manage that?' she pouted again and ushered me inside.

The house was large and airy. The front room was stuffed full of hundreds of trophies, the walls covered in framed prints that looked like they had been cut from strips of seventies wallpaper. The trophies dominated the room, displayed proudly on a series of gold trimmed glass shelves. 'Skittles trophies,' announced Mrs H proudly. 'From Ascension Island,' she continued. Mr and Mrs H, as with so many Saints, had spent many years living on Ascension, where they earned a British wage working for the military. The Harrises had worked and lived there for more than twenty years before they returned to St Helena.

Mrs H was a busy woman. As well as running the guest house, she also doubled as one of the island's restaurants, 'catering for up to twenty', she announced proudly, explaining that they were a popular venue for office parties, particularly in the run-up to Christmas. As if that weren't enough to keep her busy, they also acted as a bakery, selling fresh baguettes and croissants, and supplying the island's pubs with 'bar' food. The Harrises were St Helena's very own Terence Conran, creating their own little business empire and monopolizing the island's Cornish pasty market.

I got the feeling Mrs H was always trying to impress me. She would appear as I was tucking into my bangers and mash or gammon and pineapple. 'Look at this,' she would say, producing an enormous marrow, 'isn't it impressive? We're the envy of Jamestown, you know, we grow bananas, papayas, oranges and lemons,' she would say as she produced examples of each one. Sometimes she would appear with a fresh loaf of bread. 'Feel this,' she would say, handing me the loaf, 'not bad, eh?'

On one occasion she appeared with a briefcase. 'Guess what this is,' she said as she laid the case in front of me like some secret agent. I half expected to find a ticking bomb or a pile of gold bars – certainly not a full set of cutlery neatly arranged in its customized compartments. 'Take a look at these,' she announced proudly, dipping into the collection. 'These are the only ones on St Helena,' she said, holding a spoon with an unfeasibly long handle. 'They are perfect for puddings,' she explained, 'you know, knickerbocker glories from tall pudding glasses. Everyone's terribly envious,' she smiled, packing the briefcase away and beckoning me to finish my roast beef and Yorkshire pudding.

I was woken early by a rooster, and after a full English breakfast that included the local favourite, black pudding, I set off for my appointment with the law. Opposite the police station was HM Prison, a surprisingly large building with a handful of 'guests' staying at Her Majesty's pleasure. The island prison seemed impenetrable and yet back in the eighties the incredible escape of a Dutch prisoner made the international headlines. It was a feat not even Napoleon had managed to accomplish, and is a story still talked about on the island today.

The Dutchman had arrived aboard a yacht from Cape Town, with a cargo of Amsterdam's finest. The island police had been alerted by the South African authorities and the man was promptly arrested. Sentenced to imprisonment, he spent several years incarcerated below Jacob's Ladder, until one day he disappeared. The island was searched but he was never found. It wasn't until a year later that the Dutch authorities confirmed that he was back in Holland. The man had become something of a national hero amid claims that he escaped from the island on a small raft, on which he crossed the South Atlantic to Brazil, from where he found onward passage to Europe. Locals scoff at this tale as impossible, but the man has escaped completion of his sentence because of Holland's relaxed drug laws and the government's refusal to hand him over.

While he had managed to escape from the island undetected, people have been known to smuggle themselves on to the island. The first case was in 2000. The RMS was half-way into her voyage from Cape Town when a young boy was discovered hidden in the ship's funnel. It transpired that the sixteen-year-old was from Burundi and had been looking for a way to Europe. He had wandered the docks in Cape Town and spotted the 'London' emblazoned on the RMS. He had sneaked aboard one night and had somehow managed to escape detection for three days, sneaking into the kitchens for food in the middle of the night before returning to his smoky hideaway. Upon discovery, it was decided to continue to St Helena before deciding what to do with him. Sympathetic passengers gave him clothes and he was provided with meals and even his own cabin.

Naturally the young boy was delighted by this generosity. He was slightly less thrilled when he discovered that 'London' was in fact St Helena. Despite his disappointment at 'London's' lack of opportunities, he applied for asylum. The *St Helena* agreed to look after him while his case was debated. Once again, the generous islanders provided him with clothes, toys, pocket money and even his own house, but nothing could allay his disappointment at the smallness of 'England', and more significantly his home sickness, and so several months later, before his case had been completed, he decided to return to Africa.

Naturally the RMS had stepped up its vigilance as regards stowaways after the incident, but another young boy managed it on the voyage before mine, though this time the island had lost its patience with asylum-seekers and he was held aboard the ship until he could be 'dropped off' in Senegal on the ship's return passage to the UK.

Napoleon isn't the only person to have been imprisoned on

St Helena. The island was used during the Boer War for more than 6,000 South African Boer prisoners. This historic association with prisoners has attracted several of the world's most famous one-time prisoners to the island, including Terry Waite, who has become a regular visitor.

Naturally, where there are prisoners, there are judges, and while the island has its own dedicated courtroom, those sentenced can still appeal. I met the court of appeal on Ascension while waiting to board the RMS *St Helena* for the voyage to her namesake. They had been horrified to learn that I had flown down on the same flight as the Princess, as they had been told that no one was to travel on the same flight as HRH as she would be boarding the ship immediately and there was to be no delay. The judges had to take an earlier flight and had been 'bored senseless' for nearly a week. The irony in waiting again for the royal who was now breakfasting with the administrator on Green Mountain did not pass them by. They were, in their own words, 'not amused'.

I had the great fortune to be seated at the same table as them for the two-day passage to St Helena. I don't think I had ever met a judge before and certainly not one as theatrical as these. They reminded me of the actors that used to visit mummy at our house in central London when I was a child, with lots of hysterical giggling and endless displays of theatrics.

The Honourable Justice Appleby QC, the Honourable Justice Benson QC and the Honourable Justice Woodward QC were on their way in what was the second 'expedition' by the court of appeal to the island. They would be spending eight days on the island, during which time they would be hearing six appeals. Justice Appleby was the president of the group, had visited the island once before and had also, incidentally, been the other two judges' teacher.

I had been greatly entertained by the three judges during the voyage from Ascension. I could always find them by smell, enveloped as they always were in a plume of smoke from Appleby's regular cigars. Appleby cut quite a figure as he wandered around the ship in a pair of pyjamas cut into shorts and a panama hat, his walking-stick in one hand, his pluming cigar in the other. The three judges would hold court out on the sun deck.

They had invited me to watch one of the appeals. Thankfully I have never been in a courtroom as either a defendant, a witness or an observer, so St Helena seemed as good a place as any to lose my courtroom virginity.

The court was next to the castle in downtown Jamestown. Outside were two cannons from a ship wrecked in James Bay. They had been decorated with flowers and festooned in bunting to celebrate the royal visit. The courtroom was bright and airy with a high ceiling. Two fans hung down, slowly spinning like tired geriatrics. The judges' bench dominated one half of the courtroom, while several rows of leather-covered benches provided the public seating area.

A pretty young Saint was busy polishing the court table when I arrived. She looked at me confusedly when I asked where I might sit. They don't get many spectators in the public gallery but eventually she pointed to the row of benches. I was disappointed to learn that there would be no manacled convict in the dock charged with picking too many breadfruits, and the plaintiff was working in Amsterdam.

The prosecutor and defence soon arrived, as did an elderly man who looked like Rumpole of the Bailey. 'Please rise,' announced a voice. I stood up, the only spectator. I was staggered when the three judges entered the room; I barely recognized them with their wigs and gowns. They had lost their mischievous twinkle and looked serious and scary.

It surprised me how 'unsaintly' the court was. The three judges were from Nottingham, the policeman guarding the door was from Scotland Yard, the prosecutor was from Barbados, the defence lawyer was a Scotsman, the plaintiff a Swede, Rumpole of the Bailey was anything but a St Helenian and there was me, a Londoner.

The case involved a Swedish teacher called Olson, who had left the island aboard the RMS for medical treatment in Cape Town. Mr Olson, in the absence of his own personal medical insurance, was invoicing the Saint government for all the costs. It was obvious from the outset that it was a lost case, but the court went about the due process of law with aplomb, interrupted just once when Justice Benson capsized a cup of water over his two colleagues, giving them all rather unfortunate wet patches in their laps.

During a pause in the case the three QCs took a quick cigar break. It was an odd sight to see the three judges in gowns and wigs, puffing on cigars, incontinent stains on their trousers, with Jacob's Ladder soaring high above.

During this fag break, Mrs Bollox walked past. She stared at the QCs with astonishment. I watched her as she looked them up and down before she came closer. 'Hello,' she said with her Scots burr. 'So what is it that you do?' she said, addressing Appleby. His eyebrows met his wig, and I could see the twinkle of amusement in Benson and Woodward's eyes. 'I'm a judge,' boomed Appleby. 'Oh, how interesting,' she said before wandering off to find Mr Bollox, leaving the QCs in a fit of hysterical giggles.

St Helena is roughly divided into the city, Jamestown, and the countryside, the rest of the island. Saints would talk of spending the 'weekend' or 'holidays' in the countryside, and some even had weekend cottages 'out of town'. I heard one rumour that there were still a handful of Saints living in the countryside who had never been into Jamestown, but most people I asked seemed to agree this was unlikely, though there are plenty of Saints who have never left the island's shores.

St Helena is only ten and a half miles by six, though it seems much larger because of the steep mountain peaks and the deep valleys. The day after the court hearing, I decided to hire a car and explore the rest of the island. I would do this in a 1980s red Ford Capri, complete with a dangly die (there was only one), but before I headed off to the island's interior, I decided to find my bearings on St Helena's only island tour.

Colin Corker's 1929 Chevrolet charabanc is something of an institution on St Helena. It has no doors or roof and the eighteen seats are made of wood, with a slightly newer engine and a plastic awning that could be raised in the eventuality of rain. The charabanc tour has become as synonymous with St Helena as Napoleon himself, so I felt it my duty to tour the island, with the Bolloxes and an American couple. I was the youngest out of the car and passengers by about fifty years.

The first stop on the tour was the Briars, where Napoleon lived for his first weeks on St Helena. The chocolate box house was a few miles inland from Jamestown and had striking views across the hills to the sparkling water of James Bay below.

Henry Porteous's house had proved to be unsuitable for Napoleon and his entourage. The French were astounded at the meagreness of the house, and felt that Longwood House would make a more suitable 'venue'. After a night in the cramped quarters, Napoleon, Sir George Cockburn and Bertrand (one of Napoleon's servants) rode the five miles to inspect the location of Bonaparte's future residence.

They had been bitterly disappointed by what they found at Longwood House. The ceilings were low, the walls damp and the garden bare. Napoleon was assured that it would be transformed into a home fit for an . . . emperor. Until this point the house had been used as a summer residence for the governor. It was on the party's return to Jamestown that they passed Briars hamlet. It was here that Napoleon spotted the Balcombes' house. The family offered Napoleon their house, but he declined and chose instead to occupy the small pavilion, just next to the house, from which he had views down to James Bay.

Napoleon spent two months at Briars. I had read that he became friends with the two Balcombe boys. They would clamber over him like a climbing frame, examining the rings on his fingers, his clothes, the embroidery on his jacket, his medals and of course his hat. He became friendly with the rest of the Balcombe family and was especially fond of their thirteen-year-old daughter, Betsy. Apparently she even taught him how to play blind man's buff as she was the only French-speaker.

Betsy once told Napoleon how little English children who did not behave were warned that Boney the bogey man would come and get them. One day she is even reputed to have produced a mechanical children's toy, made of wood by a London manufacturer. It showed a fat-bellied Napoleon in his trademark hat, standing on the bottom rung of a ladder. You pressed a button and the little figure mounted jerkily up the steps, each one of which was marked with the name of a country: Russia, Spain, Italy. And the top step was called St Helena. When he reached the top his legs crumpled under him, and he toppled from the ladder and hung there like a spider suspended on a thread.

These two months were considered the most enjoyable of Napoleon's stay on St Helena. At the beginning of December, work had progressed far enough for Napoleon to move into Longwood House. It was with reluctance and sadness that he departed the Briars, to continue his life of exile at Longwood.

Longwood Old House was originally a cowshed, which was later transformed into a five-room house. In preparation for Napoleon's stay, a sixth room was added, which was used as the billiards room. In the bathroom there was a large copper bath tub panelled in oak. Napoleon used to soak in the bath for hours on end, reading, chatting and even lunching. The valets would sleep on the sofa in the adjoining room, ready to respond when Napoleon rang the bell.

Although the house was enlarged to accommodate the number of occupants, it was still cramped. More than twenty people at a time were living within its limited walls. Napoleon was allowed to walk outside in the garden and he was given freedom of movement. If he went beyond the boundaries of the property, however, he had to be accompanied by a British officer.

Napoleon and his entourage complained bitterly about the inadequacies of Longwood House, and so plans were drawn up for an alternative building to be constructed. Longwood New House was built and brought out from England and assembled opposite the existing building. Napoleon died before he could ever move in. The building was demolished just after the Second World War.

Napoleon's life at Longwood House followed the same day-to-day routine for most of the seven years. There was always the fear that he might try to escape and the governor felt compelled to have two warships continuously circling the island, while more remained anchored at James Bay. Not only was the sea heavily patrolled, but the island itself was manned by many thousands of soldiers. Two camps were formed, at Deadwood Plain and Francis Plain. During the day, sentries patrolled outside the boundary walls of Longwood, but in the evening they took up their watch in the garden as close to the house as was possible. Napoleon resented being so closely observed. He felt like a zoo animal and he eventually cut peepholes into the shutters so that he in turn could observe the peeping sentries.

Governor Hudson Lowe loathed Napoleon and was haunted by the prospect of his escape. Every attempt was made to treat Napoleon as a prisoner and to demean him. Lowe refused to address him as 'Emperor': he was to be called General Bonaparte, a law which travelled all the way to the grave. The governor personally censored all correspondence and a strict curfew of 9 p.m. was imposed across the island. An orderly officer had to report daily that he had physically seen Napoleon and a log book was used to record each and every movement.

From the start of his governorship in April 1816 Hudson Lowe had an acrimonious relationship with Napoleon Bonaparte. The last time the two men met was on 17 August 1816. The following October, the area in which Napoleon was allowed to go out unaccompanied was reduced by a third. He was also forbidden to speak to anyone unless in the presence of an English soldier, and the sentries posted outside were ordered to take up their post outside the house at sundown rather than at 9 p.m. as previously.

Little by little Napoleon's entourage grew smaller and smaller. Marquis de Las Casas, who thought of himself as Napoleon's closest confidant and to whom Napoleon dictated his memoirs, was arrested, and in January 1817 he was sent back to France. His crime: that he attempted to evade the censorship of all correspondence by the government by dispatching secret letters to London through his former servant. The next to leave Longwood was General Gaspar Gourgoud. During Napoleon's exile, Las Casas and Gourgoud jealously competed for Napoleon's attention. Even after the departure of Las Casas, Gourgoud's jealously still flared and he seemed to take out his frustrations on everyone. He became quarrelsome and self-absorbed. In February 1818 Napoleon and Gourgoud had a huge row. This resulted in the general's asking to leave the island. Only after a letter was written claiming illness as the reason for departure did Governor Lowe permit him to leave Longwood House.

The year 1818 was not a good one for Napoleon. He was plagued by illness and he became moody and irritable. Francschi Cipriani, the major at Longwood House responsible for the smooth running of the household, died after a four-day illness. Around the middle of that year, four other members of staff all left with their families. On 2 August, Napoleon's personal and trusted physician, Barry O'Meara, left the island after a row with the governor. Dr O'Meara had an arrangement for a time with the governor to report on Napoleon and his entourage. He soon tired of the governor's strict restrictions and he stopped his reports. He resigned before the governor could fire him. Napoleon was without medical care for more than six months and his health deteriorated further. By this time it had been determined that Napoleon was most likely suffering from chronic hepatitis. The governor was worried that people might attribute his ailments to the unsuitable conditions on St Helena and he decided to suppress the information. A naval surgeon brought to the island after Napoleon suffered one of his painful bouts of illness confirmed this diagnosis. Lowe was incensed and had him court-martialled. Napoleon was once again left doctorless. During the time of his illness, Napoleon was weak and in bad spirits. He took little exercise and he seldom went into the garden. It seemed he was losing interest in life. On 20 September of that same year a new team arrived to take over the running of the house. Napoleon was unimpressed with his new servants, but his health began to improve and in March of the following year he took a keen interest in the gardens. Longwood House was situated in a wind-swept plain and the gardens had been little more than open scrub land on which the donkeys grazed. By May work had been completed, and the exile now had a vegetable garden, lemon and orange trees, and even a Chinese pavilion where he could shelter from the elements and hide from the ever-present sentries.

Napoleon was unable to enjoy the gardens for long. His health worsened again. Napoleon's last excursion was on 4 October 1820, when he and his servants, Bertrand and Montholon, rode the five miles to Sandy Bay to have breakfast on the lawn of Sir William Doverton, the estate's owner. After this the ailing Napoleon was restricted to just short, slow rides by carriage. In mid-March 1821, Napoleon became house-bound, because his health was so poor. His sickbed was moved from his bedroom to the drawing-room. His condition worsened, and on 5 May 1821 Napoleon died. The body lay in state in the drawing-room, the walls covered in black muslin.

The controversy surrounding Napoleon's death continues even today. A post mortem was carried out immediately after he died and the official cause of death was said to be stomach cancer and a perforated stomach ulcer. However, there has been speculation about traces of arsenic found in his hair, and the chance that he was slowly poisoned to death by arsenic-treated wallpaper.

Napoleon was buried in a simple tomb in the rather aptly named Sane valley, a place chosen by Napoleon himself as his final resting-place. Close watch was kept on him even after death, and sentries were stationed to guard the burial site. And there he remained for nearly twenty years, until 1840, when his body was finally returned to France.

Longwood House was much larger than I had first expected. Although, apart from the stone front steps, the house is a replica, as the original was destroyed by damp, termites and years of neglect, its structure remains much as it was. But the rotting wooden walls have been replaced by solid breeze blocks, giving the overall impression of a much warmer, friendlier place than it would have originally been.

The trade winds hit the east of the island, where Napoleon's house was situated, just above an area called Deadwood Plain, which is where prisoners were kept during the Boer War, and where a military camp was established during Napoleon's stay.

The French *tricolore* snapped angrily in the cool wind, its halyard clanking like the mast of a ship. Longwood has been maintained by the French government since 1858 and Michel Martineau is the French vice-consul on the island. Both Michel and his father before him have been responsible for maintaining and renovating the house. It seemed incredible that an island so very English should have a tiny landlocked French enclave hidden in its hills. Longwood even smelt French, with its musty old polish fusing with the smell of cooking that emanated from Monsieur Martineau's private apartments hidden in the depths of the house.

When we first arrived at Longwood House, we found the gates and doors firmly locked. 'Typical French,' cursed Colin, 'they're always late.' It made me smile that even here, in the farthest corner of the earth, there existed a firm Franco-British rivalry. I had even heard locals telling French jokes in Donny's.

St Helena seemed too small to need a French vice-consul, but Longwood received a steady stream of visiting French tourists and academics alike. I had sailed aboard the RMS from Ascension with four Parisian history professors who had travelled all the way from Dorset on this academic 'pilgrimage' to Bonaparte.

It must have been a gloomy existence for Napoleon. Longwood seems to have its own microclimate, consisting of rain, cloud, mist and wind. I returned to the house every day that I was on the island, hoping to catch Longwood in the sunshine. Instead I was invariably met by a thick wall of mist that appeared to linger over the house like a depressing spell. Set on open plain, firmly in the island's damp interior, Longwood is exposed to the full force of the wind that sweeps across the valley. A light mist hangs in the air invading every corner, with a cool damp lick.

J.J. was my guide around the house. A young South African in his mid-thirties, he was, I later learned, Michel's boyfriend. I wondered what the islanders thought about this couple? J.J. had obviously conducted the tour many times before. I watched his eyes roll upwards as he was asked for the umpteenth time about the poisoned-wallpaper theory. 'We do not subscribe to that theory here,' he said with his thick South African accent. He went on to explain that the presence of arsenic in wallpaper was normal at that time, as it was used to create the colours, and that the small trace in his hair could have been from his medicine.

The rooms where Napoleon and his entourage lived have been decorated with exact replicas of the furniture, curtains and even wallpaper. Napoleon's billiard table is still there, as is his death bed and even a copy of his death mask.

I asked J.J. about the latest theory published in the British tabloids, nearly two hundred years after his death, that it is not the body of Napoleon that now lies in Les Invalides in Paris, but that of his servant.

France's ministry of defence turned down a request to test the DNA of the body assumed to be that of Napoleon after claims by a French legal expert and historian, Bruno Roy-Henri, that the body was not Napoleon's at all but that of his loyal butler, Jean-Baptiste Cipriani.

Roy-Henri speculated that the British swapped the body to conceal evidence of neglect or of poisoning, and to avoid upsetting diplomatic relations with France. Napoleon's body was supposedly taken and hidden in a crypt in Westminster Abbey while his butler was buried in full pomp in France.

Monsieur Roy-Henri's theory is based on inconsistencies between accounts of Napoleon's first burial on St Helena and his exhumation and reburial in Paris in 1840. Napoleon was said to have been buried in the innermost of three coffins placed one inside another. At his exhumation, there were said to be four. His teeth, notoriously yellow and rotting during his lifetime, were said to be gleaming white when he was dug up.

J.J. rolled his eyes again at this latest hypothesis, news of which hadn't had time to filter through to St Helena. He shook his head and lifted a limp wrist. 'Impossible,' he said, 'the bodies couldn't have been swapped, too many people would have been involved.' J.J. explained that records were probably less scrupulous in the nineteenth century than they are today. That Napoleon can still make the headlines so many years after his death is a measure of his enduring appeal, though his name is synonymous with great power and battles and remains one of the most evocative in the world. It still has a mesmerizing effect on me. As a child I used to imagine him on St Helena, sat on his school trunk, his trademark hat on the floor, his head buried in his hands.

But while the rest of the world continues to be fascinated by Napoleon, Saints have a tendency to roll their eyes at the mere mention of his name. 'Not another book about Napoleon?' they would say. 'Why must every reference to St Helena include a mention of Napoleon?' This seems churlish, because St Helena would probably have been abandoned if it weren't for him. Bonaparte is arguably the only reason that St Helena is still populated today, and is certainly the main attraction for at least half the island's visitors.

I had met two French couples on the RMS, who certainly weren't visiting St Helena for anything other than Bonaparte. I was told of one Frenchwoman who visited several years before who had come dressed as Josephine, Napoleon's wife. She had spent a whole week wandering around Longwood, wailing and sobbing uncontrollably.

An American film crew had recently been to the island to film the exterior shots for a new costume drama about the emperor. The filmmakers had used locals as extras, although in the end they had used only the island's expats, as they were the only ones that could pass as British soldiers. Perhaps unsurprisingly this had further inflamed the islanders, blackening Napoleon's name even more.

St Helena without Boney is like the Vatican without the Pope, or Britain without the Queen.

From Longwood we continued to Sane valley, Napoleon's original burial place. The guard's shack is still standing where it was. The site had been chosen by Napoleon himself, although some have suggested he asked to be buried next to the Seine, not Sane Valley. It was a peaceful site, surrounded by tall pine trees. I wondered whether Napoleon had deliberately chosen to be buried out of sight of the ocean that imprisoned him.

★

The last stop on the charabanc tour was Plantation House, the official residence of the governor and his wife, although it is also home to the island's oldest resident, Jonathan the giant tortoise. So famous is Jonathan that his image and name adorn the front of the island's 5p coin. You really have it made when your face decorates a currency.

No one knows how long he has been on the island or how old he really is, although it is generally agreed that he is between 150 and 200 years old, which would mean that he may have met Napoleon, or rather Napoleon may have met him.

Jonathan lives on the lawn in front of the impressive residence. I sat on the grass in front of him and stared into his dark eyes. His face had been well lived in, was weathered and wrinkled. Maybe Bonaparte divulged secrets to Jonathan, like I sometimes do with my dog Inca, whispering secrets into her ear? What did he know? In the absence of a Dr Doolittle moment, I left Jonathan to his ruminations, and he wandered off, chewing the cud. He'd seen it all before. We returned to Jamestown in time for tea.

'The radio station called,' said Mrs H as she poured me a hot cuppa. 'They say they want to talk to you,' she continued, before disappearing off for the milk and sugar. Surprisingly, most milk on St Helena is Longlife, as there is no dairy on the island. Surely an isolated population of 4,000 could justify a small dairy? I had asked a Saint about this, and he had explained quite simply that no one could be bothered, and that it was easier to import Longlife milk. And so they ate their Corn Flakes with UHT.

Mrs H was itching to find out why they had called. She returned with a plate of homemade scones and jam, which she placed in front of me. It wasn't long before curiosity got the better of her. 'What they want to talk with you 'bout?' she asked, hands on hips, lips pouting. 'They mentioned something about *Castaway*,' she said.

I explained that I had been part of the BBC's *Castaway*, and how I had lived on a small island for a year, at which point she turned her head away. 'Oh,' she sighed, 'and there was me thinking you were an actor from the film with Tom Hanks.' She snapped her flip-flops unimpressed and disappeared into the kitchen to prepare dinner for that evenings's hen party. Which part did she think I had played? The basketball?

Mrs H was particularly excited about the new curtains and electric fireplace that had arrived aboard the RMS. She had waited nearly a year for the arrival of her home improvements, and her husband wasted no time in installing their new drawing-room feature.

Mr Harris was much quieter than his wife. He would walk around the house bare chested, in just a pair of trousers over which his pasty-rich stomach hung, screwdriver in hand, ready for a spot of DIY. He was also the chief baker, rising at 3 a.m. each morning to bake the daily bread in their oil-burning Aga.

I watched as he struggled with the electric fire. He was sweating heavily in the humid air. 'What do we need an electric fire for in Jamestown?' he said agitatedly. 'The temperature never gets below 20 degrees.' The 'missus', however, had set her heart on the fireplace after seeing a picture of it in a magazine, and it seemed Mrs H was having one whether they needed it or not.

That evening, Mrs H was cooking for an island hen night, and I had been invited to dinner with Doug Patterson and his family. St Helena certainly seemed to have its fair share of Scotsmen. I had met another Glaswegian in Donny's who was working in the island's medical laboratory, having previously been assigned to Saudi Arabia and Somalia. The court's defence lawyer had also been a Scotsman.

Doug Patterson had been a social worker on St Helena for eighteen months. One of the disturbing aspects of St Helena society is that a huge proportion of the island's children are growing up without their parents. It is estimated that over a hundred children on the island are being cared for by adults who are not their parents. The economic situation and the high rate of unemployment mean that Saints are forced to work offshore in order to support their families, and invariably this means that children are forced to live with grandparents, who are often unsuited to the needs of these teenagers. Some people, including Doug, have argued that this has led to behavioural problems, and more significantly to a high rate of heavy drinking and underage sex.

I asked Doug what it had been like for his sons to integrate into this new society. He explained that one of the reasons he was keen to integrate his sons into the island's education system was to expose them to 'minority issues': 'I felt it was important for them to know what it feels like to be a minority group.' Most surprisingly of all, Doug explained that the boys had been the subject of substantial racist bullying.

The irony is that the Saints represent a mixture of many different nationalities and influences. The people themselves tell the story of the island's history. The first settlers were Portuguese; then came the British and Dutch, bringing with them slaves from the Far East. Later came the Chinese labourers and then the Boer prisoners. St Helenians are a mixture of all these.

I could never really establish whether or not the Saints enjoyed their UK status. A feature of the island is that nearly 70 per cent of the population is employed by the government, and employees are forbidden to criticize their employers by law.

I asked a group of young Saints in the White Horse pub what they thought about their UK status. 'Pile o' shit,' mumbled one drunken islander to the amusement of his friends. 'We should be part of South Africa,' he slurred. Somehow I doubted his commitment to the idea. In any case, South Africa's slumping economy meant that the likelihood of it subsidizing this money pit was slight. Nearly every Saint I spoke to agreed that the island could never be totally independent.

Throughout the years, various attempts at self-sufficiency have been tried and tested. Perhaps the most successful was the attempt to introduce the flax industry in 1874. More than a hundred acres of New Zealand flax were planted by the Colonial and Foreign Fibre Company. This first attempt was a failure owing to high transport costs, but a second attempt in 1907 was successful and it became the island's main supporting industry, supplying the British Post Office with flax fibres with which letters were bound. For more than fifty years, the flax industry thrived, until 1966, when the British Post Office made the decision to change from flax to cheaper synthetic materials. The flax industry collapsed, 250 people lost their jobs and the island economy faltered. The remnants of the flax industry are still evident across St Helena, where the crop grows in abundance, in places offering protection and shelter from the wind that lashes the island.

This insecurity seemed entrenched in the island's history of colonialism. Doug explained that the island and her history ignores the importance of the Saints themselves. He pointed out that there are no memorials, plaques or busts in memory of any Saints. 'It is as though they have been excluded from history,' he explained.

As if to prove the point, Doug voiced his opinion that the royal visit had been organized very 'colonially'. 'It was like something from the Raj,' he continued, 'with all the whites sitting on the stage with HRH Princess Anne, while all the natives looked on.' He also explained that the royal function at the governor's residence had been a thoroughly 'white' affair as well.

I had certainly been surprised by my thoroughly 'white' experience in the courtroom, and the podium for Princess Anne had been bursting with sunburnt white faces.

I returned to Jamestown, along the dark, narrow roads. The sky was blanketed with a trillion stars.

Next day I set off on my own tour of the island. A steep road bisects the mountain and leads from Jamestown up to Half Tree Hollow. From here I lurched and spluttered through a succession of hairpin bends. St Helena is sometimes described as an emerald set within a brooch, the stone representing the rich green interior, the gold, her rocky fortress-like cliffs. The interior was like another world. Pine trees lined the road, while rich green pastures spread out like a patchwork. I passed two farmers leading a pack of donkeys along the road. Suddenly St Helena felt like another planet, another era.

The landscape was a rainbow of greens, as lush flora stretched for as far as the eye could see. St Helena was a positive Garden of Eden in the middle of the vast aquatic desert of the South Atlantic, and its lushness hadn't gone unnoticed by sailors throughout the years, who used the island as a sort of giant larder.

St Helena is located in the tropics, but her climate is kept mild by the south-east tradewinds. The year is roughly divided into two seasons, the warm summer and the cooler winter. There is, however, a significant climatic change between Jamestown on the northern coast, which tends to remain warmer at between 20 and 30 degrees, and the interior of the island, which is between 10 and 20 degrees. Interestingly, her climate is perfect for growing coffee. St Helena coffee is much sought after by connoisseurs for its unique flavour and rarity. It is sold in Fortnum & Mason's in London, where it costs a staggering £12 a kilo, making it one of the most expensive coffees in the world, and certainly the only coffee produced on UK land.

St Helena is haunted by its past. I could almost taste its history as I explored the island – it seemed to drift in the mist, invading every pore of the land. But it was the story of one young man that haunted me more than any other, Fernando Lopez.

Lopez was a Portuguese nobleman. He set off on a voyage with General D'Alberquerque in search of new lands to conquer and claim for the Portuguese Empire. In 1510 they crossed the Indian Ocean from Arabia, and arrived in Goa on the south-west coast of India. After a brief battle they captured the ancient port town, and claimed ownership of this unknown land. There weren't enough men in the expedition to hold their claim, so D'Alberquerque returned to Portugal to mass an army of warships with which to defend his new world. Fernando Lopez was left to guard the city and await the General's return.

It took D'Alberquerque nearly two years to return with reinforcements, upon which he discovered that Goa's charm had rubbed off on Lopez and his men, who had immersed themselves in the local cultures and even adopted the Muslim faith, an unfathomable crime at the time. The traitors were rounded up and were punished for their sins. Lopez was to receive the harshest punishment because he had been considered the most responsible of the group, with his noble Portuguese background. His punishment was severe even for the 1500s. He lost the fingers and thumb from his left hand, and his whole right hand. His nose and his ears were cut off and all his hair was plucked out in a practice known as 'scaling the fish'. When his torturers had finished meting out their punishment, Lopez was left to hide the shame of his betrayal and of his hideous wounds in the countryside.

D'Alberquerque died several years later and it was only then that Lopez emerged and sought a passage home to Portugal. While his wounds had healed, leaving terrible scars, his conscience had not. It was during this passage home that the ship stopped at St Helena for fresh water and supplies.

At that time St Helena had only recently been discovered and was known only to the Portuguese. The island was still uninhabited, and Lopez, having lost the confidence to return to his family, sought refuge in the interior forests. The ship waited, but eventually set sail without him, leaving Lopez to become St Helena's first castaway and resident.

With a minimum of supplies, Lopez set about creating his own little island home. He dug a hole in which to sleep and thrived on the island's rich flora and fauna. It was a year before another ship appeared on the horizon, and Lopez, still ashamed at his body, for ever marked with his betrayal, hid himself once again in the thick interior forests.

As the island was still known only to the Portuguese, and the crew, upon discovering his crude little camp, agreed that whoever lived there could only be Portuguese. They left him some supplies and a letter telling him that he was in no danger, and that he shouldn't hide the next time a ship came by.

As time went on, Lopez became less timid and he learnt to appear when ships anchored. It wasn't long before Lopez became a bit of a celebrity. The first celebrity castaway.

Each sailor that met Lopez must have been overcome with horror and compassion for this lonely man who refused to leave his island home. With compassion came gifts, lots of them. They gave him seeds of vegetables and fruits so that he could grow gardens of lemons and breadfruits. They also gave him living creatures: ducks, hens, chickens, goats, peacocks, cows, pheasants, dogs and cats. And so Lopez became a farmer and a gardener. He overcame his disabilities, and turned his solitude into productive ends. He transformed the landscape, digging lazy beds and tending to his gardens. St Helena became a true island oasis amid the watery desert that is the South Atlantic.

Tales of this paradise soon spread, and with it the legend of Lopez and his awful mutilations. People talked of the man who ruled over this kingdom, and it wasn't long before word reached the king and queen of Portugal. The royals were touched and intrigued, and Lopez was summoned to their palace in Lisbon. His Portuguese nobility had the better of him, and he came obediently. The king offered him anything he might desire, and Lopez, still reeling with Catholic guilt, asked for permission to visit the pope in Rome so that he could confess to his sins, and put an end to the mental torture that so plagued him.

After his audience with the pope, Lopez begged to be returned to the island, and asked the king of Portugal to give him written permission to remain there and never again be called from his 'home'. And there, in the steep gully which runs down to the sea, Lopez continued to live; happily tending to his gardens and to the animals which now roamed the island freely; content to live in splendid isolation, alone except for rare visits from the ships journeying between Europe and India.

Lopez died in 1545, after living on St Helena for nearly thirty years.

I continued along the road to Blue Hill – not because I wanted to, but because I had become totally lost amid the heavy landscape. I crept up a steep incline and into the mist. The wind began to pick up and I could hear it whispering through the trees. The road reached a high peak, with deep valleys slipping away on either side. A dozen trees had been beaten to a stoop by the wind, another cowered against the incessant punishment. The mist and cloud were being driven by the wind, billowing in long fingers over the road.

It is startling, the change in terrain, as one crosses the island. From the damp mists of Blue Hill I headed for the arid region of Sandy Bay, just two miles away, and the island's only 'beach', made from black sand and rock.

From Diana's peak, in the centre of the island, I had been told, a naval officer had calculated that, on a very clear day, it is possible to see 54,000 square kilometres of ocean stretching out 360 degrees around you.

I continued along to the proposed airport site at Prosperous Plain. It was only a few minutes' drive from Longwood House, past the golf course and next to the island's new Millennium Forest, in which islanders have planted thousands of gumwood trees. The stakes in the soil clearly marked the proposed runway.

It was hard to imagine a Boeing roaring up and down this plain that looked anything but prosperous. It was like a desolate moonscape. The wind bit hard as it raced across the wide valley. A fairy tern danced above me, floating on a thermal, spying as I walked across the barren soil past cacti forced into a crouch. It was gypsum from Prosperous Plain that was used to make Napoleon's death mask.

It was as hard to imagine St Helena with an airport as St Helena without a ship. The significance of the RMS became more and more striking throughout my stay on the island. I noticed how every home I visited seemed to have an effigy of the ship, whether it be a painting, a postcard or a photograph. I saw small models of it, and the children had created an exhibition of cardboard cut-outs of the ship in the island's museum.

I began to notice how people glanced at the ship as they went about their daily chores along Main Street. People in Donny's would angle their chairs around so that they could keep one eye on it, as if they were replenishing their memory of it. Ours was the first visit in more than six weeks and the islanders had been starved of her image. I watched as a group of teenagers sat on the top of Jacob's Ladder, smoking and drinking bottles of South African beer. They all seemed to keep one eye on the ship and one on their cigarette.

The importance of the RMS cannot be underestimated. She is the island's lifeline, but there was more to her than that. She seemed to be the heart of the island. When she is there the tempo of life increases, when she leaves it drops. I was told of the low spirits that sweep across the island when the ship leaves. Donny's closes down and the party finishes.

The agricultural fair had been absent from St Helena's social calendar for several years, but the arrival of Her Royal Highness had geed up local enthusiasm. Francis Plain was the chosen venue for the proceedings, a large, open, green area that doubles as the Prince Andrew School playing-fields.

Legend has it that it was on these playing-fields, during a friendly game of cricket, that a fielder went to make a catch and tumbled over the side into the deep ravine below. His departure from the game was for ever immortalized in the scorebook as 'retired dead'.

Each of the island's 'regions' had entered the fair, competing for the coveted prizes for best papaya, best-kept chicken and the all-important best loaf, for which Mrs H had entered no fewer than six different loaves.

At one end of Francis Plain was the livestock ring in which cattle, sheep and goats were all paraded to the great applause of the crowd. The islanders seemed to transform themselves into cowboys. I noticed a huge number of stetson hats and cowboy boots, and even watched one young Clint Eastwood sit atop a thoroughly fed-up-looking bull – although an infinitely more fortunate bull than the one Tristan da Cunha used for golf practice.

Each region of the island had submitted a display to show off its wares. It was here that I spotted my very first St Helenian breadfruit. Breadfruit had first been brought to the island over two hundred years before by Captain Bligh. Fresh from his epic open-boat ocean journey after the infamous mutiny on the *Bounty* that led to the settlement of Pitcairn in the South Pacific, Bligh had returned to the South Seas aboard HMS *Providence*, on which he completed his original mission to collect breadfruit for export to the Caribbean, where it was to be used as a cheap and efficient food for slaves.

Bligh had stopped off at St Helena on his return voyage, where he supplied the island with a dozen of the fruit trees, the crop of which still flourishes today.

It seemed that most of the island had turned out for the agricultural show. Dozens of barbecues provided hamburgers and fishcake butties, while a temporary bar was doing a flourishing business supplying bottles of South African beer.

'You must be the writer,' enquired a friendly Saint, who introduced himself as Basil George. He was selling copies of his St Helenian novel. He explained that he was the head of St Helena's Commission on Citizenship, responsible for campaigning for the return of their British citizenship. I was surprised that he had referred to me as the 'writer', but then again this was a small island, and I had mentioned it to Mrs H.

Basil had the familiar warm Saints features. With their dark skin and hair, and their big wide smiles, the Saints have that ability to make everyone around them happy. They exude friendliness whether they mean to or not. Walking down the street could take hours on St Helena as each person stops to swap pleasantries and talk about the weather. I found myself crossing the road on occasions simply unable to cope with saying hello to the same person for the fifth time in a single day.

I sat down for a cup of local coffee and a jammy dodger, while the Princess wandered around in her sunglasses, closely watched by her ever-vigilant bodyguards and half a dozen over-excited Saint Police.

Much to my disappointment, and to Mrs H's horror, none of her loaves won a prize. 'It must have been fixed,' I overheard her complaining to her husband, who, catching my eye, smiled and shrugged his shoulders.

The following day I had been invited to Sunday lunch with the Robertsons. Dulcie, a Saint, had fallen in love with and married Bobby, a Scotsman. They had lived in Glasgow for nearly forty years, and had finally retired to St Helena in the early nineties.

Dulcie spent her days painting while her husband had become a local councillor.

The Robertsons lived in Rosemary Hall, just across the valley from Scotland. Their house looked out on to the plains below; the sea twinkled in the distance. Lush green forest surrounded their secluded lot. Across the valley in Scotland (ironically the driest and most wind-free part of the island), a stereo blasted Eminem from a small farmhouse. His staccato rapping boomed out around the hills. It didn't suit St Helena, it sounded too alien. 'Shut the f*** up,' shouted Bobby in his strong Glaswegian accent.

Sunday lunch on St Helena meant Sunday lunch: roast lamb, chicken, roast potatoes, gravy and Yorkshire puddings were served alongside the St Helenian Sunday addition of curry.

Bobby, I soon discovered, was a rather outspoken figure on the island, as popular with the islanders as they were with him. 'They're lazy,' he announced with a mouthful of island spuds. 'They have been given too much and have become lethargic. Where else in the world do you have to pay schoolchildren to attend school?' Apparently, Saints are paid £17.50 per week to attend classes. This had been deemed the only way to ensure full attendance.

'The only reason they entered the agricultural show was because they were paid to,' he continued. Bobby explained that the reason the awards presentation had taken so long the previous afternoon was because every person was given a cash prize. 'That was the only way we could get anyone interested in taking part,' he said, rubbing his thumb and forefinger together.

I noticed that Dulcie remained silent, refusing to defend St Helenians. Instead she kept spooning more food on to my plate and pointedly avoided the subject. 'I love John Craven,' she cooed on learning that I worked on BBC's *Countryfile* with the former *Newsround* presenter. 'I remember watching him as a child, so sexy in those jumpers.'

The RMS *St Helena* had been chartered to sail Princess Anne to Ascension Island for an onward flight to the UK a few days earlier than scheduled as she had an important court appearance involving one of her dogs. The RMS would be gone for several days before collecting me and the rest of the passengers and continuing on to South Africa.

I had arranged to meet Governor Hollamby in his castle office the day after the Princess departed. The spacious room had wood panelling and a large portrait of a very young-looking Queen Elizabeth. The walls were decorated with photographs of previous governors, peering down to keep an eye on things, and dozens of ship's crests donated by visiting vessels. Two sizeable windows opened out on to James Bay.

His big wooden desk was piled high with paperwork. A copy of the Falkland Islands weekly paper the *Penguin Post* lay open on his desk, alongside a two-week-old copy of the *Guardian*. Hollamby wore an open-neck short-sleeve shirt, his cheeks were flushed red from the elements, and his eyes looked tired.

'Were you pleased?' I asked the rosy-cheeked governor.

'Thrilled,' he replied, with a broad smile. I asked him if he was disappointed at the lack of press interest back in the UK, where the Princess's impending court appearance had dominated Fleet Street. In fact, her trip to St Helena had been ignored altogether.

The governor explained that they had hoped to generate a little interest in the 'unknown' island, but that the visit had been 'a success'. 'You know she is due in court tomorrow,' explained Hollamby. 'And she still came all the way to our island,' he said, obviously touched by the gesture.

Hollamby considered the airport his little baby. In fact, much to the disappointment of his wife, he had extended his tenure for another two years in order to secure the deal. His El Salvadorian wife had long tired of the island and had chosen to live in Cape Town.

I had been told by one Saint that the governor had even mooted the idea of naming the airport after himself, Hollamby International Airport. Ingenious, I thought. If you can't find a new island, mountain or valley to name after yourself, then simply build an airport.

I asked him how he felt about the rejection of Shelco's proposal. 'DFID feel that their plans are too ambitious,' he explained. I asked if they were likely to find another company willing to undertake such a vast commitment of time, money and resources. Shelco had already invested many millions of pounds in their proposal. Hollamby explained that one of the problems is the worry that the two-phased approach was too risky. He explained that if Arup were willing to put their name to the project, then the proposal would probably be accepted 'tomorrow'. He explained that DFID would be sufficiently impressed by Arup's pedigree designing and building such celebrated projects as the Millennium Dome and Japan's new international airport, but that Shelco was Sir Nigel's retirement baby, and a project 'too small for Arup'.

The airport was certainly an ambitious project for an island with just a few thousand inhabitants. Seventy-two per cent of the islanders had voted in favour of the airport. The majority of the objectors were 'expats' who felt they had found their utopian paradise and didn't want it spoilt by the buzz of passenger jets and flocks of tourists, but the fact is that St Helena could never be a Majorca. The island lacks the package deal essentials, like beaches and sunshine. St Helena could and would only ever appeal to a select few tourists interested in the island's ecology and history.

I had been struck by the island's absolute dependency both economically and politically. The airport débâcle was a mani-festation of the island's total inability to sustain itself. Without this ability I doubted the islanders could or would ever feel any real sense of identity or heritage. St Helena was like an empty box of chocolates. She looked good from the outside, but she was hollow within.

Leaving St Helena was poignant. I felt a sadness for the people and the island. The Saints had shown me great generosity and warmth, and the island had impressed me with its beauty, but it lacked the resources and infrastructure to be self-sufficient. The airport decision would remain in the hands of the Foreign Office and the RMS *St Helena* would continue to serve and shape the island.

I sat at the railings and watched as the island disappeared over the horizon. Donny's would be closed now until the ship returned in four weeks' time. People would look out on to James Bay and see just the small fishing-vessels. The ship had gone and St Helena had lost her beating heart for another month.

For four days we beat into the wind on our way to Cape Town. The ship was full of Saints visiting family or taking an annual shopping trip to the South African city. I stood at the rails as we approached the Cape. The lights twinkled and sparkled in the balmy night air. A mother, her daughter and her granddaughter stood at the rail.

'Look, mummy, look,' squealed the young girl, 'a skyscraper, a skyscraper.' She was jumping up and down, flailing her arms wildly. For the young girl, this was her first adventure away from St Helena and the first time she had seen a city larger than Jamestown.

'I've never seen so many lights, it looks like a giant Christmas tree,' exclaimed the grandmother, mouth ajar. Suddenly I realized that this was the first time off St Helena not only for the young girl, but for Granny too.

'How long are you staying?' I asked her, astonished at the realization that she was seeing the outside world for the very first time in her seventy years.

'Four days,' she replied, returning her wide-eyed gaze to the skyline.

'This is your first time off St Helena, and you're only staying for four days?' I stammered.

'Exactly,' she smiled.

'But don't you want to spend more time exploring?' I implored.

'Not really,' she shrugged. 'To tell you the truth, I only really came for the boat trip. I've always wanted to sail on the RMS,' she smiled.

4. The Falkland Islands

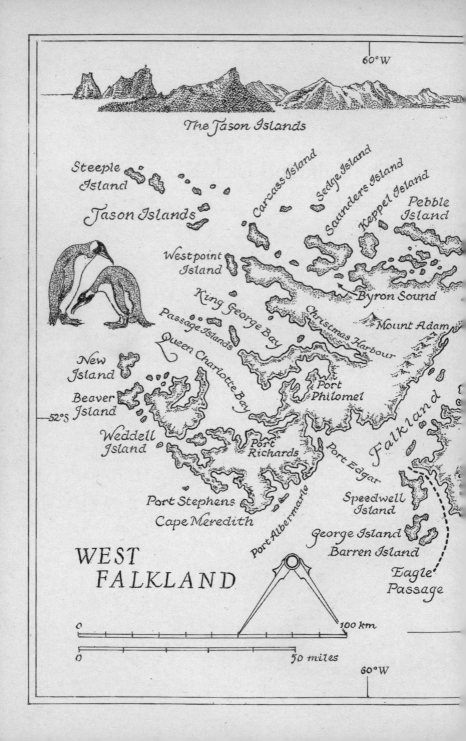

60°W

The Jason Islands

Steeple
Island

Jason Islands

Carcass Island

Sedge Island

Saunders Island

Keppel Island

Pebble
Island

Westpoint
Island

King George Bay

Byron Sound

Mount Adam

Christmas Harbour

Passage Islands

Queen Charlotte Bay

New
Island

Beaver
Island

Port
Philomel

52°S

Weddell
Island

Port
Richards

Port Edgar

Falkland

Port Stephens

Cape Meredith

Speedwell
Island

George Island

Barren Island

Port Albemarle

Eagle
Passage

WEST
FALKLAND

0 _____ 100 km

0 _____ 50 miles

60°W

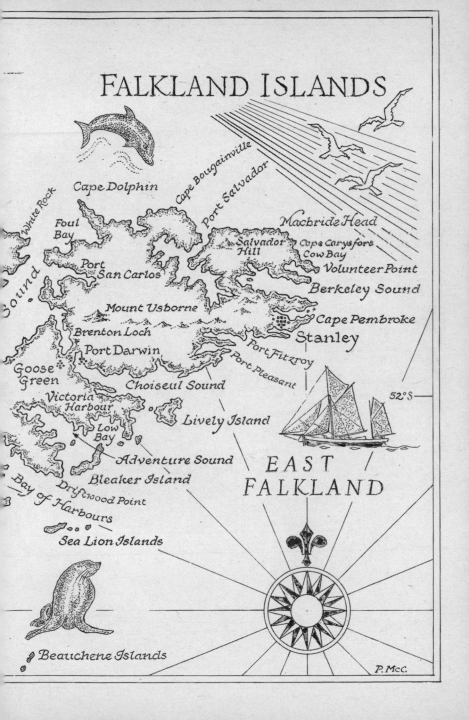

FALKLAND ISLANDS

White Rock
Cape Dolphin
Cape Bougainville
Port Salvador
Machride Head
Foul Bay
Salvador Hill
Cape Carysfort
Cow Bay
Port San Carlos
Volunteer Point
Sound
Berkeley Sound
Mount Usborne
Cape Pembroke
Brenton Loch
Stanley
Port Darwin
Port Fitzroy
Goose Green
Port Pleasant
Choiseul Sound
Victoria Harbour
Lively Island
Low Bay
52°S
Adventure Sound
Bleaker Island
EAST
Driftwood Point
FALKLAND
Bay of Harbours
Sea Lion Islands
Beauchene Islands

P. McC.

'Oi, you're that f****** bloke off the telly,' guffawed the guard at the main gate. I smiled and handed over my documents. 'What the f*** you doin' 'ere?' he continued.

'I'm off to the Falklands,' I replied as politely as possible.

'Who sentenced you to that?' he said in between mouthfuls of Cornish pasty. 'It's a shite hole. I spent four months there, and I 'ope I never see that f****** place again,' and with that he stamped my papers. 'Enjoy yourself,' he said with a broad grin across his face, 'I didn't.' At which he broke into gales of laughter.

The Falklands experience begins in a fashion that, given their history, is entirely appropriate. Check-in is at one of the UK's largest military airbases, RAF Brize Norton in Oxfordshire.

Brize Norton isn't exactly your Heathrow or Gatwick. The terminal consisted of a large hall. Gone are the shops and duty-frees, replaced by a battalion of imposing vending machines that cough and sneeze out rather nasty-looking plastic cups full of Cup a Soup and dishwater tea. The two check-in desks are staffed not by smiling check-in girls with pouting red lips, but two thoroughly fed-up uniformed RAF personnel.

The flight board was also a reminder that we weren't in your average airport. Instead of Los Angeles, Miami, Barbados or Madrid, the flight board read as follows:

AFGHANISTAN
DIEGO GARCIA
GIBRALTAR
CYPRUS
DECIMOMANNU
BELIZE

ASCENSION
MPA (FALKLANDS)

I queued up in the austere hall, conscious of my uncropped hair and uncamouflaged bag. 'The Falkland Islands?' stuttered the check-in assistant as he read my ticket. 'You sure?' he laughed mockingly. 'Why would you want to go to that cold pile of shite?' he asked sincerely. 'Haven't you had enough of cold wet windy islands?' I could tell it was going to be a long journey.

The RAF rather euphemistically call their passengers 'walking cargo'. The load on my flight could be broadly divided into two camps, the happy and the utterly miserable. The former tended to be dominated by returning islanders and visitors like me, while the latter seemed to be made up entirely of soldiers weeping into their cans of Coke at the prospect of a Falklands winter.

My name was called and I marched out on to the busy tarmac and towards the huge grey hulk of the RAF Tristar aeroplane.

Apart from her grey livery, the Tristar didn't appear very different from any other plane. The interior was fitted in the same way as most commercial airlines, except that there was slightly more leg room as some of the rows of seats had been removed to make way for military stretchers. Contrary to what I had been told, there were loos. However, a few tell-tale signs throughout the flight gave us gentle reminders that we were not on a conventional flight.

Absent were the stewardesses and in their place half a dozen surly-looking RAF men wandered up and down the aisles in their green jump-suits without much enthusiasm. I don't suppose any of them joined the air force to become Air Stewards, offering 'coffee, tea, tea, coffee'.

I sat back in my seat and explored the contents of a white paper bag that had been dropped on my tray. Meals were a little like stepping back in time to the days of shorts and Aertex shirts: a sausage roll, some egg and cheese sandwiches, wrapped in clingfilm, a small carton of orange squash, a banana, a KitKat and the *pièce de résistance*, a Wagon Wheel. I hadn't seen one of those since the good old days of my imaginary expeditions. Somehow it seemed like a good sign.

Nearly twenty hours after leaving rainy Oxfordshire, I caught my first glimpse of the Falkland Islands. Through the rain-streaked window, I watched as the colourless ocean turned to colourless land. There was no sign of life; just bleak hills and rocks and sodden earth, dotted with rugged-looking sheep.

As I gazed I became aware that I was being watched. In a scene straight out of *Top Gun*, I followed the small glass canopy of a fighter plane as it appeared above our wing. The pilot waved his gloved hand. The soldier next to me waved back. 'What's 'e still doing 'ere, must be 'is second deployment, poor bugga.'

The RAF Tornado shepherded us into Mount Pleasant Airbase. This routine escort service has long been a way of keeping bored pilots entertained, like giving a child a colouring book on a rainy day. What staggered me was how close they flew. I could practically see the old packet of Polo mints on the dashboard, and the tax disc in the window.

The Tornado disappeared as effortlessly as it had appeared and the Tristar touched down at Mount Pleasant, which with its rows upon rows of dull barracks is rather misleadingly named.

Mistakes, misnomers and misunderstandings seem to characterize the Falklands. This can be best exemplified by the opening sentence of the Bradt travel guide to the islands: 'The Falklands lie some 300 miles off the west of southern Argentina.' This may sound unremarkable except for the fact that the islands are off the east coast, not the west, placing it in the wrong ocean and off the coast of the wrong country. These aren't the only inaccuracies or misconceptions about the Falklands. Another that so irks the locals is that the capital is not Port Stanley, as was so often reported during the conflict, but Stanley – there's a difference. For those who may have other misconceptions or possibly no conception of the Falklands, here is a short geographical synopsis.

Situated in the South Atlantic, the Falkland Islands lie between latitude 51 and 53 degrees south and longitude 57 and 62 degrees west (about the same latitude south as London lies north). They are

400 miles from the South American mainland. The Falkland Islands comprise two main islands (East and West Falkland) and some 700 smaller islands, a total land area of about 4,700 square miles, covering an area the size of Wales. The distance from Stanley, on the extreme east, to New Island, on the extreme west, is some 148 miles.

No one really knows when the Falkland Islands were first discovered, but they began to appear on maps of South America from about 1507, although their name and the number of islands varied from map to map, while their latitude varied between 49 and 51 degrees. Their most common name seemed to be the Sanson Islands.

The first British claim to the discovery of the islands was on 14 August 1592, by Captain John Davis of the *Desiree*, which had been part of Thomas Cavendish's second expedition. Two years later, another English captain, Sir Richard Hawkins, sighted the islands and renamed them Hawkins Maydenlande after himself and Queen Elizabeth I. The islands were named a third time after a Dutch captain sighted them in 1598 and called them the Sebalines. The islands got their current name after Captain John Strong, aboard the *Welfare*, landed on the islands in 1690 to replenish his ship. He named them after Viscount Falkland, who was the then treasurer to the Admiralty. And the islands have been known to Latin America as the Malvinas since the 1600s.

'Welcome to MPA,' announced the pilot. 'Due to gale force winds we are unable to offload you as normal,' he continued in military speak, as the plane was buffeted around the runway by the force 10 wind. The Falklands weather is notorious for diverting the Tristar and I had been advised to get inoculations for a possible landing in Brazil, Montevideo, or even Dakar in Senegal, all of which are regular diversions for the Tristar. Some sceptical islanders noted the frequency with which the plane tended to be diverted to the warm beaches of Brazil or stranded on tropical Ascension during holiday periods.

I first travelled to the islands at the invitation of the Falklands government to write a magazine feature. I had been asked to become travel editor of a glossy magazine and write reports from around the world. I suspect the magazine had been expecting a series of jolly jaunts to Polynesian paradises and tropical Caribbean islands. Instead they got East Timor, Zambia, a rhino relocation project in Nepal and the Falklands.

At least we had landed in the Falklands, although as I listened to the wind and rain hammer against the side of the plane, the attraction of the Caribbean was obvious. Eventually we started to move forward towards one of the enormous hangars along the runway. The gigantic doors had been opened and to my astonishment we drove in as if we were little more than a Mini. The doors were closed behind us and the pilot informed us that it was now safe to disembark.

My surreal introduction into South Atlantic culture continued as I wandered through the gloomy halls of the air terminal to the baggage reclaim belt. We all crammed into the tiny hall as two soldiers in army fatigues mounted the console and called out for everyone's attention.

'It is very important that you all listen to these safety instructions from the Bomb Disposal Office,' boomed one of them. 'Ordnance recognition,' hollered the second soldier before they took it in turn to hold up a dazzling array of mines and grenades, with a little description of where each could be found and what it could do to you. It was like a briefing for the dangerous-birdspotting society. 'THIS ONE IS DESIGNED TO EXPLODE AT KNEE LEVEL AND WILL REMOVE BOTH YOUR LEGS,' boomed soldier one. 'THIS ONE BLEW A CAR OFF THE ROAD,' warned soldier two. After scaring the life out of every civilian in the hall, and handing us all maps detailing the whereabouts of the 25,000 live mines in over a hundred different minefields, they wished us all a pleasant stay.

I had noticed a number of unusual passengers on the flight. They had appeared removed and distant. Their eyes faraway. I noticed them again as I searched for my luggage under a mountain of camouflaged kit bags. Some appeared to be accompanied, escorted even, and it was only after I overheard one of their conversations that I realized who they were. It was the twentieth anniversary of the conflict, and a number of former soldiers had chosen to return to the islands for the first time since the war, a chance for them to lay their ghosts to rest. Some, it appeared, had come with their psychiatric nurses to help them through the traumatic ordeal. It was a sobering experience for me, and one that was never far from my mind during my stay.

Outside the terminal a flock of Land-Rover Defenders stretched as far as the eye could see. There were Royal Navy Land-Rovers painted grey, Army Land-Rovers in green, and government Land-Rovers in red. There were white ones, yellow ones; I even spotted a pink one. Some were brand new, while others looked older than my grandfather. There were convertible Land-Rovers, six-wheel Land-Rovers. Some had been souped up like boy racer cars with booming stereos and even dangly dice, while others looked sad and depressed. Dozens and dozens of the cars spluttered and vibrated, spilling diesel fumes into the first fresh air I'd breathed for nearly twenty-four hours.

A study has estimated that there are more than 3,000 Land-Rovers in the Falkland Islands, which, given a total population of just 2,300, is more than one per person.

I was escorted in a Land-Rover by Falkland Islanders Debbie, Becky and Emma Jane. They looked as if they had just returned from a shopping trip on the King's Road. To my shame I'd been expecting dungarees and wellies.

Falkland Islanders are predominantly of British background. Historically farmworkers were recruited from the rural areas of Scotland and Southern England. There are also a number of families of Scandinavian descent, their forbears having remained in the Falklands after being shipwrecked in the eighteenth and nineteenth centuries.

'The Falkland Islanders come of a hardy stock, content with a decent life of personal achievement, proud of their strength of character, their origins, and their family ties . . . of such outstanding qualifications and hardiness for work, in as often as not, the harshest weather in this distant colony of the British Commonwealth,' explained the *Falkland Centenary Booklet* in 1951.

These three pretty girls who met me had been charged with the unenviable task of promoting the Falkland Islands as a tourist destination. It is difficult to imagine how the Falklands could have received any more negative publicity since the world learnt that they weren't in the Outer Hebrides of Scotland but in the South Atlantic Ocean, when Argentina tried to relieve the UK of them twenty years ago.

The Falkland Islands had been the setting for the last great colonial war, in which Britain fought an army of 10,000 Argentinians on a territory 8,000 miles from home. It was an epic feat of arms, but was it worth the deaths of 255 British servicemen and 655 Argentines? For many it seemed incredible that Britain should take such a risk to retain a territory that the government had been trying to wipe its hands clean of for years. For many it was a battle fought by Thatcher for Thatcher, but for the islanders, the war was about liberty and the freedom to live in their homeland.

On 2 April 1982, the Falkland Islands went from blissful obscurity to a PR disaster as Fleet Street's finest descended on the remote islands that had now become a battlefield and a graveyard for hundreds of soldiers. Falkland Islands Tourism must have thought long and hard about their strategy. Their trump card was to hire Debbie, Becky and Emma Jane and send them around the world to promote their homeland.

My childhood recollections of the Falkland Islands are limited to the powerful words 'gotcha' and 'yomp'. The image of a marine with a Union Flag attached to his rucksack. The face of Simon Weston. But above all it was those images of a bleak winter landscape of mud and snow that endure in most people's minds.

The Falkland Islands have spent the last twenty years trying to counter this popular perception, and they were struggling against a tide of twentieth-anniversary publicity. I had been invited out to the islands for *Hello!* magazine on one understanding: 'Whatever happens,' I was told, 'Don't Mention the War.'

The 1982 w★★ of course had been brewing for years, and was the climax of years of tension. Discussions about the islands' sovereignty have raged from the 1500s to the present day.

The islands were discussed by a United Nations committee on decolonialization in 1964. The Argentinian claim was based on the sighting of the islands in the 1500s, while the British claim rested on the first recorded landing on the islands in 1690, and the settlement and administration of the islands since 1833. Britain agreed that the islanders would be granted self-determination and argued that Argentinian control would create a new colony rather than remove one. Talks continued for many months until a number of incidents brought negotiations to a head.

In September 1964, a light aircraft circled Stanley before landing on the racecourse. The pilot hopped out of the plane, planted an Argentinian flag into the ground, handed over a letter stating Argentinian sovereignty over the islands before jumping back into the plane and flying off again.

Soon afterwards a DC4 on an internal flight in Argentina was hijacked by twenty nationalists calling themselves the Condors. The plane flew up Stanley Harbour before landing on the racecourse, missing the grandstand but hitting some telegraph poles before eventually sinking into the mud. The Condors took four hostages before being overwhelmed by the islands' local defence force and handing themselves over to a local priest. They were collected by an Argentinian naval ship and each given nominal sentences.

Later that year another landing took place, though this time it was a small detachment of Argentinian marines aboard a submarine. They surfaced near Stanley for a few hours to recce potential landing beaches near the capital. The second officer on board, Juan José Lombardo, rose through the ranks to chief of naval operations, and was responsible for masterminding the 1982 Argentinian invasion.

Relations between the two countries settled until 1976, when a British research ship, the *Shackleton*, was fired upon by an Argentinian gunboat. Argentina even set up an illegal military base on Southern Thule, an uninhabited dependency of the Falkland Islands.

The climax of the frosty British–Argentinian relations, of course, came in 1982. It began with the landing of an Argentinian scrap metal merchant on South Georgia. He was accompanied by military personnel. On 26 March, the head of Argentina's military junta, General Galtieri, decided to invade. The first land forces reached the islands on 2 April and took control of Stanley after a short battle with the handful of Marines who were garrisoned on the islands.

These soldiers and the governor, Sir Rex Hunt, were flown to Montevideo in Uruguay the following day. Rex Hunt, in defiant dignity, refused to shake hands with the conquistadors. He donned his full colonial governor's uniform, complete with sword and plumed hat, and drove in his 'official' car, a maroon London taxi complete with the Union Flag.

Over the following days the Argentinian troops consolidated their position in the islands, also landing troops on South Georgia and the South Sandwich Islands. The United Nations passed Resolution 502 calling for the cessation of all hostilities, the withdrawal of Argentinian troops from the islands and the resumption of talks between the two countries. In London, the House of Commons was convened in an emergency session on 3 April and informed that a task force would be sent to liberate the islands.

The first British naval convoy left the following week for the South Atlantic, and Britain declared a 200 mile exclusion zone around the islands. Argentina landed more than 10,000 troops on the islands. And for a time Wideawake airfield on Ascension became the busiest airfield in the world as Britain massed the task force.

Hostilities increased and the British task force landed on 21 May, on the western side of East Falkland at San Carlos Water. Several of the warships were damaged, or in the case of the *Ardent* sunk, but the land force were able to get ashore unscathed. By 24 May 5,000 British troops were entrenched on East Falkland. They advanced towards Stanley, and by the end of May special forces had the capital surrounded. The fighting eventually reached Wireless Ridge and Mount Tumbledown on the outskirts of the capital. The capitulation of the Argentinian forces meant that these were some of the last battles of the war, and over the following few days more than 10,000 Argentinian prisoners were brought into Stanley.

Britain formally declared an end to hostilities as soon as the South Sandwich Islands had been reoccupied on 20 June 1982.

The three Falkland babes had organized for me to spend my first night in Darwin, a mile away from Goose Green, an hour's bumpy ride from the airport. There is only one all-weather road in the Falkland Islands, and that is the one that runs from Stanley to Mount Pleasant Airbase (or vice versa, depending on whether you ask native or military). This road is the longest in the Falklands, at 35 miles long, though it is only tarmacked in places, the rest being loose gravel. The road is notorious for the high incidence of accidents on it, a result of it being the only road in the islands where motorists can grind their ancient Land-Rovers out of first gear. And the abnormally deep drainage ditches on either side of the road lead to several fatalities a year, a huge number given the islands' population of 2,300.

There are a number of theories and myths about the reason for the excessively deep drainage ditches, but the most popular is the story that the construction engineers asked for meteorological data for the islands. Brainwashed, like me, by the images of 1982, they had misinterpreted the data, muddling inches for feet. The ditches had been designed accordingly to deal with the annual rainfall of 12 feet rather than 12 inches that they had assumed deluged the island. The result is a narrow road built up several feet from the flat valley, with sheer slopes on either side.

The rest of the Falklands are traversed cross-country, hence the small army of 4 × 4s.

We bounced our way along the rough track as barren moorland stretched into desolate valleys. Big skies reminded me of the Scottish Highlands. Along the side of the road was a stark reminder of the war that once raged here. Dozens of rusty red signs painted with the skull and crossbones marked one of the islands' hundred minefields. Mine clearance had been attempted, but more injuries had occurred during this attempted clean-up, it was decided, than would be caused by simply leaving them in the marked-off areas. While many of the minefields were nothing more than moorland, one of the islands' most beautiful beaches had also been mined, and was now closed for ever.

Goose Green has become one of the most famous names in the islands as a result of the battles that raged there in 1982. The community hall, in the centre of the settlement, still bears the scars of the 114 people incarcerated there during the war. Almost a month after the initial invasion, all the residents imprisoned in the hall scrawled the letters POW on the walls. In contrast to this rather bleak reminder, Ken Greenland runs a cosy lodge just down the road.

Ken reminded me of a First World War fighter pilot with his plummy accent and his handlebar moustache. The lodge was filled with all the accoutrements for a rainy day. There were board games and jigsaw puzzles, and even a complete collection of old magazines all neatly stacked in chronological order alongside an even larger collection of Falkland Islands War books.

Only about 400 of the population live outside Stanley, or in 'camp', as it is known. Living in camp has never been easy in the Falklands. Even today the communications and transport infrastructure is difficult for those outside Stanley. There is even an hour's time difference between 'camp' and Stanley.

The islanders have always had to be incredibly self-sufficient. The only fuel was peat and each settlement had its own store and its own school. Living off the land according to the season was integral to camp life. November was 'egging' time, which involved the collecting of penguin and albatross eggs to supplement their diet.

My first 'experience' of Falklands hospitality had been at Goose Green, where, still jet-lagged from the long flight from the UK, I had been offered a penguin with my cup of tea. I knew that the islanders had once collected penguin eggs, but I couldn't believe that they still indulged in eating these endearingly comic creatures as an alternative to a scone or a hot cross bun. Oh, the indignity of it. I knew the Falkland islanders were going to be strange, I thought to myself and was about to launch into a tirade about their insensitivity when I noticed the familiar markings of the chocolate biscuits in my host's hand. 'I'd love one,' I smiled with a blush.

★

Falkland Islanders are called 'kelpers' by Argentinians, although the military call them 'Bennys', after the *Crossroads* character with his woolly hats and jumpers. After locals complained about this 'racist' remark, officers banned the use of the word, so the wily troops decided to call the islanders 'stills', because they were still Bennys. The islanders call the military personnel 'when I's', because of the number of times they begin a sentence with, 'When I was in . . .'

Farming on the Falkland Islands is largely a monoculture based around wool, which is generally exported to the United Kingdom. Farms on the islands used to be huge, with as many as 700,000 sheep. These farms were eventually broken up and subdivided into eighty-eight still large farms. The sheep-shearing shed at Goose Green remains the largest in the southern hemisphere. Today there are nearly a hundred owner-managed farms, with an average size of 33,200 acres.

From Darwin in East Falkland, I headed to Port Howard in West Falkland. The islands' poor infrastructure means that the only practical way of getting around them is aboard the world's smallest airline, the Falkland Islands Government Air Service. The tiny red eight-seater propeller planes connect a network of forty landing strips around the islands, of which only one, Stanley airport, is tarmac. The rest, like the roads, are simply fields of sheep.

Goose Green's airfield consisted of a small terminal 'shed'. Landing procedures in camp involve a number of comic and rather unusual pre-flight checks. First the field must be cleared of any sheep or geese. This involves driving up and down tootling the horn and waving arms frantically out of the windows. The wind sock is then raised, allowing the details of wind direction and speed to be called through to the approaching pilot from the Land-Rover's VHF radio. Then the same multi-purpose Land-Rover becomes the airfield's fire engine by attaching a mobile fire extinguisher to the back.

It was half an hour to Port Howard. The settlement is one of the most picturesque in the Falklands and is also one of the few remaining large farming settlements in the islands. The farm is nearly 200,000 acres with more than 50,000 Corriedale sheep.

Port Howard, I had been told, was one of the most popular places to visit in the Falklands, with visitors staying at the lodge, run by the magnificently eccentric Hattie Lee. Hattie, originally from Cumbria, had run the lodge since she arrived in the Falklands, five years ago. She had been working as a tour guide in Mongolia, where she cooked for people on yak holidays. She had come to the Falklands to work at Port Howard lodge for a season, but had fallen in love with a popular local called Robin Lee. The two had a whirlwind romance before marrying. Tragically, Robin died just a few months later, leaving Hattie to run the lodge and his estate.

Hattie's house was a happy one. She fussed over her guests and was regarded as the best chef in the islands. During my stay at the lodge, the peace and quiet of camp life was broken on a number of occasions by the violent cacophony of Sea King helicopters ferrying officers from MPA for a few days' R&R at the lodge.

Hattie drowned me in tea and scones before offering to take me on a grand tour, beginning with Mount Maria, the 2,000-foot mountain that dominates the pretty settlement. She agreed to take me to the summit, deciding to drive me up in her cooking-apron. It was a gloriously sunny day as we edged our way over steep pastureland. The Land-Rover coughed and shuddered its way up the ever-increasing incline, stopping every few minutes for another one of the gates that infest the islands. There were gates everywhere. I imagined a farmer looking at the blank spot in the middle of the field and saying to himself, 'Good place for a gate, that is.'

The meadows were home to both sheep and upland geese. In the early twentieth century the government classed the geese as a pest and introduced a bounty payment for goose beaks, as they were perceived to be in direct competition with the sheep for pastureland.

Hattie told me about one of her visitors, an American called Brad who was on a recce for his travel company, the fantastically named Blast 'n' Cast, specializing in 'huntin' and fishin'' holidays. He had been very impressed at the lethargy of the upland geese, which made them particularly easy targets, and much to the horror of locals was planning on returning with clients, 'to catch the little critters'.

As we ascended the mountain, Port Howard disappeared in the valley below, and the rolling Atlantic Ocean appeared on the horizon, sparkling in the late-summer sunlight. The higher we chugged, the softer and boggier the ground became. We squelched through the soft mud until the Land-Rover could go no further. The engine wheezed heavily as the back wheels spun deeper and deeper into the soggy earth. It wasn't long before they'd been completely swallowed and the tail-gate kissed the pastureland. 'We're bogged,' huffed Hattie, crawling on her hands and knees attempting to dig away at the clingy soil.

Bogging, explained Hattie, is a common occurrence in the islands, and one to which she was particularly prone, much to the amusement of everyone else in Port Howard. 'How do we debog ourselves?' I asked. Hattie explained that 'boggers' call up on the open channel of the VHF radio, allowing all 2,300 residents of the Falkland Islands to hear their SOS. The nearest Land-Rover in the vicinity then comes to the rescue. Hattie blushed as she imagined the reaction across the Falklands to her call: 'Not again.'

While we waited for help, Hattie suggested that we continue up the mountain, its grassy slope strewn with granite outcrops. We sat atop Hattie's favourite rock, where she had come with her late husband Robin, and gazed out to sea. I felt sure if I stared hard enough I would see the Argentinian coastline.

Two hill-walkers soon appeared, descending the steep slopes in giant leaps. They looked like tropical frogs as their bright-red coats appeared and disappeared as they dipped in and out of the large boulders and tall pinnacles.

'Good afternoon,' they chirped. I noticed that they weren't wearing red jackets at all but T-shirts and shorts. I peered down at my thick fleece and jumper and my heavy trousers and suddenly felt rather over-dressed. I hadn't been sure how to pack for my Falklands adventure. I had been told that it was the islands' summer, with the addition that it was quite the norm for the Falklands to experience a summer, winter, autumn and spring all in one day.

I had been surprised by the warmth and particularly the strength of the sun, which had left me permanently beetroot, but here, half-way up a mountain, was certainly not the place or the weather for shorts.

'We're making the most of the summer,' smiled the man with a thick beard and baseball cap. 'We don't get weather like this at home,' added the woman turning her face to the sun.

'Where's home?' I asked.

'South Georgia,' he replied.

'Oh,' I nodded, 'you don't sound very American.'

'That's because we're not,' he said irritably, 'we're from South Georgia.'

Gordon Liddle and his partner were both employees of the British Antarctic Survey and the two of them had been living down in South Georgia for nearly two years. They were in the Falklands for a quick holiday before returning 'home'. 'It's amazing who you bump into on a Falklands island,' smiled Hattie as the two South Georgians disappeared into the meadows below.

Our saviour arrived in the form of an ancient blue Land-Rover, a rope and some good old-fashioned elbow grease. We were back in Port Howard in time for tea.

While Port Howard is now the most important sheep-farming area in the islands, sheep weren't introduced until the mid-1800s. In the first half of the nineteenth century the Falkland Islands were becoming a popular place for whaling and sealing ships, many of which used the islands as a base for their trade. By this time Argentina had gained independence from Spain and made her own claim of sovereignty over the Falkland Islands, dispatching David Jewett, commander of the *Heroina*, to assert her ownership. Argentina soon appointed the first governor to the islands and land was granted to the first two settlers, Louis Vernet and Don Jorge Pachero. This first attempt to colonize lasted less than a year, but Argentina persevered and a second expedition was sent to the islands in 1826. A garrison was eventually settled at Port Louis, and Vernet, who was eventually made governor, had three American schooners arrested for alleged illegal sealing. Word soon reached the United States when one of the ships managed to escape, but the captain of the *Harriet* was taken to Buenos Aires for trial. The US responded by sending the USS *Lexington* to the islands, destroying the settlement of Port Soledad and declaring the islands free of government.

The British eventually arrived on the islands in 1832, when Captain Onslow gave the occupying Argentinian settlers notice to vacate the British Crown land. The governor was exiled back to Argentina, but the new British governor was murdered just a year later by a group of mutinous gaucho cowboys from South America. The gauchos were arrested and taken to Britain for trial. They were eventually released and returned to Montevideo.

In 1840, the Colonial Land and Emigration Commissioners declared the Falkland Islands suitable for colonization. A new town was built in the sheltered bay of Port William and named Stanley after the then secretary of state. The islands prospered during the California gold rush. Ships that had rounded Cape Horn used the islands as a place for repair and retreat from the severe Cape weather. Stanley became one of the busiest ports in the world towards the end of the nineteenth century. The boom lasted until the completion of the Panama Canal in 1900, which dramatically reduced the number of ships needing to use the islands, and sheep farming assumed an increasingly important role.

By 1880, the Falkland Islands Company had more than 100,000 sheep and several thousand cattle on East Falkland alone. Attempts were made to export frozen carcasses, but the frozen mutton was deemed to be of an insufficient standard for the European market, and two meat canning factories were built in 1910. The market flourished during the First World War but it soon dropped as fresh meat became more readily available, and wool became the islands' main export.

Shearing-sheds dominate the small harbour. Today wool is collected by the islands' only ship, the *Tamar*, and shipped to Stanley for onward passage to the UK.

Like most of the larger settlements across the Falklands, Port Howard has a small community school. Although the school has had up to twenty children, when I visited there was only one, a rather lonely Guy Morrison, who would ride to school each day on his quad bike before returning home to help his dad on the farm. Guy, however, was one of the lucky camp children who lived within commutable access of a school.

For several dozen children in the islands, school means classes over the phone and on the internet. Classes are run by a crack team of teachers based in Stanley's secondary school in the 'camp education department'. Radio classes take place daily and are augmented by visits from the teachers, who fly out to live with the families for a few months each year.

The following day, I was leaving Hattie's nest for the rugged shores of Carcass Island, a 45-minute plane hop to the north-west. Carcass Island is situated to the west of West Falkland. The present owners are Rob and Lorraine McGill. The tiny settlement has well-established hedges and trees, giving the place more the feeling of some Sussex estate than one of the Falklands' remotest islands. The oldest house is Valley Cottage, which was built in 1870 and is now used as one of the islands' self-catering properties.

Rob had the typical weather-hardened features of the Falkland Islanders, with his rosy-red cheeks, his dishevelled mop of white hair and his oil-splattered jeans, which seemed to be de rigueur outside Stanley. His Land-Rover looked like it was older than him. Its doors were held closed with bale twine and the back was stuffed full of old animal-feed sacks, spare parts for a wind turbine and wooden fencing stakes.

Rob's house could have been anywhere in the UK. The drawing-room was filled with the by now familiar 'rainy day' jigsaws and board games, and old copies of *National Geographic*. An open fire danced around the wallpapered walls, while Gary Lineker's soothing tones introduced *Grandstand* on the TV.

A green Aga pumped heat into the cosy kitchen, while huge bay windows offered views out on to the English country garden beyond. The shelves were stocked with familiar-looking packets of Corn Flakes and Porridge Oats, and jars of marmalade and Marmite. It could have been a house straight from the pages of *Country Life*, except, that is, for two small details: the first was the VHF radio that sat in pride of place between the Aga and the cat basket.

The VHF radio is the lifeline to the outside world for many camp-dwellers, and I could practically watch Rob's ears twitch as he walked around the kitchen listening to the Falkland Islands news, which included the comings and goings of every passenger travelling aboard FIGAS. Surnames are read out on air, though passenger weights are thankfully censored.

More curious, though, was the neatly stacked pile of mugs on the shelf next to the door. This may not sound like an unusual spectacle for a British home except for the fact that there weren't five but five hundred of them.

'They're for our guests,' Rob beamed. I struggled to register. I had flown for nearly twenty-four hours to get to Stanley, followed by a further hour's flight aboard a minuscule aeroplane, and a final hour trampolining around the back of a Land-Rover to get to this place. Just how often does he get five hundred visitors?

By my rough calculations, the FIGAS plane, which could take up to eight people, would need to make over sixty round trips to the island to complete a tea party of this size.

'Take a look in the larder,' he teased. I padded across the wooden floor and pulled the pantry door open. I was met by a patisserie-ist's fantasy. Dozens of shelves were stacked high with every cake, pastry and chocolate imaginable, thousands of them: éclairs, meringues, Black Forest gâteaux, profiteroles, handmade truffles, scones, Danish pastries, flapjacks – it was a scene from Willy Wonka's chocolate factory.

Rob explained that the island and the house with its pretty gardens had become popular as a tourist stop for cruise ship passengers. 'We've got 250 coming in on the *Marco Polo* on Monday,' he smiled. 'Aunty and I have been baking since last Monday.' Cruise ships had started to include a tea visit in their South Atlantic itineraries: Antarctica, South Georgia, Stanley and Rob McGill's kitchen.

Rob McGill has lived on Carcass Island for nearly thirty years, and is largely self-sufficient, with organic vegetables, meat and dairy produce. The island is also one of the Falklands' most water-rich islands, with eighteen different water sources. Electricity is now produced from one of the increasingly popular Proven wind turbines, identical to the one we used on Taransay.

During the war, Rob had stuck it out on the remote island, cut off from the rest of the world and removed from the heavy fighting on East and West Falkland. He was also cut off from news and supplies. Rob told me of one occasion, several weeks after the invasion, when he had been sat in the kitchen one evening and heard a knock at the door. Now this may not sound particularly unusual until you remember that Rob was alone on an island many miles from anywhere.

He brazenly opened the door only to discover several men dressed in full diving-gear, their faces painted black. 'SBS,' they announced, informing Rob that they were all commandos from the Special Boat Squadron, the naval version of the SAS, and that they had come to 'sweep' the island to ensure it was clean of Argentinians. Rob invited them in for tea and they ended up staying for several days. An SBS plaque sent to Rob after the war thanking him for his help now had pride of place on the kitchen wall.

Until now I hadn't really noticed how few trees there are in the Falklands, but as I wandered around the mature gardens full of cypress trees, I suddenly realized how stark the rest of the islands had been. The same had happened on Taransay, where there had been no trees at all. We had become so used to a landscape void of trees, that it wasn't until I left the island and returned south that I noticed how much I had missed them.

Apart from the draw of the pastries, Carcass Island is also a popular stop for naturalists, and indeed some of David Attenborough's documentaries have been filmed from these very shores, which are bustling with gentoo and Magellanic penguins, seals and, most amazing of all, elephant seals.

These are some of the most odd-looking creatures on earth and seeing one for the first time is a little like an encounter with ET. They look more like slugs than elephants, but of course slug seals doesn't have the same ring. They get their name from an inflatable proboscis. The males are humongous creatures reaching up to twenty feet in length and up to five tons in weight – that's more than five Minis.

I spent hours watching them as they bellowed and farted and squabbled among themselves. They reminded me of old men arguing as they lay sunbathing in the late-summer sunshine. Their bodies were heavily scarred from fighting over territory and females.

At the time of my visit a team of Italian scientists were busy undertaking a study into elephant seal phonetics. This involved holding microphones as close to their vocal cords as was possible. It was an extraordinary sight to watch these two Italians with their microphones attached to sticks creeping up on the sleeping elephant seals, who would respond in the same way every time, by lifting their heavy heads up and screaming at the mad scientists who would then poke the microphones as close to their mouths as they dared.

I had a close encounter with one of these grumpy beasts myself. I had been snooping around the tall grasses next to the dunes, where, unknown to me, I had been spotted and was being watched. Elephant seals can raise their heads up to 10 feet above the ground, just high enough to peer over the tall grasses. As I peeked into the dunes, the furious beast lunged, screaming at me in a shower of spit. I could have sworn it was saying, 'Oi, you're that bloke off the telly,' but my senses had been incapacitated by its incredibly smelly breath.

It fell asleep again where it landed. Its skin was heavily scarred from fighting over the ladies. I was just glad it was as lazy as it was moody, or Rob could have served me to the next visiting cruise ship as a pancake.

From Carcass Island, I headed south-west to the largest privately owned island in the world, Weddell Island. And Weddell, I soon discovered as we came in to land, has its own unique landing hazards: not sheep, or even upland geese, but penguins, thousands of them.

The island is home to huge colonies of gentoo penguins. Tall elegant birds, gentoos are also the most comical of the penguins, waddling around like waiters from *Mary Poppins*, tripping up over tufts of grass and always using the same route to and from their rookeries. I spent hours staring at their antics, frequently laughing out loud.

Weddell is the third largest island within the Falklands group and is named after the Antarctic explorer Captain James Weddell. The island was used to experiment in processing seals for their oil in 1923. Samples were sent to Britain to assess whether they would be a suitable base for paints. However, a trial in which 384 seals were boiled down produced only eleven barrels and the venture was deemed a failure. Today the island is owned by Mr Visick, a London-based businessman who has attempted to broaden the island's horizons. In May 2002, *Heat* magazine reported that 'Robbie Williams is considering hiring out one of the Falkland Islands, Weddell, as a location to make his first Hollywood movie.' The story went on to suggest that he must have chosen the remote island because he wanted to keep away from the prying eyes of the paparazzi.

When I visited Weddell it couldn't have seemed a more unlikely story, and it was one which locals dismissed as Visick's 'PR spin'. The permanent island population was just two, a farmer and a brassy young woman from South Shields on Tyneside, Karen Taylor, who had come to the Falklands after answering an advert in a newspaper. She had been working at the Halcyon hotel in London's Holland Park at the time, when she spotted the vacancy for someone to run the island and its 54,000 acre farm.

Karen had strived to make Mountain View House as British and homely as possible, creating a small pub in the front room called the 'Weddell in, waddle out', and even organizing games of cricket on the lawn and high tea at 4 o'clock.

I shared the flight from Weddell Island back to Stanley with the flying doctor. It meant a number of diversions on the way home. Inaccessibility and remoteness mean that for some settlements their only chance to see the doctor is during his twice-yearly house call visits, and I was lucky enough to escort him to a number of the islands' smallest communities.

The Falklands are at their most stunning from the air, like some organic Pollock painting, a green canvas speckled with white and grey. The Atlantic Ocean spreads between the islands in a rich palette of blues and whites, streaked with the brown stains of the kelp beds just below the surface. I was staggered at the number of dazzling white sandy beaches and the remoteness of some of the small hamlets, many of which are now deserted.

Our first stop was a small isolated community of half a dozen living in a number of old farm buildings. As we bounced along the lumpy field, the temporary fire truck trundled along beside us. As we came to a halt in the windy field, a burly farmer in denim Osh Kosh dungarees covered in oil and blood stains ambled over to the plane and poked his head around the door. 'Hello, Ben,' he said with a West Country burr. 'The missus would like to invite you in for tea,' he smiled with his heavily lined face. This from a man I had never met on an island to which I had never been before.

What I soon learned was that BBC's *Castaway* had been shown in the Falklands on BFBS (British Forces Broadcasting Service), a composite channel made up of highlights from all the UK's terrestrial channels and then beamed to British soldiers all over the world. The programme had been incredibly popular in the islands. While the doctor went off to examine Granny and take aunty's blood pressure, I went in for tea. The kitchen was buried under a mountain of old magazines and copies of the *Penguin News*, the islands' only weekly newspaper. The Rayburn was busy heating the house, filling the hot-water tank, cooking the lamb and drying the half-dozen pairs of Y-fronts hanging above it.

The VHF radio fizzed into the smoky air. I sat at the old wooden farmhouse table, most of which was taken up by a giant computer, on which a young girl was busy surfing the web.

'Homework?' I asked.

'No, shopping,' replied the bespectacled young girl. As with so many remote corners of the world, the internet had revolutionized life in the Falklands.

I was presented with a steaming cup of tea and a mountain of homemade cake, while I was interrogated about *Castaway*. When the doctor had completed his checks it was time to move on to the next settlement.

In total, we stopped at four settlements, and each time, I was invited to sample the family's baking. I had become aware of the islanders' tendency to stuff tourists full of food at every opportunity. I confronted Hattie about this worrying trend. 'It's because we're all terrified about visitors going hungry,' she explained simply. 'We don't have corner shops out in camp, so we make sure we feed you whenever we can.'

By the time we reached Stanley, I waddled out of the small plane, my tummy sloshing with tea and cake from the islanders' irresistible hospitality.

Stanley felt like a sprawling metropolis compared to the sparsely populated camp in which I had spent the last week. It even felt strange and unnatural touching down on a tarmac runway. 'Where are the sheep?' I thought as we taxied in to a smart terminal building where Councillor Richard Cockwell was waiting to meet me.

Stanley must be one of the most extraordinary capital cities in the world. It grew dramatically during the California gold rush in the mid-1800s. The islands were used as a victualling point on the long journey from the United States' east coast to the west coast via Cape Horn. The capital city has continued to be the commercial centre of the Falkland Islands, with nearly three quarters of the islands' population living there. The port experienced a huge influx of traffic after the Argentinian invasion, when floating accommodation blocks known as 'coatels' were used by the military prior to the construction of the military base at MPA.

Stanley has not always been the capital of the Falklands, however. Until 1843 the seat of government had been Port Louis, in the north-east of East Falkland. Port Louis, or Fort Saint-Louis as it was originally called, was the earliest settlement on the Falklands, founded by the French when Louis Antoine de Bougainville came to the islands in April 1764. He was an idealistic young Frenchman who had fought in Canada and witnessed the loss of Quebec to the

British in 1756. He had dreamed of founding a new settlement for the Acadians, who had been expelled from Canada to Saint-Malo. He established a colony and renamed the islands the 'Îles Malouines', derived from Saint-Malo, which is also the derivation of the Argentinian name: 'Islas Malvinas'.

The French occupation did not last long as the British had established a settlement of their own at Port Egmont, on Saunders Island off West Falkland. Although relations between the two communities were fairly cordial, the remote settlers got dragged into the complicated web of European politics. Spain objected to the French settlement in a land that they considered part of their South American portfolio. France was anxious not to upset relations with either Spain or England and eventually agreed to vacate the islands for a fee of £25,000 from Spain.

The British settlement was also evacuated under pressure from Spain, though it was the use of warships as opposed to cash that persuaded them to abandon the islands. The British left behind a flag and a plaque representing their claim to ownership. It wasn't long before the Spanish also left the remote islands, leaving for the nearby United Provinces of Rio de la Plata, which later became Argentina. The Spanish also left a plaque and flag registering their claim to the islands.

Stanley is probably the most remote capital city in the world, and it seems apt that it should be twinned with Whitby, a windswept port town on the north-east coast of England. It is situated on the north-facing slope in order to catch as much sun as possible throughout the year. Stanley's history has been punctuated by the shipwrecks which lie along the harbour. The *Capricorn* was a Welsh barque dating from 1859. She was carrying a cargo of coal from Swansea to the west coast of South America when her cargo caught fire. She was scuttled to put out the fire and moved to her present position, where she was used as jetty.

The largest wreck is that of the *Lady Elizabeth*. The three-masted barque was returning with her cargo of guano bound for England when she was damaged rounding the Horn. She pulled into Stanley, where her crew refused to continue owing to her unseaworthiness. She was scuttled in the harbour, where she remains to this day.

'Rush hour,' lamented Richard as we drove into Stanley, 'blast.' He scrunched his face in anticipation. The road ahead of us seemed perfectly clear. We drove past the public jetty and Jubilee Villas, a row of terraced houses built in 1887 and named to commemorate the Golden Jubilee of Queen Victoria. They are a perfect example of English nineteenth-century brick terraced houses that could have come straight from the set of *Coronation Street*. The only difference is that instead of a traditional slate roof, they have the mandatory Falkland corrugated iron, known locally as 'wriggly tin'.

We continued down a nearly deserted Ross Road. 'I thought you said it was rush hour?' I asked.

'It is, we'll hit the traffic down by Barrack Street,' he sighed. We continued on our whirlwind tour of Stanley, past the Whale Bone Arch, which is made up of four enormous jawbones from two blue whales. It was a gift to the islanders from the whalers of South Georgia in 1933.

'Blast, blast and double blast,' blurted Richard, 'look at that traffic.' Ahead of us were four Land-Rovers all waiting for a further three Land-Rovers to ascend the hill. There are no traffic lights in the Falklands and priority is given to cars ascending and descending the hill. Four cars hardly felt like a traffic jam in the London sense of the word. And the fact that Richard recognized every car and knew who everyone was and where they were going didn't seem to help him cope with the fact that he had driven smack bang into the centre of Stanley's rush hour, and now we would surely be stuck for at least a minute.

I was staying in the Malvina House Hotel on Ross Road, just overlooking the harbour, where I had received a message summoning me to see the Falkland Islands government for an urgent meeting. I was puzzled by the summons and even more surprised to discover the reason: 'I am afraid that the RAF are refusing to let you fly with them again.' Given that the RAF are the only means of getting on and off the island, this would have left me with the option of either swimming or emigrating to the islands for good, neither of which I was particularly keen to do. 'They say that due to conduct unbecoming, but expected from a minor Z celebrity like yourself, you have been banned from flying with them.' I was staggered, what had I done? Was it the second cup of orange squash I had dared ask for? Or perhaps I had snored? Did I forget to put my hand up before going to the loo?

I learnt that the RAF had complained about my 'disgraceful' behaviour at Brize Norton in England and specifically my 'demand to sit in the VIP area at the front of the Tristar with Secretary of Defence Geoff Hoon'. The RAF explained that they had only relented in allowing me to sit up front with Hoon because 'they didn't want to make a scene', but that on reflection they had decided to make a complaint to the Falkland Islands government about my 'abhorrent' behaviour, and had decided not to allow me on one of their planes again.

I was baffled; I had behaved impeccably, and moreover had sat at the back of the plane with everyone else. I had never even seen let alone met Mr Hoon. I explained this to a blushing secretary, who apologized that the RAF can sometimes be a bit 'uppity'.

A message was sent back to Brize Norton advising them to check their systems to confirm that I had indeed been seated at the back of the plane with the hoi polloi and not up in the VIP area with the defence secretary. I could only hope that they kept such records, or I risked spending slightly longer than I had at first anticipated in the South Atlantic islands.

Determined not to let this bizarre affair ruin my day, I spent the afternoon exploring the windy city by foot, visiting the post office and catching up on my e-mails in the Hard Disc café. I was struck by the number of souvenir shops, which seemed to outnumber everything else in Stanley. There were dozens of them, all selling a multitude of penguin merchandise. Penguin T-shirts and sweat-shirts, penguin umbrellas, penguin teddies, penguin figurines, glass penguins, fluffy penguins, paintings of penguins, squeaky penguins, penguin hats, penguin snow domes, penguin slippers – you name it, one of the tourist shops sold it. Like Rob's crockery, the number of tourist shops was soon explained when the *Marco Polo* pulled into the harbour, disgorging nearly a thousand passengers into the town, nearly doubling her population.

Stanley must be one of the most colourful capital cities in the world, with brightly painted wood and corrugated iron roofs, and her Smartie box of identical Land-Rovers. Many of the houses were brought down in kit form and assembled on the spot. Today, the Scandinavian kit house has become a popular design around Stanley.

Some of the best-preserved of the older houses are those on Pioneer Row, two streets up from Government Jetty. In 1849, thirty prefabricated cottages were brought and erected by thirty married pensioners from Chelsea and Greenwich in London. They were to form a garrison and be part of the colonization of the islands that was being encouraged at the time.

The small island museum was crammed full of artefacts and memorabilia from the period and included an exhibit dedicated to the 1982 conflict which consisted of a small mock-up of an Argentinian trench featuring a note passed to a local woman from a young Argentinian conscript:

We're sorry but we're hungry
Please buy only for me, Micky and Juan
When you see a man with stars or red lines you can't speak with
us
Please if you can, buy us these things
2 Toothbrush
3 Wafer Cadbury's
4 Mars
3 Ragal Cadbury's
3 Orange Sandwich o L'orange Cadbury's
8 Whole Nut Cadbury's
A piece of ham
And if you can buy other things for eating. Thank you

Quite how Argentina ever hoped to win a battle using these pathetic young conscripts is something only Galtieri will ever know, but the note was a sad reminder of what a waste the war had been.

Inevitably the war's twentieth anniversary had seen a wave of journalists and film crews descend on the islands for special anniversary newspaper supplements, and television documentaries. The islanders were understandably twitchy about the renewed interest in the w**, and the renaissance of all the old archive footage. They had struggled for twenty years to change public opinion about the islands and improve their image from battle-ground to tourist destination.

It was a difficult balancing act for the islanders. On the one hand they were forever grateful for the bravery and sacrifice made by all those who fought for the islands, and on the other they had to face the nearly universal Fleet Street opinion that the war should never have happened, and that it hadn't been worth it for the sake of a handful of Brits on some windswept rocks in the remote South Atlantic.

Many critics, including Max Hastings, were furious at Thatcher's government for the £2 billion it spent after the war creating 'Fortress Falklands' to defend a 'strategic interest in something Britain never acknowledged before the war . . . post facto to justify fighting for it'. Many feel that the estimated £25,000 per year per Falklander spent on the defence of these islands is unjustifiable.

I was told of Hastings's most recent visit to the island, where he was looked after by John Fowler, manager of Falklands Tourism. Max Hastings, former war correspondent, first 'liberator' into Stanley (à la Simpson) and editor of the *Telegraph*, had visited the islands in 2001, when he had returned with a film crew to make a documentary about the conflict. Hastings and Fowler hadn't seen eye to eye, partly because of Hastings's anti-Falklands sentiments. It was with great glee therefore that on 11 September 2001 Fowler mumbled something to Hastings about the attacks on New York and Washington. Hastings threw a tantrum when Fowler informed him they couldn't reach a telephone or a television until that evening, and so it was that Hastings missed one of the biggest events in his lifetime because he was stranded on a remote island he had no love for. It certainly didn't improve his opinion of the Falklands.

While I was there Stanley was gripped by its own hot news story – a murderer still on the run. The residents were divided between those in favour of pursuing the criminal and those who felt he should be left to whatever fate nature had in store for him. The murderer was not some stir-crazy Falklander but a bloodthirsty sea lion preying on unsuspecting penguins down at Gypsy Cove. The sea lion had been waiting for tourists to gather before sneaking up behind sunbathing Magellanic penguins, decapitating them, then horrifying the tourists by juggling with the headless corpses for hours, tossing a lifeless body into the air and catching it in its sharp teeth.

The Falklands, of course, have their own journalists to record such events, and I had even been asked for a radio interview by the world's most unfortunate media acronym, FIBS – the Falkland Islands Broadcasting Service. I had also been interviewed by the islands' only newspaper, the *Penguin News*, which boasts a world record by having the highest per capita sale of any newspaper anywhere in the world, with 100 per cent readership on the islands, a figure sure to turn Rupert Murdoch green with envy.

The sea lion story was headlining the local news both on air and in print.

The governor of the Falklands, Donald Lamont, and his wife had invited me for afternoon tea at Government House, their official residence. The house originally dates from 1845, but each governor and his wife have added their own unique touches, giving the place a homely feel. The huge conservatory at the front of the house is home to one of the most successful grape vines on the island. Outside the west entrance are a pair of brass guns dating from 1807, and elsewhere is an old harpoon gun, like the whale jaws donated by the South Georgia whaling station.

Bullet holes still visible in the walls mark the most dramatic period in the history of the building, the war of 1982, when the Argentinians arrested the Marines, famously recorded on camera, and made them lie face down on the lawn outside the house while the Argentinian flag was raised.

Inside, the walls were decorated with various paintings, including a number of watercolours donated by Prince Charles. Lamont was a genial man who had a genuine love of the Falkland Islands, and he enthused about them and the islanders over tea and scones.

While the war raged between Argentinian and British soldiers, the islanders themselves conducted their own war. They were under the control of a foreign dictatorship, and the invading force was keen to make its mark on the islands. Road signs and street names were all changed to their Spanish equivalents, and the Argentinian anthem was broadcast over the local radio station. While some islanders contented themselves with the clandestine printing of prep school prank posters to tease the 'occupiers', some islanders took a much riskier stance.

Over dinner in the Upland Goose, Terry Peck, with his gruff voice, told me how he had spied for British Intelligence. Terry had been the islands' former police chief, and when the war started he dressed himself up as a builder, stole a motorbike and drove around the islands taking photographs of key installations, using a camera hidden in a drain pipe. His photographs of anti-aircraft missile sites were smuggled out and later appeared in the hands of army and navy intelligence officers.

Terry spent weeks in camp, sleeping under the stars, and evading capture by persuading the young conscripts that he was a builder or a plumber on his way to repair damaged buildings. Terry was awarded an MBE for his bravery during the conflict, although, rather bizarrely, he was later charged with stealing the motorbike on which he carried out his daring mission. 'They had to.' He shrugged his shoulders. 'The chief of police couldn't be seen getting away with stealing.'

Terry told me the story that after he had been to collect his award from the Queen at Buckingham Palace, he had lost his briefcase containing his medal. He had been 'devastated', not for the loss of his MBE, but for the loss of the shiny *Blue Peter* badge he had also been awarded. 'That was the proudest badge I ever received,' he smiled as he chewed on his roast lamb and Yorkshire pudding.

In the years following the 1982 war the islands' infrastructure changed considerably. The Falkland Islands Interim Conservation and Management Zone was introduced to protect fish stocks around the island, with an extended zone 200 miles from the island. Any vessel wishing to fish within this zone now requires a licence from the Falkland Islands government. Nearly 75 per cent of the catch is squid, and nearly £20 million is contributed to the islands' economy every year from the sale of these licences.

Today, almost all the calamari we eat in Britain, Spain, Japan and South Korea is from Falklands-caught squid. As a result of this Falklands-run operation, the local yearly GNP has risen from £4m to £55m, reserves from zero to £140m, the population from 1,800 to 2,300, and personal income from £5,000 to being one of the highest in the southern hemisphere. Even the rate of exam passes is higher than in the UK, and one in five residents own their own business.

The squid, of course, may migrate, and the prospect of oil-drilling, once touted by the media as an opportunity to create 'another Kuwait' and make every islander a millionaire, has proved inconclusive, though studies continue.

Becky from Falkland Islands Conservation invited me to Long Island, a small farm ten miles north of Stanley as the crow flies, but a good deal longer by rickety old Land-Rover. It took us a bone-rattling two hours to reach the remote farm of Glenda and Neil Watson, who run one of the last farms in the Falklands still to use steers to herd their sheep.

Neil and Glenda had already headed off by the time we arrived, so we set out on foot to catch a glimpse of them herding the horses across the spit from the island to the farm. I heard the horses before I saw them. I could hear a pack of hooves crashing into the shallow surf that was lapping across the spit, and then, in a scene straight out of a spaghetti western, dozens of horses galloped across the white sand, their manes a blur of hair. Neil and Glenda were close behind, their long wax jackets protecting them from the shower of sea water created by the herd as they galloped along the beach.

It was a breathtaking sight. I had never seen such a large herd of horses galloping. I was overwhelmed by their grace and beauty as they thundered towards me.

The noise was visceral as the horses galloped past us, snorting and neighing with pleasure. Neil pulled hard on his reins and his horse rose on its hind legs before settling. It was foaming at the mouth, and its skin was sweaty. 'Do you want to help?' asked Neil with his slight antipodean burr. 'Do you ride?'

'Of course,' I smiled.

'Good,' he said, 'you can take Glenda's steed.'

I turned to Neil as I settled into the unusual saddle. 'Is this an Argentinian saddle?' I asked without thinking. I noticed Neil's face bubble up red. I could practically see steam coming out of his ears.

'No, it is not a f****** Argentinian saddle,' he spat. 'It's a Falkland saddle,' he fumed before galloping off at speed.

Not a good start, I thought as I raced to catch up.

Argentina is still a hot potato on the islands. I had failed to notice the sign posted at the entrance to Neil's farm that read: 'Long Island. No access to Argies, 7 councillors or Argie supporters. God Save the Queen. Neil Watson.' I had, however, noticed how, as with the war, islanders refrained from mentioning Argentina. The supermarket had been stocked with various products from Chile and even Uruguay, but had been free of Argentinian products. The islands' freight vessel, the *Tamar*, ferries between Stanley and Punta Arenas, at the southern tip of Chile, to stock up on produce. That is a little like London using Athens as its main trading port with continental Europe, but the islanders preferred to buy from Chile than to eat the fruits of their arch enemy. The islands were dry of Argentinian wine.

The outstanding sovereignty dispute with Argentina over the islands remains politically sensitive. Many of the islanders still feel Argentina is a threat to their security, and a state of alert had been called shortly before I arrived after a member of the Falkland Islands

Falkland Islands

Catching up on the gossip on the MPA road. Land Rovers are the only car here

FIGAS – Falkland Island Government Air Service – landing on one of the island's airstrips

Port Howard airport's departure lounge

Memorial to the 1982 Falklands War

Atop Mount Maria, Port Howard

Beach on Caracass Island

Elephant Seals
BEHIND THE TALL DUNE GRASSES ON
CARACASS ISLAND

*Helping Rob McGill ready the airfield on Caracass Island —
the ubiquitous Land Rover has been improvised into a fire engine*

Penguins on Weddell Island

FALKLAND ISLANDS BROADCASTING STATION

Steve Johnston
Station Manager
Programme Controller

Broadcasting Station,
John Street,
Stanley,
Falkland Islands.

Tel: 27277
Fax: 27279
e-mail:
fibs.fig@horizon.co.fk

Baking bread for Karen Taylor, sole inhabitant of Weddell island

Penguin News

FALKLAND ISLANDS

5 Crozier Place, Stanley, Falkland Islands • Telephone: 22684 Fax: 22238 • pnews@horizon.co.fk • Every Friday • Price: 60p

Friday, March 16, 200_

V12 No. 50

Foot and mouth update:

Wool sales OK

WOOL entering Britain will be subject to rules concerning Foot and Mouth disease, but so far the sale of Falklands wool has not been affected.

It was also announced this week that British wool deliveries into the European Union, notably Belgium, which is the main market for UK carpet wools, have resumed.

...alklands wool yes-... Hall of Falkland ...Ltd. told *Penguin* ...d wool and tops are ... OK to our special-...ase." adding, "since ...n February 20 we ...ve not experienced ...,000 kilos of greasy ...o far and we are not

...ised that the sterling ... had crept upwards ...drawback was the ...ustralian dollar Mr ...mand is good and the ... just beginning to go

...red Islands wool grow-...ree ships have arrived ...position is as we want

...o local job cuts

...NG an announcement ...onal communications ...able and Wireless that ...approximately 4,000 employees ...will lose their jobs, Steve Baker, General Manager of the Falklands branch, has confirmed the cuts will not affect employees here.

Mr Baker told *Penguin News*, "The job losses are in Cable & Wireless Global which looks after Group's business in the USA, UK, Europe and Japan. The job losses in UK are estimated at around 2,700. The redundancies arise mainly as a result of rationalisation and efficiency measures in these operations.

●Castaways' Ben Fogle bonds with *Smokie* at Long Island Farm.

HELLO! Ben and Ken

CHARMING Castaways star Ben Fogle (27) was a hit with Islanders during a visit to the Falklands last week.

Ben, a popular character in the real life BBC television series *Castaways*, spent eight days discovering the Camp and Stanley and meeting Islanders in the company of *Hello!* magazine photographer Ken Lennox.

Jo Morrison of the Falkland Islands Tourist Board explained what brought them to the islands: *"Hello!* has a new young editor who asked Ken for some ideas. Ken who already knew Ben, suggested contacting him and it was decided that the two would undertake travel features involving destinations that

could be reached but were very uncommon.

"They have already been to Lapland and will be rounding up rhinos in Nepal next."

Ken Lennox has been to the Falklands three times before, once with 1982 war veteran Denzil Connick.

Jo (who along with Manager of the Tourist Board John Fowler and the Falklands Office in London, organised Ben and Ken's itinerary) said, "The trip exceeded all Ben's expectations; he had worked in South America and really wanted to visit the Islands but hadn't had the chance. They really enjoyed getting out to Camp and thought Stanley was amazing."

■continued page 3.

■continued page 3.

No SG licences fo_ Falklands vessels

NO Falklands flagged vessels ha_ been licenced to fish in South Ge_ gia waters next season.

Enraged by the decision are Te_ Blake and Mike Summers, direc_ of two companies that own Fa_ lands flagged vessels that have f_ waters for the last three to four ye_ They say the South Georgia gov_ ment promised licence priori_ Falklands and British flagged ... sels.

According to Russ Jarvis fo_ South Georgia Government, a ... reduction in the Total Allow_ Catch (TAC) as recommende_ CCAMLR* and a greater em_ on conservation measures has the two vessels being filtere_ during the licensing process.

Mike Summers, speakin_ Quark Fishing, whose *Jacqueline* has fished in Sout_ gia Waters for four year_ mented, "I am extremely su_ that South Georgia has dump_ Falklands flagged vessels no given that the Falkland_ has assisted South Georgi_ civilianisation process."

Tony Blake Director of ... ing (owners of *Lyn* who ha_ SG waters for three years... was, "...very disappointed b_ could be the difference betw_ viving and not surviving.

"We were given to b_ British and Falklands fla_ sels would have priority ... ously not.

Asked if he would b_ representations Mr Blak_ would not expect the Forc_ to change its mind but want reasons and want it won't happen again."

Mr Jarvis told *Pen_ "CCAMLR and the Sou_ government are workin_ towards the managemen_ ery. The TAC for toot_ duced dramatically to_ problem that we could_ many licences.

"There are now two fishing (pots and long_ reduced longline licenc_ only about nine - there_ 40 applicants.

"The vessels are th_ pending on their con_ CCAMLR conservation Mr Jarvis who_ cally flagged vesse_ licences, knock..._lined in wanti_

New BAS station official opening

THE British Antarctic Survey will inaugurate a new station at King Edward Point. South Georgia next

Lamont, Councillor Richard Cockwell, Operations Manager SGSSI Gordon Liddle and Corina Goss News Editor (FIBS).

Falklands Election 250 days

Becky Ingham, me and Neil Watson at Long Island

HMS Endurance (Tim is 3rd from left)

The Trough in Stanley with Fighting Pigs, wearing an honorary T-shirt

Stanley Harbour at dusk

Pitcairn

Mangareva

Dramatic sunset at Mangareva in French Polynesia

The incriminating breadfruit plant and the 'Blue' parcels for Len Brown

Debilitated by days of seasickness after three days on the Pacific Ocean, I emerge to find Adamstown off the ship's beam

The 'Antigua' flag signifies our arrival off Pitcairn's northern shores

Didier with Mahi Mahi, caught on a hand line and hauled aboard by hand

Didier, 'the ship's goat', fillets the fish aboard his self-designed, self-built yacht, the Sauvage

Pitcairn at last

Foreign &
Commonwealth
Office

London SW1A 2AH

From the Parliamentary Under Secretary of State

Dear Ben Fogle,

I have seen copies of your letters of 8 November to Alan Huckle and Kate Joad. I am replying as Minister responsible for the Overseas Territories.

I am aware of your interest in the Overseas Territories, and I am sorry to learn that you were recently unable to spend time on Pitcairn. It must have been frustrating to be refused entry given that you had travelled such a long way and had thought that you had obtained approval for your visit.

The decision as to who may or may not be granted permission to land on Pitcairn rests with the Pitcairn Island Council, on advice from the Commissioner, not HMG nor indeed the Governor. However, had you given us specific forewarning, we might have been able to help, at least in alerting you to the necessary procedures and explaining the background to your interest to the Council.

I hope nonetheless that this has not coloured your view of this fascinating island and resourceful community.

Yours sincerely,
Valerie Amos

AIR TAHITI
GMR
GAMBIER
NO. 06-50-57

Pitcairn Islands   WEAVING Official First Day Cover

Ascension

Georgetown

The island's post office at Georgetown

Ascension's shopping mall, Sue Ryder boutique and the island's turtle nest, the DIY shop (both closed)

Ascension Island's Detachment of the Saint Helena police force in Georgetown

Georgetown's church

The White Hill letterbox walk on the eastern shore off the
island with Johnny and his godchild Danielle

Dr Nicholas 'Johnny' Hobson with one of the island's
land crabs, which once threatened to overrun the island.
They have one enormous pincer

The island's resident donkeys threatened with
castration. Green Mountain is obscured in cloud cover

Paddy in Green Pond, home to the
'muddy' mountain goldfish

Drainage basin atop Green Mountain

View of Wideawake airfield from Green Mountain

USS Pathfinders anchored off Georgetown

Red Lion farm's now-derelict buildings

Tunnel leading to Dampiers Drip atop Green Mountain

Ascension's lava field. The island was once described as 'Hell with the fire put out'. I thought it looked like an old ashtray

Ben with Buffalo, tuna-fishing off Ascension

BBC Ascension

FAO: MR BEN FOGLE

FAX No. 00 44 20 7723

One of the island's ubiquitous
radio masts beaming
'The Archers' to West Africa

English Bay

The Garden of the Administrator's residence on Green
Mountain. An oasis among the island's black lava.

Defence Force discovered an upturned military dinghy floating in the surf. The dinghy contained a gun and an Argentinian flag, along with a number of provisions all from Argentina. A thorough search was conducted and the entire vicinity scoured, and it was eventually assumed that it must have been an Argentinian fanatic who had planned to plant a flag on the islands. The dinghy was swamped and he was presumed dead, although some islanders claimed conspiratorially that he was picked up and 'disappeared' by the military.

One of the reasons the islanders remain so sternly pro-British, with their fading portraits of a young Queen Elizabeth II and the dozens of Union Flags fluttering from garden masts, is this insecurity and mistrust. When President Menem recently offered each islander £1 million a head in exchange for Argentinian sovereignty, the islanders dug their heels in and refused the cash.

The experience of galloping along the beach behind fifty horses must be rated as one of life's most breathtaking experiences. A huge smile cracked irrepressibly across my rosy-cheeked face as we thundered towards the farm. 'Now this is what it's all about,' I thought.

That evening we decided to dine at Stanley's newest and most fashionable eatery, the Brasserie, a large modern restaurant with wooden floors and minimalist decoration. It was the type of restaurant normally found in Notting Hill Gate rather than a remote island chain in the South Atlantic.

Still swaying from the bouncy journey home, Becky, Emma Jane, Debbie and I all sat in the Brasserie enthusing about the day's riding at Long Island, when I heard a voice behind me. 'Ben Fogle, what on earth are you doing here?' It was Tim, a university friend from my Naval Reserve days. Unlike me, he had enlisted and was now a sub-lieutenant aboard HMS *Endurance*, the Royal Navy's Antarctic survey vessel that had just arrived in the Falklands. It's often said that the planned withdrawal of her predecessor convinced the junta in 1982 that Britain had lost interest in her islands and would do nothing to reverse an invasion.

I had learned that the military's plan to withdraw a permanent troop base from South Georgia had been shelved on the grounds that the present government, under extreme economic and political pressure, might make another similar assumption.

Tim invited me to visit the ship at MPA. Mount Pleasant Airbase, like most places in the Falklands, is in the middle of nowhere, which hasn't helped to endear it to the soldiers who rate the Falklands as almost the worst placement, second only to Northern Ireland.

In an effort to make soldiers warm to the islands and entertain troops during the long, damp winter days, MPA is not only home to the islands' only bowling-alley, but also the only cinema and until recently the only swimming-pool.

MPA is home to as many military personnel and contractors as there are islanders. The base consists of a series of bunkers and hangars interspersed with heavy rolls of barbed wire and green military vehicles. Security was high, and I found myself escorted by several burly-looking soldiers.

The deep-water port is contained within the base, and the huge red and white bulk of HMS *Endurance* stood out from the bleak landscape. It was aboard the *Endurance* that a Royal Navy petty officer had spotted an uncharted island near South Georgia, where she was currently bound.

The ship had made international headlines the year before, after a local newspaper ran a story about a team of scientists aboard who were heading to Antarctica to study the effect of helicopters on the local penguin populations. According to the report, each time a helicopter flew overhead the penguins would all crane their necks upwards, and eventually tumble on to their backs as they strained to keep an eye on this strange 'bird'. The story was picked up by the world's press, and the ship deluged with calls from every continent of the world. 'Sadly the story wasn't quite correct,' lamented the captain. 'We were studying humans' effect on penguins, and that did include the effect of helicopters,' he explained. 'But the stuff about penguins falling over was nonsense,' he chuckled.

I asked Tim what he thought about the Falklands as he took me on a tour of the ship. 'I love it,' he blurted as he showed me the ship's windsurfing boards and jet skis. HMS *Endurance* seemed to have more in common with a cruise ship than a military vessel, but then her primary role was as a hydrography craft, surveying the uncharted waters of the South Atlantic, primarily around Antarctica.

It was heartening to meet someone from the military who openly admitted a soft spot for the islands. I had become increasingly despondent about the services and was still concerned about the dispute with RAF bureaucracy that remained unresolved. I still wasn't certain whether or not they would let me leave the island.

During what I hoped would be my last day on the islands I had been invited to visit one of the islands' schools. Stanley has two schools, the primary school for children aged 5–11 and the Falkland Islands community school for those aged 11–16; I had been invited to the latter.

The school was built at a cost of £10 million and has the feel of an American high school, with its long corridors and lockers; the only clue that this is not any old school was the dozens of explicit acrylic paintings of the Falklands War that lined the walls of the long hallway. The school certainly didn't seem to lack facilities, with the islands' only library, sports hall and squash courts, and now a swimming-pool as well.

While the school has the facilities to educate up to GCSEs, for those students wishing to continue their education to A-levels and beyond the islands have an agreement with Peter Symonds sixth-form college in Winchester, where a number of Falkland Islands students board each year.

After my tour of the school I was asked to start the annual Tumbledown Run, a school race around Mount Tumbledown. Winter was fast approaching and the warm sunshine had been replaced by a cool drizzle. It seemed odd standing atop this mountain that it had been the site of one of the war's bloodiest battles just twenty years ago. But it is a sign of the Falklanders' determination rather to look ahead that today the children use it for their annual fun run.

While I had been enjoying myself, word arrived from London.

The RAF had checked their records and discovered that it hadn't been me but a BBC newsman accompanying Hoon who had thrown a hissy fit. The RAF, it seemed, had picked on me as the most visible representative of the BBC, although in truth my journey had nothing to do with the corporation. It was a decision someone knew was wrong when they made it, although they did, graciously, change their minds about flying me home on my £1,000 ticket.

I was invited to a Falklands barbecue for my last night on the islands. In tune with the islands' rather erratic weather, a huge blue tarpaulin had been draped across the garden, creating a temporary cover from the torrential downpour. Food was also suitably Falklandish: Benny kebabs made from mutton with baking soda, wine and herbs.

The night finished at the Trough, the Falklands' answer to the London Hippodrome. The islands' no. 1 band, the Fighting Pigs, had volunteered to put on a special gig in honour of my visit, 'CASTAWAY PIGS' posters had been plastered all over town and word had soon spread. There was a queue of people waiting by the time we arrived. The Trough, in keeping with its name, could best be described as a very large trough, with a very small bar. The walls were stark and dark, except that is for a drum skin hanging in pride of place above the bar. A spotlight illuminated the signatures of Status Quo, who had visited the islands in the eighties.

There was a buzz of excited anticipation as the Fighting Pigs took to the stage and started their set. The Trough, I noticed, was divided between the military, who sat binge-drinking in one corner of the room, and the islanders, who were boogying around the dancefloor doing their mimed rendition of 'DISCO' with their arms.

On the other side of the divide a female soldier shouted over the noise of the electric guitar, 'Why did you come to this awful place?'

'Do you mean the Trough or the Falklands?' I asked.

'Both,' she shouted, before offering me a beer.

'Don't you like it here?'

'Like it?' She looked like I had just told her she had a fatal disease.

'I loathe this place, with its awful people. You can't actually like it here?' she added.

I looked around at all my new friends throwing shapes on the dancefloor. The military cannot be praised enough for their bravery and courage during the 1982 conflict. They suffered huge casualties for the liberty and freedom of the Falkland Islanders, in a war that many critics, including the military, feel should never have happened. Twenty years later, they still have a major presence in the Falklands, almost doubling the population of the islands. Naturally the army, navy and RAF provide an essential defence barrier against any future Argentinian threat, and I have no doubt that the islanders respect their importance. But I was beginning to wonder how they cope with the constant dourness of the military towards life in the Falklands, a little like a grouchy relative, always doing their best to depress the rest of the family.

Having enjoyed nearly four years in the naval reserves myself, I am not an instinctive critic of the military. On the contrary, I respect and admire the work they do, but I was disappointed at their behaviour in the Falklands. I was fed up with their contemptuous remarks and their undignified disdain for the Falklanders and their home.

'Actually, I love this place,' I said, 'and you can shove that drink.' And with that I smiled and walked back to join my new friends.

I had been captivated by the magic of this remote island chain. I had been heartened by the spirit of the islanders and enchanted by the beauty of their land, but I'd been frustrated by the attitude of the military. The Falkland Islands are like a jar of Marmite, I thought. Love it or hate it, there's no in between.

Slightly inebriated by the Falklands' finest, I stumbled into the four-wheel-drive taxi. I smiled brightly as I thought about my island adventure and of the people I'd met. I looked out at the full moon of the southern hemisphere that was reflecting off the calm waters of Stanley harbour.

'So, did you get to do everything you wanted?' asked one of the Falkland babes who had ended up in the same taxi.

'I think so,' I slurred as we passed the bomb disposal office.

'Have you tried everything?' she implored placing her hand on my knee.

Well, if you insist, I thought.

5. Pitcairn

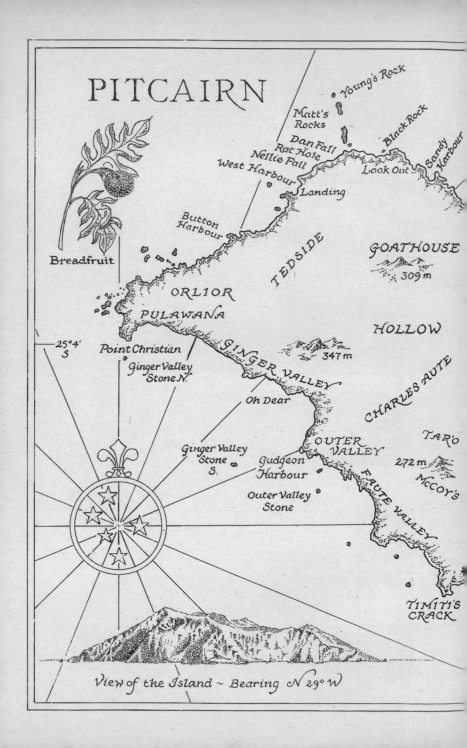

PITCAIRN

Young's Rock

Matt's Rocks

Dan Fall
Rat Hole
Nellie Fall
West Harbour

Black Rock

Sandy Harbour

Look Out

Landing

Breadfruit

Button Harbour

TEDSIDE

GOATHOUSE

309 m

ORLIOR

PULAWANA

25°4' S

Point Christian

Ginger Valley Stone N.

GINGER VALLEY

HOLLOW

347 m

CHARLES AUTE

Oh Dear

Ginger Valley Stone S.

Gudgeon Harbour

OUTER VALLEY

TARO

272 m

McCOY'S

Outer Valley Stone

FAUTE VALLEY

TIMITI'S CRACK

View of the Island ~ Bearing N 29° W

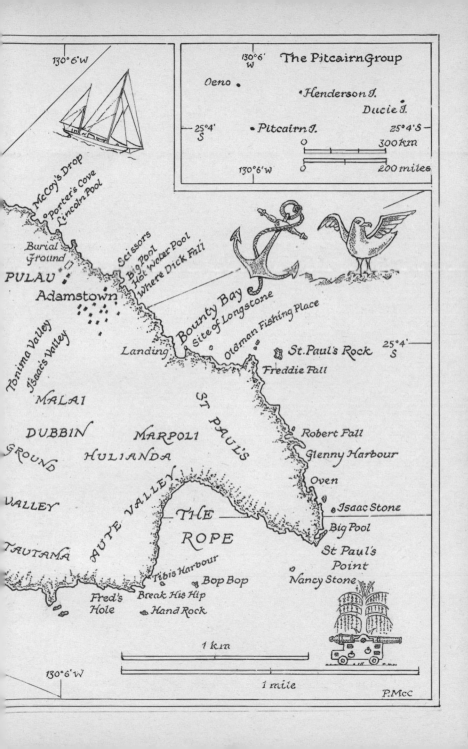

130°6'W

The Pitcairn Group

Oeno

130°6'W

Henderson I.

Ducie I.

25°4'S

Pitcairn I.

25°4'S

300 km

130°6'W

200 miles

McCoy's Drop

Porter's Cove

Lincoln Pool

Burial Ground

Scissors

Big Pool

Hot Water Pool

Where Dick Fall

PULAU

Adamstown

Bounty Bay

Site of Longstone

Oldman Fishing Place

Landing

25°4'S

St. Paul's Rock

Freddie Fall

Tonima Valley

Isaac's Valley

MALAI

DUBBIN

MARPOLI

ST PAUL'S

Robert Fall

GROUND

HULIANDA

Glenny Harbour

VALLEY

AUTE VALLEY

THE

Oven

Isaac Stone

ROPE

Big Pool

TAUTAMA

St Paul's Point

Tibis Harbour

Bop Bop

Nancy Stone

Fred's Hole

Break His Hip

Hand Rock

1 km

130°6'W

1 mile

P.McC

The inhabitants of Pitcairn couldn't even fill a bus. It is one of the most distant of the few remaining outposts of the British Empire, and one of the most remote places in the world. Incredibly for an island steeped in maritime history, the area around it is one of the only parts of the globe to remain uncharted. The story of this tiny population began in the docklands of London's East End in 1787, aboard a ship called the HMS *Bounty*, captained by one William Bligh.

The story of Captain Bligh and the *Bounty* is as coupled to modern day Pitcairn as Yorkshire pudding is to a Sunday roast. The story has created, moulded and shaped the lives of Pitcairners for over two hundred years, and to understand the island one needs to understand the events that brought them together.

In October 1787, HMS *Bounty* set sail from London. Her mission was to sail to Tahiti, where she was to collect a large number of breadfruit trees and transport them to the West Indies.

The breadfruit was reportedly 'a fruit in such abundance, as seems almost to exempt man from the original doom of earning his bread by the sweat of his brow', and a committee of West Indian planters suggested the translocation of this fruit to the West Indies as a cheap and efficient way to feed the slave labour.

Captain William Bligh was chosen as the man for this important expedition that was to be part financed by the Royal Navy. The ship chosen for the voyage was the *Bounty*, an ex–merchant ship of 215 tons.

It took nearly a year before the *Bounty* finally reached Tahiti on 25 October 1788, and there she anchored for twenty-three weeks. It has often been suggested that it would have taken just two weeks to collect enough breadfruit trees to fill the *Bounty*'s hold, although it has also been claimed that Bligh was waiting for the favourable trade winds in order to continue their journey. But it is impossible to ignore the allure of the highly liberal local women for the sailors, and the attraction the women felt to these exotic-looking white men, who were certainly not looking forward to their long passage back to the hardships of life in Victorian England.

The mutiny and its causes have been the subject of much debate, but it is generally agreed that it erupted as a result of a personal conflict between William Bligh and Fletcher Christian. Some experts have hinted at the possibility of a homosexual relationship between the two men that went sour. Whatever the cause, on 27 April 1789, Captain Bligh and eighteen of the *Bounty*'s crew were lowered into a 23-ft launch and cast out to the ravages of the South Pacific. The *Bounty* sailed on with the new captain, Fletcher Christian.

Under Christian's command the mutineers returned to Tahiti, where they attempted to settle on the nearby island of Tubai, but meeting local resistance the mutineers split into two groups and eventually Fletcher set off aboard the *Bounty* with nine mutineers, six Polynesian men, twelve women and a baby. They faced a daunting future. They had to discover an uninhabited land that was unlikely to be found by the Royal Navy, who were certain to send out a search party. The ship was undermanned and the seas heavy as they searched for a new land. It was during this long and arduous passage that Christian discovered a reference to Pitcairn Island in Bligh's log book.

Pitcairn lies in isolation in the South Pacific, on the outer edge of south-east Polynesia, roughly half-way between South America and Australia, and close to the line of the Tropic of Capricorn. The island was first recorded in 1767, when Philip Cartaret sailed by aboard HMS *Swallow*. Cartaret decided to name the island after Major Pitcairn of the Royal Marines, whose son had first spotted it.

Luckily for the mutineers, Cartaret mischarted the island in both latitude and longitude, placing Pitcairn 200 miles out of position, and therefore confining it to the vast and largely unexplored South Pacific for many more years.

Pitcairn was a rough oblong about one mile wide and two miles long, with very mountainous terrain rising to over 1,000 feet. Most parts were heavily wooded, with thick undergrowth. The island was on the edge of the world, and was to be an ideal new home to the mutineers.

When I was a child my eyes had been drawn to the islands like a smudge on a window. I can remember watching Marlon Brando playing Fletcher Christian, in the 1962 film *Mutiny on the Bounty*. If I stared at a map for long enough I could almost hear Brando's familiar voice resonating from the South Pacific. The little splodge far off the coast of South America was my only evidence that the story was true. Was Brando really still living on this minuscule island?

My first real insight into Pitcairn came about during my year on Taransay. It transpired that Roger Stephenson, the doctor, was something of an 'isleophile'. Apart from spending a year as the doctor on St Helena in the South Atlantic, Roger had also been the doctor on Pitcairn.

I had been mesmerized by his tales of this remote island. He often used to refer to them as 'real castaways', and us as fakes. I can still remember my envy when one day Roger received a letter addressed to: Roger, Taransay, North Atlantic. On the reverse it had the return address: Betty, Pitcairn Island, South Pacific. The whole world suddenly seemed smaller when I looked at that envelope. It was also my first real proof that Pitcairn really did exist – the story wasn't just a figment of Hollywood's imagination, the island not an erroneous printing smudge on my wall map. If Roger could get there then so could I.

My Pitcairn adventure began in a busy London showroom. A crowd had gathered to gawp at the object of my desires, a key to Pitcairn's history. I gazed at its rounded body with its soft contours and its coffee coloured skin. It was a thing of beauty, a fruit of life.

'Where shall we begin?' asked a man with a monocle. 'Fifteen,' he announced. 'We have 15, 20, 25, 30, 35 any more? any more? 40, 45 to you, sir, 50, 55, 60, is that my final offer? going once going twice, £60,000 to the gentleman in the corner.' His little hammer snapped against the wooden brick.

The small engraved coconut had gone for a staggering £60,000, but of course this was no ordinary coconut, and this no ordinary market. I was at a Christie's auction and this was Captain Bligh's coconut, used during his long voyage to Timor after he was cast adrift during the 'mutiny on the *Bounty*'.

It seemed staggering that someone was willing to pay such a high price for *Bounty* memorabilia, but I was after something much more valuable. I wanted to visit the *Bounty*'s descendants first hand, an adventure that would take me to the ends of the earth.

It is believed there was a Polynesian settlement on Pitcairn between the twelfth and fifteenth centuries, and there may have been an earlier settlement as much as 2,000 years earlier. As the mutineers were to prove, small though it was, Pitcairn provided all the basic necessities of life. For the Polynesian settlers the island had the only quarry in the region at which they could flake off the sharp-edged stones needed to make adzes and other cutting-tools.

Today, the island has a permanent population of just thirty-six, all descendants of the mutineers, and understandably a rather shy and suspicious community.

'It's not quite a fatwah, but she is not welcome back,' had been the Pitcairn islanders' response to the last person to write about them. Dea Birkett, a travel writer, had spent several months on the island in the early nineties. *Serpent in Paradise* had been her candid account of her stay.

I couldn't imagine my jolly attempt to visit Pitcairn ending so unhappily. However, just as I had discovered on Tristan da Cunha, my literary predecessor had left islanders wary of any nomadic scribes. In fact, since her visit, the island had passed a strict law to prohibit any writers whatsoever. Oh, Dea!, I thought as I looked at the challenges pitted against me.

I knew that getting permission to visit Pitcairn would be hard enough, but actually getting to the island would really test my mettle. Pitcairn has no airport, no proper harbour, no safe anchorage and no scheduled boat service. As if this weren't enough to deter would-be visitors, she also happens to be in the middle of the South Pacific ocean, 1,300 miles from Easter Island to the east, and 3,300 miles from New Zealand in the south-west.

One of the few ways of getting there is on a container ship sailing the Panama–New Zealand trade route, as Birkett did. This can be difficult in itself as the infrequent ships are often either full or unwilling to stop off at the minuscule island. For those who successfully find a ship, negotiate a berth and survive the two-week ocean voyage, they must then face the prospect of living on the island until another ship happens to pass, prepared to stop and take them back home again. Dea Birkett spent three months on the South Pacific island, not so much because she wanted to but because that's how long it took for another ship to arrive.

Unfortunately I had no such luxury of time, trying to visit six of the most remote islands in the world within a year. This wasn't going to be easy, but I was confident I could do it.

I set about trying to obtain permission. Pitcairn has its own government website, which contains facts and figures about the island, including a brief history. The site also has its own 'shopping mall', allowing cybercastaways to buy anything from stamps and postcards to the island's home-produced honey. It also contained advice for would-be travellers and an application form for those wishing to visit.

The notice to applicants for permission to land reads as follows: 'A licence to land and reside in any of the islands may be granted by the Governor. It is usual to consult with the Pitcairn Island Council before issuing a licence.'

I sat down with a steaming cup of Earl Grey and worked my way through the lengthy form. The application asks the usual name, address, profession, etc., but rather more interestingly it also asks for purpose of visit and religious denomination. A notice reminds applicants that 'licensees must be in good health, free from all infectious and contagious diseases, and that would-be visitors must not import any flora or fauna to the island'.

Reason for visit? I thought long and hard before settling for a lengthy epistle about my time living on Taransay with Roger Stephenson. I waxed lyrical about small-island life and how I had become infatuated with islands, and I concluded that to visit Pitcairn had been a life-long dream (as is true) and that I hoped they would allow me to fulfil my childhood aspirations.

It was only when I had completed my application that I saw a problem. How do I get the form back to the island? There was no messageboard or return e-mail address, and if I posted it to Pitcairn, I could very well end up being on the same boat as the letter and delivering it myself by hand.

The site also had a section titled 'Contacting Pitcairn', in which it explained that the island had recently installed a new Inmarsat 'A' and Inmarsat 'mini-M' phone through the British Telecom Earth Station in New Zealand. It all sounded rather complicated to me. 'The station is usually unattended,' continued the information, 'but the answering machine is checked at 20.00, 00.00 and 05.00 GMT. But if you are lucky,' it teased, 'there may be someone there.'

I considered the message I might find on the answering machine: 'Sorry we can't get to the phone just now'? On an island just over half a mile square, one had to wonder why not.

Curiosity, and the fact that I still didn't know how to get my application to the island, got the better of me, so I picked up my mobile and typed in the 10-digit number. For some reason I was a little nervous. I'd never spoken to a mutineer – okay, a descendant of a mutineer – before.

Beep beep, beep beep . . . the line was engaged.

I tried again, and this time I got a ring tone. 'Hello,' the voice crackled down the line.

A real-life Pitcairner just said 'hello' to me, I thought incredulously, lost for words. 'Um, hello,' I blushed, 'do you have an e-mail address to send in an application to land?' I asked timidly.

'Yes we do, my dear.' And with that she read out the address and bade me good luck, and with a click of the receiver she hung up and disappeared back into the realms of my consciousness. How terribly unoriginal, I thought to myself. I had just fulfilled a lifelong ambition to talk to a Pitcairner, and all I asked was if she had email.

I sent off my application and set about the even more important task of working out how I was going to get there. On the basis that a container ship was simply too unreliable and would take too long, I looked into the possibility of finding someone somewhere with a private boat who was willing to make this unusual voyage.

Chile and New Zealand, the two nearest land masses, were simply too far away from Pitcairn to contemplate chartering a boat. Both would involve many weeks' sailing and would be prohibitively expensive.

French Polynesia's five archipelagos cover an expanse of ocean larger than Europe. Even if I found a yacht in Tahiti, thousands of miles still separated the capital from tiny Pitcairn. Even Easter Island was nearer. There was no simple answer.

Classified as a part of Polynesia, the Pitcairn islands are actually an island group that encompasses four isles: Oeno, Dulcie, Henderson and Pitcairn. The nearest inhabited island to Pitcairn is Mangareva in French Polynesia, some 150 miles away.

The islands have always had a close connection with Mangareva in the Gambier Archipelago, and at one time a Polynesian trading route existed between Pitcairn, Mangareva and Easter Island. Mangareva's lagoon had abundant supplies of black-lipped pearls (I call them Gothic pearls because of their deep black colour), which could be cut to make fish hooks, while Pitcairn had the only stone quarry in south-eastern Polynesia. Open boats would ply their trade between the three islands.

Mangareva seemed like the most logical place to begin the ocean passage, but I soon discovered that this remote island group with a population of just a thousand was well off the tourist trail and without potential boats to make the journey to Pitcairn.

Salvation eventually came in the rather unlikely form of London's Groucho Club, a central London media haunt. I had been celebrating a friend's recent engagement, when I mentioned in conversation that I was trying to find someone with a boat in French Polynesia who would be willing to make the long round trip to Pitcairn. I was unexpectedly put in touch with a French couple, Sophie and

Didier Wattrelot, who according to my matchmaker Jeanne owned a yacht called the *Sauvage* that was somewhere in French Polynesia.

Soon after I made contact with the *Sauvage*, a reply finally arrived from Pitcairn:

> Dear Ben, thank you for your response to our questions. As you will be leaving on the same vessel on which you arrive at the first opportunity it leaves Pitcairn you are not required to hold a licence to land or reside. You will need to pay NZ$25 to come ashore and if the use of any Pitcairn vessel is required that must also be paid for. Your payments are to be made to the immigration officer of the mayor of Pitcairn upon arrival. We wish you a safe journey and hope you enjoy your short stay on Pitcairn Island. Kind regards, Shirley Dillon, Pitcairn Government

I had found my transport and now had the blessing of Pitcairn.

The difficulty though was in trying to synchronize everything. I had to get from London to Tahiti and then onwards to Mangareva in the Gambier Archipelago, which was served by just one flight a week. At the same time Didier had to sail six hundred miles from the Marquesas Islands to join me in Mangareva. This all had to be carefully planned around my busy schedule and Didier's prior bookings, not to mention the area's hurricane season. For nearly six months we corresponded, until finally we settled on a date in November when I would meet Didier in the Gambier Archipelago of French Polynesia.

It was dark by the time we touched down in Papeete international airport, Tahiti. It had been a gruelling flight from London via Los Angeles, a long flight that hadn't been helped by my horrible hangover. Charles Veley, still attempting to 'conquer' the world, had stopped off in London before 'doing' West Africa. He had organized a little party in London, and as with all 'little' parties, it had ended with me passing out in a cab home.

I had woken up an hour and a half before my Air New Zealand flight was due to depart. Several frantic calls, half a dozen Paracetamol later I grabbed my bag and caught a speeding cab to Heathrow. In my disarray I had forgotten something so important that my entire trip would depend on it, but I wouldn't discover what that was until I was in the depths of the South Pacific.

Three happy Tahitian men welcomed us from the plane. They all wore Hawaiian shirts and one of them played the ukulele, while the others sang their traditional island songs. Nothing particularly untoward except that it was three in the morning.

A pretty young girl handed me a small carnation. It made a nice change to receive a flower rather than the poker-faced stare that seems to be the standard UK issue. 'Bonjour,' she smiled seductively. Blimey, I thought. Even at three in the morning this young Polynesian seemed genuinely happy to see me, a bleary-eyed traveller with a tongue like sandpaper.

At immigration I waved my burgundy passport at another smiling Polynesian with a flower behind his ear. 'Bonjour,' he smiled, ushering me through without even looking inside, as if this were Calais rather than a distant island in the South Pacific. The reason for this apparent informality is that French Polynesia is a French overseas territory, in much the same way as Pitcairn is a British territory, and technically therefore part of the EU. In a strange twist of geopolitical fate, 10,000 miles from either country I would cross from French waters into the South Pacific's English waters.

The best thing about arriving in a new place at night is the strength of the impressions and feelings one has the following morning. Normally one's senses are diluted by the gradual integration into a new country, but by arriving at night one could be in practically any part of the world, the landscape hidden and veiled by the shadows, until the morning, when you get to experience the full impact for the first time without the hindrance of airports, traffic jams and fatigue.

I used to savour those moments as a child arriving in Canada for the summer. I would invariably arrive at my grandfather's cottage late at night. The only proof the lake was still there was the gentle sound of water lapping against the shore. I would lie restless in my bed, until the first sign of light signalled daybreak. I would dash from the cottage still wearing my pyjamas.

There are few places that can genuinely take your breath away, but my first morning in Papeete, when I pulled the curtains back to reveal the image before me, I felt like I had been winded.

French Polynesia is better known by the name of its main island, Tahiti. These islands are the epitome of everything the Pacific island paradise is supposed to be. The dream made reality.

Polynesia's white reef-fringed islands with vivid blue lagoons and soaring green smouldering mountains look like the exotic movie locations they are. I can still remember the first time I saw a photograph of Bora Bora. It struck me immediately as the most beautiful place I had ever seen. I thought these colours only existed in my paintbox. The image leapt from the page and singed itself into my consciousness, to be summoned whenever I heard the words tropical, island or paradise.

I must admit that when I first read about the BBC *Castaway* project in the *Guardian*, 'island' had been the first word to catch my attention. In a split second the image of Bora Bora landed in my mind.

The image that appeared in my window was no less spectacular that morning. The ocean sparkled like a bed of diamonds, while on the horizon Moorea soared from the water like some child's painting. The island was fringed with a dazzling white line of beaches. Gauguin, I decided, didn't do it justice.

I had a day and a night to explore the island's capital before my flight south. I knew about Tahiti's status as an overseas territory of France, but I was staggered at how much Gallic influence there had been on this Polynesian paradise. I walked past boulangeries where islanders were busy queuing for their fresh baguettes and croissants. I sipped espressos and snacked on a croque monsieur.

In the sidewalk cafés I watched as women teetered past in unfeasibly high heels, dressed from head to toe in Chanel, clutching their Louis Vuitton handbags. One woman swept past in a fur scarf. It was nearly a hundred degrees.

The shops were no less Parisian: Cartier, Pierre Cardin and

Versace. I bought a copy of *Paris-Match* from the corner tabac and even popped into one of the island's many hypermarkets to pick up some provisions for Pitcairn: Burgundy and Chablis – Pitcairn is a dry island, so I felt I could indulge during the passage.

The evening in Papeete sees the arrival of 'Les Roulottes', vans and buses that have been converted into mobile restaurants. Each day from 6 p.m. until 1 a.m. they convene on the quayside. Each has been heavily modified. The sides can be lowered and made into temporary counters, while plastic tables and chairs provide emergency overflow seating. I walked past mobile pizzerias with their 'in van', wood-fired pizza ovens. Pizza le Romain supported the side flaps with a handsome pair of Roman columns. It even had a cut-out centurion to keep an eye on diners. There were dozens of Chinese vans and even a Hong Kong truck specializing in chow mein. There were American diners complete with neon lights and juke boxes. But by far the most popular dish seemed to be 'steak frîtes – even the Chinese and Italian vendors offered their own versions of this classic French dish.

Little barbecues shrouded the entire waterfront in a blanket of smoke. Each roulotte had rigged up a little fan to blow the drifting smoke away from their customers. The smoke was funnelled from fan to fan before soaring free in the small gaps between vehicles. Generators whirred and fires hissed and cracked, giving the place the feel of a fairground. I sat at Chez Roger and tucked into a rather chewy plate of steak and chips.

Four hours' flying time from Tahiti, the Gambier archipelago is the most remote French Polynesian island group, and the one closest to Pitcairn. I set off early the next morning on the second leg of my adventure.

I was surprised by how full the plane was. My neighbour soon explained that last week's flight had been cancelled, because someone had stolen the plane's return petrol from the airport in Gambier. The flight had been suspended until replacement fuel could be shipped to the remote atoll.

Thibault was a pale-skinned, light-haired Tahitian. In his early thirties, he spoke perfect English and worked for ATP – Agence Tahitienne de Presse. He was on his way to Gambier after a tip-off that an American star was somewhere in the archipelago.

I told him about my attempt to get to Pitcairn. 'But no one ees allowed,' he explained, 'a French film crew was denied permission only last week, they 'ad come all zee way from Paris. 'ave you seen the New Zealand papers?' he asked. I shook my head, embarrassed by my ignorance. 'Look,' he said, pulling an old copy from his bag that was stuffed full of papers and magazines.

'Why have you got so many magazines and newspapers?' I asked.

'For research,' he replied. 'Photographs of celebrities make a lot of money, but first I need to recognize the famous person.' His little satchel was crammed with copies of *Hello!*, *Paris-Match* and various antipodean versions of celebrity gossip rags. I was travelling with Tahiti's only paparazzo.

Thibault handed me a copy of the *New Zealand Herald*: 'GOV-ERNOR GAGS PITCAIRNERS', screamed the front page. The news story explained that Pitcairn governor Richard Fell had taken the rather extreme measure of fining islanders caught gossiping with fines of up to NZ$50. An ordinance, much like the one used to evict the Ilios from the Chagos Islands, had been dispatched by boat from New Zealand and had been posted on the island's noticeboard, much to the chagrin of the islanders. The news story quoted a spokesman for Mr Fell. 'Some wild accusations about people on and off the island have gone beyond the pale. The Governor thought it was time to remind people that this particular ordinance (rule) does exist and the island becoming a rumour mill wasn't going to do anybody any good.'

Wild accusations and fines for gossiping from a governor who sounds more like a prep school teacher. It all seemed a little extreme.

The article went on to quote one islander, Betty Christian, as saying, 'On Pitcairn, when you don't have the radio or TV blasting out all day, people talk about whatever may be going on locally. It's part of our culture.'

Quite right, I thought. Gossiping and islands would be lost without one another. On Taransay we thrived on it. Gossip and rumour were like a drug. They became a part of our diet whether we liked it or not. They dragged us up when we were down and dragged us down when we were up.

I wondered if the islanders had been gossiping about their thin-skinned governor!

' 'ow long do you 'av?' asked Thibault.

'Ten days,' I explained.

'Ten days?' he spluttered. ' 'ow do you get to Pitcairn and back in ten days?' he enquired. 'What if the weather turns?'

I shrugged my shoulders and looked out of the aeroplane window at the ocean below. The surface was covered in white patches that were the heavy waves of the South Pacific. 'I'm not sure,' I confided. In just a few hours I would find out.

I landed in Gambier less confident than ever about getting to Pitcairn, but my spirits were lifted when Didier was there to meet me. I recognized him immediately, apart from the fact that he was the only person waiting in the arrivals hall: he had a deeply weathered face and wore clothes heavily faded from years on the ocean. He had a thick head of curly brown hair and had a warm face.

' 'ello, Benjamin,' he smiled as we shook hands. 'You arrive on time,' he continued with surprise. Didier had been in Mangareva for four days, having sailed from the Marquesas in just eight days rather than his predicted twelve, 'I 'ad good winds,' he explained as we boarded the water taxi for Rikitea, the island's main town.

'We 'ave company for the voyage,' he said, 'an American anthropologist and 'is Hawaiian wife. They will be our crew, no?' I had been a little worried about such a remote ocean passage with just a skipper and me, conscious of the need to operate a strict watch system allowing each of us time to eat and sleep. Even more I worried about my own ability to helm and skipper such a huge yacht in this vast ocean. It was a relief to hear that we now had a crew, if only as some extra company – two weeks is a long time to spend with a total stranger. And besides, Didier's English, I soon realized, was not much better than my own French. The two

Americans – who I was told spoke French – seemed like a happy addition to the *Sauvage*.

The *Sauvage* was a 60-foot steel-hulled yacht that had been designed and built by Didier himself. The yacht had been built in Brazil and was then fitted in the Dominican Republic.

Didier Wattrelot and his family had lived aboard the empty shell for over a year before they could afford to fit her out with cabins, galley and heads. They had cooked on a little portable gas stove and washed dishes in buckets of water brought from shore. The sea had been their bathroom for everything from washing to the loo. The family slept on mattresses on the bare floor.

I got the impression that Didier was a very very good sailor. Apart from the fact that he had the look of a salty sea dog, I also learned that he had spent his entire life on the seas, first as a fisherman and then as a sailor. I had been amazed to learn that he had sailed the eight days from the Marquesas alone and without a break.

He was from Brittany, where he had once been a fisherman before skippering charter yachts for a company. Eventually he saved enough money to design and build his own boat, on which his family now lived, seasoning between Alaska and French Polynesia. Owing to the nature of the trip to Pitcairn, Sophie, his wife, had opted to stay behind in the Marquesas and teach the children.

The *Sauvage* looked magnificent moored in the bay. She was much larger than I had expected. There was only one other yacht anchored in the bay off Rikitea and that was owned by the island's tourist officer and his wife. They lived aboard their yacht not because they wanted to, but because the island was suffering from a chronic housing shortage.

'We must leave before sunset, it is far too dangerous to sail out of the reef at night,' explained Didier as we walked along the town's tree-lined street to the police office. 'First you must clear your passport with Customs,' he explained.

Rikitea was a pretty little town built on the edge of the wide lagoon. The town consisted of a little post office, a boulangerie and a small shop. The only scar was that of the *maison nucléaire*, a fall-out shelter from the 1966–74 atmospheric testing period at Moruroa, 250 miles away. During tests, island residents would be squeezed into the windowless tomb for up to three days at a time. It is a long, grey, concrete monstrosity resembling a prisoner of war block. Half the building has now collapsed from exhaustion but the remainder is used as an island store.

The Pacific Ocean has had more than its fair share of nuclear explosions. The world's only hostile use of nuclear weapons, on Hiroshima and Nagasaki in 1945, were launched from the Northern Marianas. The French, Americans and the UK have all carried out nuclear tests in the Pacific.

France's Pacific nuclear-testing programme commenced in 1966 at Moruroa and Fangataufa in French Polynesia. Their early tests caused measurable increases in radiation in a number of Pacific countries and there have been claims on many islands, including the Gambier Islands, of a high incidence of birth defects and cancer.

In 1985, France did little to improve the image of nuclear testing when it was responsible for bombing Greenpeace's *Rainbow Warrior* in Auckland harbour, killing photographer Fernando Pereira and sinking the ship that had been preparing to set sail for French Polynesia to campaign against French nuclear tests in the region.

It saddened me, the thought of the islanders crammed into this awful tomb, and the *maison nucléaire* stood as a stark reminder of a stain on their recent history.

The police station was a simple affair: an open room with a ceiling fan and two beefy-looking gendarmes who were sat watching the French version of *Pop Idol*. With their shaven heads and burly frames they could have been mistaken for the French Foreign Legion.

A young man was sat in the corner. He had a large bandage wrapped around his bare arm, his hands were cuffed. I later learned that he was awaiting deportation to Tahiti for a custodial sentence. He had turned up in the island's hospital claiming to have been attacked by a wild dog. Doctors had puzzled over the size of the wound, and soon learned by the discovery of a tooth still embedded in his arm that it hadn't been caused by a dog at all but was in fact a shark bite, a certain giveaway that he was a 'pearl poacher', operating at night, a favourite feeding-time for sharks.

One of the gendarmes snatched the passport from my hand and examined it minutely, flicking through each page and inspecting every stamp, eyeing me suspiciously as he went. The officer asked Didier, who had completed this process earlier, how long we planned to be away. Didier answered by shrugging his shoulders and sticking out his bottom lip: 'une, deux . . . trois semaines?' he replied.

The officer stamped my passport and wished us good luck before returning to the Will Young-alike performing on screen.

'We 'ave some gifts to collect,' explained Didier as we stopped in on Rikitea's grocery store, where the grocer handed us three boxes wrapped in blue plastic and a small sapling, all addressed to a 'Len Brown, Pitcairn Island'.

The small sapling, explained the grocer, was a breadfruit plant. How very apt to be sailing to Pitcairn with a breadfruit tree, I thought, remembering the voyage of Bligh and the *Bounty*.

The grocer had spent nearly six months on Pitcairn, 'out of curiosity', a number of years before, and it was during this time that he had told a Pitcairner, Len Brown, about a different variety of breadfruit that grew on Mangareva. He had promised to send him a plant as soon as he could, and now ten years later, he was fulfilling his old promise.

Alexander and his wife Kirsten were already aboard the *Sauvage* when we arrived. It was nearly 5.30 p.m. and Didier was eager to get under way. The lagoon, explained Didier, was littered with coral banks and reefs that lay just under the surface, only discernible by daylight, appearing as dark patches and silhouettes in the otherwise turquoise expanse. We had to get out of the lagoon or we risked losing a whole night's sailing. 'The weather is closing in,' said Didier. 'A low front is due in from the east in two days.' We couldn't afford to waste any more time. The anchor was raised, and before I knew it we were on our way to Pitcairn.

Alexander was a twenty-something American studying for his Ph.D. in anthropology. He had been in Mangareva for nearly a year to study the effects of the media on the island's language and dialect. Kirsten, his wife, had recently moved down from Hawaii. The couple met Didier during his short stay and had asked if they could join as 'crew' to visit the island they had heard so much about. I asked if they knew of any other boats passing through on their way to Pitcairn. Alexander explained that he knew of only one that had left over a year ago, 'with some mad, eccentric American trying to visit every place in the world'.

We hoisted the main sail and Didier handed me the helm as he went on watch for the hazardous coral banks. It felt good to be back on the open water, and soon the mountain of Mangareva was disappearing.

Didier proved himself to be not only a competent sailor, but an excellent cook, as he took over the role of chef. Alexander and Kirsten had been bedbound since we left Mangareva, incapacitated by seasickness. He reminded me of a mountain goat as he scurried around the 60-foot yacht, happily changing sails and tacking without the aid of his green crew. He never slept for more than an hour, even at night, constantly checking his charts and tweaking the sails for maximum efficiency. Didier had the ability of commanding total control with seemingly little effort. He always seemed to smile. 'Bonjour, Benjamin,' he would say with a smile as I puked my guts over the side while he simultaneously reefed the main sail, plotted our position on the charts and cooked up a steaming bowl of rice and eggs, the only food which seemed to stay down.

I spent hours lying on my bunk, listening to the *Sauvage* as she carried us across the ocean, her steel hull the only thing between us and the ocean bottom many thousands of feet below. She seemed to be alive and I listened to her every groan and strain. Sometimes she would sigh with pleasure, other times she would creak against a head wind, her body contorted and stretched. Sometimes I could hear her breathing, short inhalations followed by one long protracted exhalation. I would find myself involuntarily miming the action, my face turning scarlet red for want of air. My imagination conjured up images to accompany the noises: a child bouncing a ball, footsteps on the hull, even mermaids singing.

Didier had rigged up three fishing-lines from the stern, each one dragging an irresistible lure in our wake. For days these lines had remained thoroughly resistible, until the afternoon of the third day.

I find the ocean mesmerizing. It is one of the few places on earth that has remained unchanged throughout time. An ocean vista today is still exactly the same as that experienced by sailors hundreds of years ago. Fletcher Christian must have seen this aboard the *Bounty* over two hundred years ago. The *Bounty* is now long gone, scuttled by the mutineers, who were worried that she might be spotted by their pursuers. I wondered what it must have been like for these 'Londoners' watching their ship sink below the waves, condemning them to a life on a tiny isolated rock.

The island may have been a paradise in terms of nature's bounty, but just like the castaways on Taransay, the settlers came with 'baggage'. Their society could not be created from a blank slate. Instead they took their cultures and histories with them, something that would mark the future of the island for ever.

When the settlement was discovered by a passing ship almost twenty years later, only one mutineer was still alive: John Adams, who was living alone with the women and children in a seemingly idyllic community. But it emerged that terrible things had happened on the island – two thirds of the men had been slaughtered within just four years of landing. Sex and jealousy had led to murder.

The first year had been a busy one, creating a foundation for their new settlement. Houses were built and gardens were planted. All the cultivable land and the women were divided between the mutineers. From the outset, the Europeans had made it clear that the Polynesian men were not equals, and thus it was that in the autumn of 1791 the Polynesian men hatched a plan to murder the whites. Little is known about exactly what happened, but the small island community was torn apart by a virtual civil war which then saw whites turn against whites.

Apart from the divisions and rivalries over the women's affections, it was the creation of a small distillery on the island in 1796 that seemed to have the most profound effect on the small, solitary community.

McCoy discovered how to make spirit from the ti plant. By 1799, under the influence of the drink, he had thrown himself into the sea with a rock tied around his neck, and Quintal had become so crazed and violent because of it that Adams and Young had been forced to kill him in self-defence. A year later Young died of asthma, leaving John Adams as the sole survivor from the fifteen men who originally landed on the island ten years earlier. This left Adams in the enviable position of being patriarch to ten women and twenty-three children.

It wasn't until Captain Folger arrived aboard a sealing ship, *Topaz*, that the nineteen-year-old mystery of what happened to Christian and the *Bounty* was solved. Fortunately for John Adams, British attention was now firmly focused on the struggle with Napoleon and there was little interest in pursuing a mutineer guilty of a crime committed nearly two decades before.

Over the following years, more and more ships began to visit Pitcairn, and the population began to increase. By 1829 Adams had died and there was increasing concern that the island was becoming unsustainable. In 1831 the British government relocated the islanders to Tahiti, but within months nearly a dozen Pitcairners had died owing to their lack of immunity, one of them being Thursday October Christian, the son of Fletcher Christian and the first child to be born on Pitcairn. Of the eighty-six people who left Pitcairn, just sixty-nine survivors returned.

Pitcairn was still not a British possession. The Royal Navy called occasionally, but it wasn't until the islanders pleaded for the official protection of Great Britain in 1838 that the island became 'British'.

'Whizzzzzzzzzzzzzzzzzzzzzzzzzz . . .' screamed the line, yanking me from my daydream. I leapt from my little nest, my heart in my mouth. I grabbed the rod from its metal holder. 'Didier,' I called. The line was still speeding from the reel like a boy racer. I gripped the rod firmly in both hands and threw on the brake to stop the line escaping.

The end of the rod became taut. I forced my legs against the stanchions for resistance, but the load became more and more unbearable. I clutched on, calling for Didier, who was temporarily deafened by the sizzling sausages he was busy frying.

The rod began to creak. I pushed the ball hard into my stomach to take some of the weight, but it was too much. The rod began to slip from my hands. It felt like I had caught 'Jaws'. The rod was bent double and soon the line started creaking too. I could hear it stretching like an elastic band. 'DIDIER!' I screamed.

PING. The line snapped with such force that I was sent recoiling back on to the cockpit floor, just as Didier emerged from the cabin clutching a steaming bowl of sausages.

'Merde,' said Didier calmly picking up the broken rod. 'Ah, we 'ave another fish.' He pointed to the hand line that he had tied to one of the stanchions. 'Try again, Benjamin,' he said throwing me a pair of gloves, ''arder this time.' The line, I discovered, was much thicker than the one that had snapped. I sat on the rail and attempted to pull it in under the guidance of Didier.

It was like trying to pull a car uphill. Each time I managed to pull up the slack, it would be snatched back from me. I struggled for several minutes before Didier offered to help. He took the line with his bare hands and with barely perceptible effort began to pull the heavy fish towards the boat.

'What is it?' I asked feeling certain it was a whale.

'Not sure,' shrugged Didier. 'Maybe it ees a tuna,' he suggested. Effortlessly he hauled the fish closer. 'It's a dolphin,' cried Didier with excitement catching a glimpse of its fin.

This was not the news I had wanted to hear. 'A dolphin,' I repeated incredulously. 'We can't eat a dolphin,' I whimpered.

'It's very tasty,' added Didier picking up speed, anxious that we didn't lose this prize fish. I felt awful, I didn't want to eat Flipper.

''elp me, Benjamin,' called Didier, struggling to pull the fish aboard. I soon realized by the vibrant yellows that streaked its long body, that this wasn't a dolphin in the 'seaworld' sense, but a dolphin fish. A prized 'poisson' also called mahi mahi, it must have weighed over a hundred pounds as I helped Didier haul it aboard.

As ever, 'superman' Didier had gutted, filleted and even salted half the fish before I could cry, 'Flipper, Flipper, faster than life.' I wondered what effect the delicious fish would have on the colour of my sick as I tucked into the freshest fish steak I have ever eaten.

For three days and nights we had beat into the easterly wind. I was incapacitated by seasickness, and my days had become nights, and nights had become long.

And then, on the evening of the fourth day, in the evening half-light, the distant silhouette of Pitcairn appeared on the horizon. The small speck was still many miles away and it wasn't until nightfall that we finally reached her stormy shores.

'It look like ze Island of Wight,' murmured Didier as he hoisted up an unrecognizable flag.

'What's that?' I asked.

'It ees the Antigua flag. It ees the nearest I 'ave to the Union Jack,' he replied logically. We were in British waters now.

Pitcairn lay to starboard, a rather ugly blob of dark imposing rock surrounded by the inky black seas. It seemed strange that we were still in the Pacific at all. We had sailed away from the sparklingly luscious shores of Mangareva just four days earlier, and had followed the seemingly endless paintbox of rich blues and greens of the Pacific Ocean for days.

The tip of a mountain rising out of the sea, Pitcairn is a high island. It has only an intermittent reef, leaving it unprotected against the open South Pacific, one reason why it remained unpopulated for so long.

The current population of Pitcairn is around thirty-six, although it peaked as high as 187 back in 1855, when the land was actually threatened with over-population. There was only limited cultivable land and water and it was agreed that an alternative island home should be sought. Some of the inhabitants were still reeling from the trauma of their last evacuation to Tahiti, and it was agreed that a similar-sized uninhabited island would be a more appropriate option for the islanders.

Norfolk Island had recently been abandoned as a penal colony and lay roughly equidistant between the north tip of New Zealand and Brisbane in Australia. It was 3,500 miles west of Pitcairn and would take over a month to reach. Norfolk had a more temperate climate and it was more than ten times as large. As well as more cultivable land it had a road network and stone houses.

So Pitcairn was abandoned once again in 1856. Although Norfolk made a good home for some of the Pitcairners, there were many, too, who were unable to settle happily. They longed for 'home'. And thus, three years later in 1859, Moses and Mayhew Young returned to the island, and then in 1864 they were joined by another twenty-seven Pitcairners from Norfolk Island.

There was intermittent contact between Pitcairn and Norfolk, and in 1872 a strong sense of family and community led the Norfolk islanders to try and reunite the two groups once again. They offered to pay the costs of the relocation and guaranteed them land. But the islanders were reluctant. Pitcairn was their home.

The safe future of the Pitcairners was eventually secured by the misfortune of others. In 1875, the *Cornwallis*, a Liverpool ship, was wrecked off the coast of Pitcairn. Her crew were saved by the bravery of the islanders. Soon afterwards the *Arcadia* was also wrecked, but it wasn't until the *Oregon* foundered on the rocks in 1883 that Pitcairn became synonymous with generosity and bravery towards shipwrecked crews. The crew of the *Khandeish* lived off the islanders' supplies for fifty-one days before their rescue. The crews were deeply indebted to the Pitcairners, and when they returned home they set about supplying their saviours with those things they lacked. Cooking utensils, buckets, clothing, flour and even an organ were sent to the islanders. Along with these exotic items were cases of books, one of which would have a profound and marked effect on the island to this day. Included in the literature was a book on Seventh Day Adventism, a religious denomination which all islanders would later adopt as their own.

'Pitcairn island, Pitcairn island, this is the *Sauvage*, over,' I spoke into the VHF handset. I still couldn't believe that anyone really lived here, and a reply seemed about as likely as a response from space.

'Good evening, *Sauvage*, this is Pitcairn, can you tell us what kind of ship you are and how many passengers and crew you carry? Over,' came the alien reply from the darkness. For all I knew it might well have been ET sitting there somewhere in the gloom, asking me whether I was a cargo ship or a yacht.

'We are a yacht with four persons,' I replied.

I could sense his disappointment by the silence. The island depends on the passing generosity of container ships for supplies and the passing trade of cruise liners to sell their wares. The effects of 11 September had been felt even here as ocean traffic dried up. A small yacht was of little use to Pitcairn.

Although the islanders are essentially self-sufficient for food they rely on many imported goods. In recent years the increase in the number of ATVs (all-terrain vehicles) and the use of the island's generator has led to a dependency on fuel which is delivered once a year by the French Navy.

Most of Pitcairn's income has traditionally come from selling the island's famous stamps, which are now sold alongside other island curios on the island's website, but ironically it is this medium, which has saved so many isolated communities across the world, that could spell the end for Pitcairn Island.

In simple terms, the increased use of the internet and e-mails has led to a huge decline in letter-writing and stamp-collecting. This has led to a steep falling off in the sale of the stamps that long provided much of the island's income. The Pitcairn Investment Fund, which used to subsidize freight to and from the island, was down to under $900,000 by 2002, a reduction of nearly 30 per cent over the past decade.

The islanders have been fighting back trying to fill the vacuum.

Their latest venture, which has been partly funded by the British government, has been the introduction of an apiary on the island. So far the project has been a success, with the islanders exporting their honey around the world.

Tourism has been cited a little hopefully as another alternative economy. In 2001 a New Zealand consortium, Wellesley, gained approval for plans for two airports, its own airline, a four-star hotel and two lodges, all on an island just a few football fields across.

Naturally there had been significant opposition to the potentially environmentally damaging project, particularly to plans to develop nearby Henderson, a UNESCO world heritage site, and coral-rich Oeno, which according to the Pitcairn Islands official website is a favourite holiday destination for Pitcairners, who 'bask in the calm waters, sun themselves on the sandy beaches which do not exist on Pitcairn and enjoy spearfishing'.

'Roger that,' came the reply, 'it is best to stand off the northern shore of the island until daybreak, we will speak in the morning, out,' and with that the voice disappeared back into space.

We spent the night sailing up and down the invisible coastline. A full moon illuminated the sky and reflected off the water. The island was a perfect silhouette. I could make out pine trees on her summit, and could even see the white line of waves crashing along her shore line. She looked beautiful and serene with her backcloth of twinkling stars.

The next morning, as dawn broke over the island, the sea had become murky and the sky dirty with streaks of heavy grey cloud. I had to agree with Didier's comparison with the Isle of Wight in the Solent. A rain squall enveloped the island. So thick was the cloud that its edge was perfectly marked by a thick black line that divided the sky like some abstract painting. Hills appeared and disappeared as the mass of heavy grey washed over the island. Waves punched against the steep cliff face. High above, the green escarpments were streaked with deep red scars as if they had been struck with a giant machete. Water cascaded down the wounded hills and into the gullies far below.

The rain squall passed and the sky became a rainbow of metallic greys with light streaks of blue, until the sun tore a peephole through the clouds, turning the entire island an orangy bronze. The sun disappeared again as the sky and the sea merged into one, and the island suddenly appeared as if it were suspended in thin air.

'Pitcairn Island, Pitcairn Island, this is the *Sauvage*, over,' I spoke into the yacht's VHF radio.

'Good morning, *Sauvage*, this is Pitcairn.'

A smile broke across my face. 'Good morning, Pitcairn. We are sorry to arrive on your Sabbath. Is there any chance that we may come ashore today? Over.'

In 1887, a Seventh Day Adventist missionary from the USA arrived on Pitcairn and converted the whole island. Adherence to the religion includes observing the strict Saturday Sabbath and the ban on alcohol, pork and any fish without scales.

'That shouldn't be a problem, we'll come and collect you, please stand by,' announced a happy voice.

'Halleluja,' I screamed in my head. I packed my small bag with a large pile of Sunday newspapers, some letters from Roger, the three boxes and the breadfruit plant.

A small orange rigid inflatable boat appeared offshore and it wasn't long before I caught sight of my first real live Pitcairn islander, Randy. His name struck me more than his appearance. I had always thought Randy was reserved for men who drive pick-up trucks and chew tobacco in middle America, not island-dwelling descendants of *Bounty* mutineers.

Randy pulled the boat alongside the *Sauvage*. 'Mind ze paintwork,' cried Didier, as the waves crashed her against the steel hull. The swell was surprisingly large, allowing Alexander, Kirsten and me just a split second to leap before she dropped six feet below.

Randy had a happy weathered face with a thick black goatee. 'Welcome to Pitcairn. You've been lucky with the weather,' he said, nodding towards a sky the colour of an elephant. I struggled to place his accent.

Although Pitcairners speak English, among themselves they lapse into Pitkern, which Alexander, the resident South Pacific anthropologist, explained was a cross between eighteenth-century seafaring English and Polynesian. And accordingly a gun is a musket, and a house has a deck. Supplies are victuals and the collective term is 'all hands'.

My knuckles went a slight shade of white as we bounded across the 'gentle swell' that now felt like a mountainous ocean. The island would disappear as we dipped down each wave, Randy reducing power so that we could ride off the next wave rather than bore through it.

Five minutes later we arrived at the small 'harbour'. It looked identical to the one on Tristan da Cunha, with its wall of 'dollases' that act as a sea defence for the small concrete wharf behind. A large crane was mounted on the thick concrete wall, behind which was a huge store with a slipway down into the thick surf.

'Welcome to Pitcairn Island,' announced a colourful sign above the store. Another hand-painted sign had been nailed to a tree. It pointed towards the ocean and read, 'HMS BOUNTY', the remains of which lay on the ocean floor several hundred feet from shore, in Bounty Bay.

A dozen faces lined the small harbour wall. They all had uniform dark hair and heavily weathered faces. Their faces were expressionless. They stared at us without a glimmer of emotion as I leapt from the dinghy on to dry land for the first time in nearly five days.

I was surprised at how lush the island now appeared. In front of me was the famed Hill of Difficulty that led up to the small settlement of Adamstown, perched 400 feet above the sea on the 'Edge'. I had spent much of the ocean passage studying my small map of Pitcairn and had been thrilled to read the island's place names. Bitey-bitey, Where-Dan-fall, John-catch-a-cow, Oh Dear, and Little George Cocknuts were just some of the names that had sent my imagination into a frenzy.

My body was still swaying and the heat felt oppressive without the natural air conditioning of the sea's breeze. 'What the f★★★ are you doing here?' asked a tired-looking man with a strong Scottish accent. 'Wrong side of the world for Taransay, mate,' he continued with an incredulous smile.

I wasn't sure whether he was a Pitcairner until he introduced himself as an MOD employee from Glasgow. He and his two colleagues were on the island as part of Pitcairn's 'ordnance' training.

The islanders have traditionally 'hunted' the island's breadfruit in much the same way we hunt grouse or partridge. They even have the 'breadfruit season'. It was William Dampier, in his 1688 *Voyage round the World*, who waxed lyrical about the wonders of this 'miracle' fruit. He noted that it was 'as big as a penny loaf when wheat is at five shillings the bushel'. As early as 1776, a Swedish botanist, Dr Solander, had praised it as 'one of the most useful vegetables in the world'.

Although the breadfruit is widespread throughout Polynesia, Pitcairn is the only place where it is picked by shotgun. A breadfruit is about the size of a rugby ball and they grow on trees as high as 60 feet. The islanders had devised a system of shooting the branch on which the breadfruit grows, allowing it to fall to earth below. A number of officials had become rather concerned about the islanders' use of firearms and these three men from weapons training had been shipped out to the island to offer proper instruction and licensing. I asked the MOD workers how long they had been on the island. 'Too long,' they answered in unison. They seemed edgy.

The harbour became a hubbub of activity as various red four-wheel quad bikes zipped back and forth. The slopes seemed much greener than they had looked from the sea.

'Hello, I'm Steve Christian, the island mayor,' announced a man in jeans and T-shirt as we unloaded the gifts. I always thought mayors wore heavy chains, I thought. 'What's that?' he asked, pointing to the breadfruit plant with suspicion. I explained that it was a gift for Len from Paulo on Mangareva. 'Can you all come with me,' beckoned Christian, leading us to the boat store which housed the island's three longboats, Tin, Tub and Moss.

'We may have a problem,' he explained before turning his back to us to have a secret conversation with someone on the VHF radio. 'What are your names?' he asked, turning to us again. We all replied, but before he had a chance to hear he added irritably, 'What do you do?'

My heart began to pound. What should I say? Should I lie? Why was he interested in our professions? What profession should I give? I thought back to the e-mails and faxes I had sent to the island asking for permission to visit on which I had stated quite correctly that I was a television presenter. That sounds harmless enough to me, I thought. It wasn't as if I had a television crew with me.

'I am a television presenter,' I said quietly.

'For who?' he continued.

Something was wrong. Where is this going? And why is he asking me so many questions, I worried. He wasn't even interested in Alexander or Kirsten, and besides they don't even have television here!

I could feel my heart pounding. My face felt flushed and beads of sweat dripped down it. The heat was oppressive and it was just after seven in the morning. I felt dizzy and disorientated. In fact I felt faint. What could I say? I had already been recognized from *Castaway*.

With a dry voice I mumbled, 'BBC.'

'Who?' he demanded, pulling his ear lobe with his finger.

'BBC,' I repeated, puffing out my chest in a weak display of confidence. 'Is there a problem?' I asked, with insecurity dripping from every pore of my body.

'Leon Salt, the commissioner, is on his way,' and with that he disappeared up the hill. More and more quad bikes were appearing from the hill above, each person arriving with the same expression-less gaze.

A sort of official-looking man soon arrived with a stern scowl on his face. He had long oily salt and pepper hair and wore tattered jeans and shirt. He hoisted himself on to the wall and stared at me angrily.

'Is that the commissioner?' I asked one of the Scotsmen.

'Aye,' he said, keeping his eyes to the ground.

'Hello, Commissioner,' I said, offering my hand, 'I'm Ben Fogle.' He stared at me intently. His eyes were blank, his face full of loathing. 'I'm not talking to you,' he grunted as he spat at the ground in a display of contempt. The pounding in my chest became even more furious, I felt light-headed, and I began to feel faint again. Christian, the mayor, had wandered back down and now whispered into Leon's ear. They glanced at me as they continued to whisper conspiratorially. I felt like a naughty child brought before the head teacher.

Leon cleared his throat. 'We have made a committee decision not to allow you on to the island, you must leave now.'

I was astonished.

'We don't want you here,' he continued, 'you didn't obtain permission, and you have tried to illegally smuggle a breadfruit plant on to the island.'

I pointed out that I had put in an application, that it had been accepted, and that the breadfruit plant was an accident, and that I had assumed it to be a solicited plant sent as a gift and delivered by us as a kind favour to the islanders.

'Bullshit,' he replied. 'I never received an application from you,' he shouted.

'But I have it –' I cut myself off mid-flow as I remembered the print-out of the e-mail that lay in my computer's printer, forgotten in my headless rush to catch my flight.

More and more islanders were arriving as word spread about our arrival.

I tried to name-drop: 'But I did this island project with Roger Stephenson.'

'You were in *Castaway* with Roger?' interrupted Leon with renewed interest.

'Yes,' I said with a smile, 'that's why I'm here. I'm travelling to the most remote islands of the UK's overseas territories. You see, I love islands and –'

'The decision has been made,' he interrupted, a scowl returning to his face, 'we don't want your sort spying on us.'

'What do you mean spying?' I replied. 'I'm not a spy,' I gasped.

Alexander and Kirsten were busy with their own negotiating and had been granted permission to stay for the day. They had even been allowed stamps in their passport. I had been denied even the request to have my photograph taken on the island, with the warning that my film would be confiscated if I tried.

'I don't suppose you have any newspapers, mate?' asked one of the MOD contractors as I skulked along the quay. I fished into my bag and handed over the pile of Sunday newspapers I had carefully packed for the news-starved islanders. (I had left the *News of the World* on the yacht for fear of offending Seventh Day Adventist sensitivities.) The most expensive newspaper round in the world, I thought. I calculated that it had cost several thousand pounds per newspaper.

I also handed over the small pile of letters from Roger. 'Can you deliver these to Betty Christian,' I asked, squeezing the words from my inverted smile.

'Don't take it personally,' whispered the contractor, thrilled with the island's first papers for more than six months, 'there's a lot of ill feeling here. I can't wait to leave,' he continued quietly, 'there's a lot of shit going on.'

'Get in the boat and take the breadfruit with you,' demanded a surly Leon. 'LOWER THE BOAT,' he yelled.

Hundreds of years after Captain Bligh had been lowered into a small boat, Fletcher Christian's descendants were doing the same to me. 'Aren't you even going to offer me a cup of tea?' I pleaded, feeling certain these hadn't been Bligh's final words. 'I FEEL LIKE BLIGH!' I shouted as the breadfruit and I were lowered into the choppy waters.

I sat with my back to the island in a display of protest at the futility of it all. I had spent weeks travelling half-way across the world to be given just fifteen minutes on Pitcairn. I hadn't even seen Adamstown. My Pitcairn dream had crumbled, all the excitement and anticipation of my long dream were dashed. I felt disappointed and humiliated. 'Bastards,' I muttered as a tear rolled down my face. We crashed across the waves to the *Sauvage*, which was once again tacking up and down Bounty Bay.

'Zut alors,' exclaimed Didier as I returned to the *Sauvage* with the breadfruit under my arm and explained that they had mistaken me for 007.

I lay in my bunk defeated and exhausted. I had defied the odds and made it to one of the most remote islands in the world. I had beaten nature and the environment only to be stopped by the islanders themselves. I had failed.

Alexander and Kirsten returned to the *Sauvage* at 4 p.m. that afternoon. They were laden with gifts and letters and had even been given the birth certificate for one of their Pitcairn-born friends on Mangareva. I had been stunned that people who had shown so little trust to me could offer so much to two strangers who had never applied for permission in the first place. 'The irony', said Alexander, 'is that if you had gone for no reason, you would have been allowed on.'

Alexander and Kirsten had been given a whirlwind tour of the island on Christian's quad bike. 'I think he was rather relieved to have an excuse to avoid church,' said Alexander with a smile.

They had visited Adamstown, where they had seen the original *Bounty* bible and anchor, they had visited the small school and met the island's two New Zealand teachers, they had passed Jonny Fall, McCoy's Drop and Dick Fall. They had experienced the island's famed mud and been drenched by the rain. They had sipped tea with the islanders and even met the seventy-year-old Mr T, a Galapagos tortoise left by a visiting yacht in the 1940s.

'You would have loved it, Ben,' they said, rather insensitively. 'We got you this,' they added, handing me a handcarved turtle, with the inscription 'Pitcairn 2002'. They also handed me a small bundle of letters. One was from Betty Christian for Roger Stephenson, and one was from one of the MOD workers for his wife, and the third was addressed to me.

'Dear Mr Fogle, We are good people, please do not tell terrible things about us. God speed.' The letter was unsigned.

That night the weather had revenge on us for all its calm. I wondered whether the islanders had called on the wind as punishment instead of a custodial sentence.

We reefed the sails, battened down the hatches and hove to. The wind's whistle soon became a cry and then a scream as it threw its almighty tantrum. I lay in my bunk listening to the wind beating its mighty fist.

A deafening roar resonated around my cabin as we heeled over. I lay awake listening to the wind tear at the tiny handkerchiefs of sail that remained. Ropes strained and the ship's steel hull creaked under the immense strain. The wind was blowing us south with all the force it could muster. The *Sauvage* remained surprisingly unruffled as she was swept from wave crest to wave crest beam first.

My imagination sailed high into the stormy sky and saw images of a vast watery wasteland whipped into a violent bubbling frenzy. In my despondency I could see our little boat, heeled to, speeding across the Pacific towards the Antarctic. Every so often I would imagine a small iceberg smashing against our hull as we hit a rogue wave that sent tin pans tumbling. I imagined a sea of tree trunks ripped from the land.

Every noise, every creak, every rumble, every clink, every clack – each noise signalled the end. How would anyone find us? How would they know where we are? Where's the liferaft? It would take weeks for a lifeboat to reach us.

I stumbled from my bunk and grabbed my life jacket from behind the door. I slipped it over my neck and tied a bow around my waist. A bow? I wasn't tying a shoe, this was my only chance of escaping a watery death! Why hadn't I paid more attention to those aeroplane demonstrations, I thought as I lay in my bunk. The wind screamed and bellowed.

Somehow, sometime, I must have fallen asleep, for I was awoken by a beam of sunlight that blazed on to my face through the small hatch. I was still wearing my lifejacket. It was back to front, its ties in a horrible tangled knot.

I climbed out on deck to find Didier coiling a rope. The sky was crystal clear, the ocean calm. I wondered whether I had dreamt the storm. Where were the great gashes from the icebergs, or the destroyed mast?

'It was quite a breeze last night,' grinned Didier, jumping about the deck like an ocean goat. 'Eet broke ze kicking strap and snapped two reef knots,' he explained with a smile.

I was still angry and hurt by my Pitcairn experience. A part of me understood their suspicion of outsiders, but I knew there was more to it than mistrust. I had known before I set out that the island was embroiled in a complicated legal case, but I had wanted to visit the island with no preconceptions, which was exactly what they had of me. I had spent an entire month travelling to one of the most remote corners of the earth, to an island that had been with me since I was a child. But the mystery of the island had become unsolvable, a mystery confined to the well-worn corner of my wall chart.

The island's mystique, however, was somewhat dispelled by some more thorough research. While I had been well aware that the island had been under investigation by British authorities, what I soon discovered, however, was a case so serious it has thrown the future of the island into uncertainty.

Kent police, who have had a historic responsibility for the island, had concluded a two-year criminal investigation, during which time they had uncovered dozens of allegations, including the suspected rape of girls between the ages of ten and fifteen.

Islanders were vehement in their protestations that the entire affair was based on misconceptions. They claimed that Pitcairn had a different set of social rules. The islanders argued that because of their part-Polynesian ancestry, the girls became sexually active at a much younger age, and therefore Pitcairn's age of consent was twelve years old. Critics have argued that their explanation is flawed, partly because some of the victims are allegedly as young as three, but it certainly reveals the degree of protectiveness felt by the islanders.

The affair began in 1997, when a fifteen-year-old islander claimed that she had been raped by a New Zealander in his twenties. The man was tried on the island and eventually sent back to New Zealand. Pitcairn first came to the attention of Kent police the same year, when Detective-Superintendent Dennis McGookin investigated the alleged rape of an eleven-year-old visitor to the island by a local man of nineteen years. He concluded that the couple had a long-term consensual relationship, but he was particularly alarmed by what he later described as 'an epidemic of alcohol- and firearms-related crimes'.

Once again the islanders rallied together and claimed that they used their guns to shoot the breadfruit from the trees.

It wasn't until a Kent policewoman was assigned to the island that the current crisis unravelled. Gail Cox was stationed on the island in the late nineties, during which time she began an investigation which has stretched from Australia and New Zealand to Britain and Norfolk Island. During her extensive investigation, police have interviewed every woman and girl who has lived on the island for the last two decades. I even discovered that police had at one point prepared to visit Taransay and interview Roger Stephenson about his short period as Pitcairn's doctor. It is perhaps rather apt then that the police named their investigation Operation Unique.

Finally, in April 2003, the *Braveheart* set sail for Pitcairn with a legal party of twelve. They arrived and promptly arrested nine men, one third of the island's adult population. Pitcairn public prosecutor Simon Moore laid charges against the nine men in the Pitcairn magistrate's court, ending more than three years of waiting by both the victims and the accused. It was the court's first sitting for 106 years.

The situation had been complicated because of Pitcairn's geographical isolation and the fact that the island had only a very basic infrastructure to support such a trial. In December 2002, the New Zealand parliament passed a law at the British government's request enabling the case to be heard in Auckland.

At the time of writing, plans were being made to allow witnesses to give evidence at the trial without leaving the island. The final decision on the exact location of the trial, however, falls to the Pitcairn governor, Richard Fell, who is also the British high commissioner in Wellington.

★

I had felt deflated and dejected at my expulsion from the island, but at last I understood the islanders' excessive suspicion and secretiveness. But the more I learned, the more sadness I felt. My Pitcairn utopia had collapsed amid a creeping cloud of desolation. This wasn't supposed to be part of my island adventure.

The romance of the Pitcairners' early story has never quite been matched by the realities of the islanders' insufferably difficult and treacherous lives. For over two hundred years the islanders have managed to cling on to their often precarious existence, but now it seemed their past had caught up with them.

I had discovered an ugly side to small-island community life, but rather than drown in the wretchedness of it all, I felt a profound sense of sadness. It shrouds these pages as I write, invading every word and every sentence.

The island community, once famed for its virtue and praised in countless Victorian sermons across the world, has been shrouded in a mist of misery. Suddenly it all seemed so futile – my Pitcairn adventure and my childhood dream had both collapsed, and now it seemed the island itself was untenable.

The island's future is in jeopardy without the able-bodied men needed to work the land and, more importantly, the longboats. Betty Christian wrote from the island: 'Our very existence is at stake. We are like one family, and whatever decision is made, we are the ones who will suffer. Regardless of our differences and problems, none of our people want Pitcairn closed down and abandoned.'

The hard fact is that Pitcairn's isolation and unique law have conspired against swift justice. Whether it's a product of their isolation, rebellious history or simply three years living under the glare of Operation Unique, many Pitcairners feel they are being not only failed but persecuted.

It was no wonder they cast me and my breadfruit away like Bligh. As one Pitcairner grumbled, in another cruel cycle of history the British, it seems, are finally getting their revenge on the mutineers.

6. Ascension Island

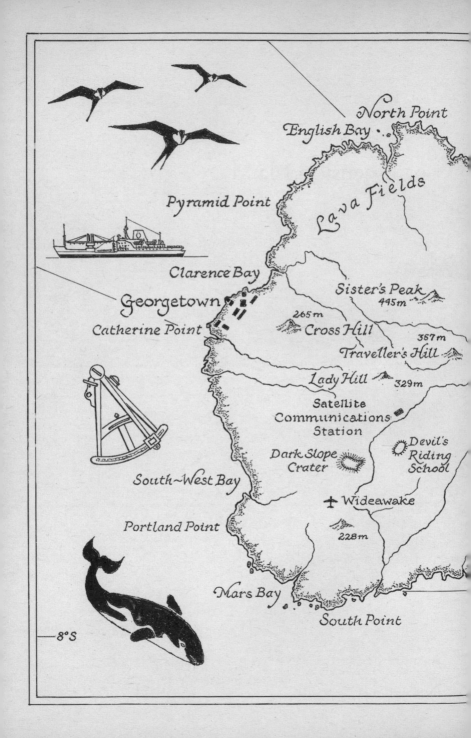

North Point

English Bay

Lava Fields

Pyramid Point

Clarence Bay

Georgetown

Sister's Peak
445m

Catherine Point

265m

Cross Hill

357m

Traveller's Hill

Lady Hill   329m

Satellite
Communications
Station

Devil's
Riding
School

Dark Slope
Crater

South~West Bay

Wideawake

Portland Point

228m

Mars Bay

South Point

8°S

14° 20' W

ASCENSION

Porpoise Point

North-East Bay

Boatswain Bird
Island

607m

Dampier

Administrator's Residence

White Hill
514 m

South-East
Head

The Peak
859 m

NASA
Tracking
Station

Settlement

South-East Bay

Green Mountain

Mount
Red Hill
544 m

Unicorn Point

White Rock

Pillar
Bay

0   1   2   3   4 km

0   1   2   3 miles

8°S

P. McC

It was just after midnight when the RAF Tristar touched down on the moon. The landscape was barren, scorched and pockmarked with craters and jagged rocks; there were no trees, no grass, no plants and no flowers. I had arrived on Ascension Island, a lunar landscape in the middle of the South Atlantic.

So accurate is the analogy that the US actually used the island to experiment with the LEM – the lunar exploration module, or moon buggy – before sending it to the moon on an Apollo mission. It has even been argued by conspiracy theorists that the LEM never left Ascension, and that the island was used as a film set for the alleged 'hoax' moon landing.

Ascension lies roughly half-way between Brazil and Angola. The nearest land is the island of St Helena, which is about 700 miles south-east. The continental coasts are over 1,250 miles east or west. The island is 34 square miles in area, and the highest point on the island is Green Mountain, at 2,840 feet. The climate is subtropical and dry, but it's the appearance of the island, not statistics, that defines it. There are a staggering forty-four dormant craters on the island. While the island's last major eruption took place about 600 years ago, basalt lava flows and cinder cones still litter the inhospitable terrain.

Although I was aware of Ascension Island from my early teatime expeditions, it wasn't until university that I discovered more about this unusual place.

Charlie had stood out from typical students: while most under-graduates had decorated their hall of residence rooms with posters of semi-clad women and treasured collections of beer mats, Charlie had turned his study into a sort of shrine to his homeland, Ascension Island.

Huge maps of the tiny island adorned the breeze-block canary-yellow walls of the 1960s building. Any gaps had been filled with dozens of photographs of his island home. Charlie had been accepted as a kind of eccentric, who preferred the rugged contours of some desolate island to those of Cindy Crawford.

I was intrigued. Charlie looked much the same as everyone else, he dressed the same and he even sounded the same. Nothing about the way he looked suggested his exotic background. This was partly explained when he told me that Ascension had no native population and that he had been living there only because his father was posted there with the RAF. It seemed amazing that a whole island could exist with nothing but a temporary migratory population.

Ascension is home to the second-longest runway in the world. Not only is it NASA's substitute moon, it is also a back-up landing strip for US space shuttle flights. Its alien nature is felt early on. Steep, bare volcanic hills, the colour of coffee, soared high above the aeroplane as it touched down.

The air was heavy when I disembarked. I had flown from a Falklands winter to Ascension's equatorial humidity. A team of tanned soldiers in khaki shorts, socks pulled to their knees, wheeled over the landing-steps, on which the words 'WELCOME TO ASCENSION' were painted alongside the Union Flag. Half a dozen red Dennis fire engines were parked at the edge of the field near the terminal building.

We had landed at the Wideawake airfield. Although Ascension is an overseas territory of the UK, the United States Air Force operates the base, which it has leased from the British government since 1956. Even the RAF Tristar I'd arrived on can land at Wideawake only with the prior permission of the US military.

I had imagined that the airfield got its name from the early southbound and late northbound flights that stopped off at the island, depositing their cargo of yawning, puffy-eyed passengers – shocked into action by a swearing parade sergeant: 'Wake up!' In fact the name comes from 200,000 pairs of sooty tern birds, known locally as wideawakes, that live on the island.

Immigration consisted of a small desk in the corner of the baggage hall, behind which the Falklands-bound 'walking cargo' were already necking the lager that they hoped would sustain them on the second leg of their journey south. The Tristar is a dry flight, and the one hour refuelling stop on Ascension is like arriving in a British pub at last orders.

I filled in my landing-form and handed over my letter of authorization from the administrator. Until just a few years ago, Ascension was the Diego Garcia of the South Atlantic, and visitors, especially writers, were *persona non grata*. Although entry requirements have relaxed, bureaucracy has not, and potential visitors must still obtain written permission before visiting.

Once through baggage control (a cordoned-off part of the car park) I was greeted by a friendly-looking man who shepherded me to a dusty white transit van, on the side of which were the letters AIAS, which stands for Ascension Island Accommodation Service. Ascension's military status had rubbed off on the island's civilians and every aspect of life was described by acronym. I had flown courtesy of FIGO from MPA in the FI to ASI with the RAF, where I would have a chance to visit the VC, the AAFB and the CSR, and have tea with the HH.

I was joined by a party of carpenters who had also flown up from the Falklands. They were on their way back to the UK after a nine-month contract on South Georgia, where they had been renovating Shackleton's House, and they were using Ascension as an opportunity to thaw out and bring some colour back into their cheeks before returning to their families.

Their faces glowed white in the dark, and they still had the 'sways' from the stormy five-day boat journey from South Georgia to the Falklands. During the previous Christmas that they had all spent on the island together, the weather had become so stormy that ships were unable to deliver their Christmas supplies. An emergency airlift was organized, and at a cost of £30,000 two bags of carrots, a turkey and a Christmas pudding were dropped on to the island by plane in time for Christmas Day.

Also boarding the bus was Martin from Newcastle. With his untucked Ben Sherman shirt, his thickly gelled hair and his heavily scented toilet water he could have stepped straight from a Geordie nightclub. Martin explained that he was a repairman, but not just any old repairman. Martin was a fruit machine repairman; in fact he was *the* Falkland Islands fruit machine man. Without him the islands would be 'fruitless'. Martin had been working on the fruits for only a couple of weeks, but there had been a problem with his work permit and he had been asked if he would mind a short holiday on Ascension while his paperwork was completed.

'F***in' crackin' to have a break from that s****y weather,' he announced. I wasn't certain whether he meant Newcastle or the Falklands. 'Noice bit a' f***in' sun, some f***in' sand, and some f***in' fishin'.' Exposure to the military seemed to have got to him. The military's propensity to swear is almost heroic. Swear words seemed to be recycled through the Tristar's ventilation system. There was no getting away from it.

We boarded the bus and set out for the island's 'capital', George-town, which lies in the north-east corner of the island, where it is dominated by a huge volcanic outcrop called Cross Hill. The town is more like a village, comprising mostly single storey prefabs. The buildings all have little flowering gardens and tend to lie along the island's main road. The hub of this small metropolis is the main square, off which are the island's only supermarket, the post office, with its familiar red postbox, and the church.

Opposite the square, on the main road, are the administrator's office, police station and HM Prison. The prison was now 'vacant', but had recently been occupied. Its most recent prisoner had been incarcerated just weeks before. He had been a passenger aboard the RAF Tristar bound from the UK to the Falklands when he had been caught smoking. He had been arrested and imprisoned before being returned to the UK for a court martial.

Accommodation on the island also betrays the island's military tradition, and while I wasn't sharing a bunk bed in some barracks, my room was simple. A tattered old mosquito net hung over a small iron bed. An old school cupboard stood against one of the walls.

The next morning I was hauled from my sleep by what sounded

like someone being murdered outside my front door. My body had been thrown into confusion by the extreme change in climate and I had been kept awake most of the night by a persistent mosquito that I thought I'd squashed about a dozen times.

The screaming continued, although it was beginning to sound more like a monkey now. Where was I? The Planet of the Apes? And, more importantly, what on earth was making that hideous noise? I struggled from my bed and pulled the door open. A dazzling beam of sunlight streamed into my room, and there in front of me was a donkey grazing on the flower box outside my door. I was well and truly up now.

I had arranged to meet Dr Nicholas 'Johnny' Hobson at 9 a.m. Everyone on Ascension knows Johnny and Johnny knows everyone. As well as being the island dentist, he was also the accommodation manager, the scoutmaster and the island's 'fixer'. In short, Johnny was the island guru and I had been advised that no visit to Ascension would be complete without meeting Johnny, and Paddy, his dog.

At nine on the dot Johnny pulled up in his white Land-Rover Defender. Paddy, a golden retriever, was sitting in the passenger seat. 'Not quite like Taransay?' Johnny said with his Irish lilt. 'I thought we'd drive up Green Mountain and look for the goldfish,' he smiled, 'they live up there somewhere.' I jumped into the Land-Rover and set off with the island dentist and his golden retriever in search of the island's famous mountain goldfish. Searching for fish atop a volcano in the middle of the south Atlantic ocean was not what I had been expecting.

The bright sunlight did nothing for the island's pockmarked complexion, only emphasized how barren and lifeless it seemed. It wasn't improved by the number of aerials, antennas, masts, receivers, transmitters and satellite dishes that seemed to sprout from the island like futuristic flowers. Everywhere I looked, their ugly frames protruded from the black volcanic rock. They were like some hideous cross between the triffids and the tripods.

Some were golfball-shaped, others looked like rotary airing-lines. I could hear a faint buzz as we drove past pylon after pylon. Signs along the side of the road warned people not to go near the aerials. I could practically see the radio beams as we headed towards Two Boats.

Ascension Island is home to a semi-clandestine organization called the CSO which is part of GCHQ (Government Communication Headquarters), the largest intelligence organization in the UK. GCHQ and the US National Security Agency jointly operate a facility in Two Boats that is part of Project Echelon, a global telecommunications-monitoring system involving more than twenty satellites. According to islanders, the CIA are frequent visitors to the island, often stopping off in private charter planes on their way to West Africa.

I asked Johnny whether there were any side-effects from living on 'aerial island'. He said that studies had concluded there was no more radiation in the air on Ascension than any big city, but he went on to admit that the island had a high rate of birth defects and cancer.

From Two Boats village the road rises sharply, winding, sometimes impossibly, up the mountainside. The Land-Rover coughed and shuddered its way up the sheer mountain bends. So tight were some of the corners that they could be navigated only by a rather scary three-point turn.

Equally startling is the change in environment. From the arid, desert-like vegetation of Two Boats, the land becomes more and more lush. The desert brush becomes denser and greener, before flowers, plants and trees become dominant. Before long I felt sure that we had accidentally driven through the sky. It was like a different world once again. The vegetation became thick and luxurious, while the air was mild and humid. It felt like we were in the Amazon, not atop a volcanic mountain in the Atlantic.

'Green Mountain Farm,' read the little sign on the gate. We had parked in a small clearing, surrounded by banana trees. On an island once described as 'hell with the fire put out', this was a surprise. In fact, Green Mountain is man-made – not the mountain itself, but its vegetation. Kew Gardens experimented with the island to increase the humidity and therefore the rainfall on Ascension. The result gives the island the overall appearance of a breast with a hairy green nipple.

We walked around the old, abandoned buildings. It had once been a thriving farm, providing vegetables and even milk for the whole island, but had fallen into disrepair, its barns and stables now derelict. We continued along a narrow path, shrouded in thick green vegetation, until we got to the entrance of a tunnel. 'Here you go,' smiled Johnny, handing me a torch, 'mind you don't slip,' and with that he and Paddy disappeared into the gloom.

My deck shoes squelched through thick mud as droplets of water dripped from the roof of the passageway. Nearly a hundred yards long, it had been built and used by soldiers of the garrison as a short-cut through the mountain for collecting rainwater. They would come all the way up from Georgetown and load up the donkeys with barrels of drinking-water before beginning their steep five-mile journey back to the settlement.

Despite the tropical climate, lack of water has always been one of the greatest threats to the island. The low annual rainfall has never been enough to maintain Georgetown. There are just two natural springs on the island, both on Green Mountain, which is subject to much higher rainfall than the lowlands. We were at Dampier's Drip.

Once through the tunnel we continued along a green valley until we reached a vast man-made bowl. Half the valley had been covered in concrete, creating what looked like a skate-boarding park. This had been built as a solution to the island's water problem. Rainwater would run across the impermeable basin and into a reservoir, from where soldiers would collect it.

We continued on, trudging through the thick vegetation. Paddy by now was just a blond tail poking up through the green leaves. The cloud cover got closer and before long our heads were disappearing into the damp mist. A steep gully meandered up the mountainside. Ropes had been tied from tree to tree along the side, creating a sort of banister up the slippery path that was awash with mud. In places the thick sludge was a couple of feet deep.

I was attempting to climb the Everest of the South Atlantic in my exhausted old deck shoes. They had seen service in some of the most remote parts of the globe, but now, it seemed, Ascension's Green Mountain was just too much for them. I struggled to scrunch up my toes and keep the shoes attached to my bare feet until my left leg disappeared into the thick quagmire. I heaved and pulled and when my leg was eventually released from the reluctant mud, my shoe was not. I dipped my foot back into the sludge, and stirred it with my leg in a vain attempt to recover the shoe. Alas, my negotiations failed. The mountain had eaten my deck shoe and I would have to go on barefoot.

'Ah, not to worry about it, there's no snakes here,' smiled Johnny in his sturdy climbing-boots, as we continued up the steep mountain. 'Those goldfish are up here somewhere,' he said, yomping on with a grin on his face.

We had been walking for several hours by now and my body was beginning to tell me so. 'Come on,' shouted the dentist, sensing my fatigue, 'we're nearly there.' It felt odd squelching through the reddish-brown mud in my bare feet. I felt naked and the mud tickled me as it squeezed between my toes. I trudged and slipped my way on up the steep path and by the time we finally reached the summit, I looked like the mud man.

Green Pond didn't look that green to me. In fact, apart from the lily leaves, it looked as brown and muddy as me, and as for any goldfish, well, I couldn't see how they moved through sludge.

Johnny assured me that it wasn't always quite so muddy as Paddy made a flying leap into the middle of the chocolate pond. His blond coat turned Dairy Milk. Several times a year, the island holds its own version of the London Marathon, and all healthy adults on the island are encouraged to take part. The race begins in Georgetown on the beach next to the turtle ponds. Runners must start with one hand in the seawater, and then race to the top of Green Mountain and dip the same hand in the dew pond. The race was originally started to keep the soldiers occupied, but like so much on the island, military tradition has become island tradition.

'Look,' pointed Johnny, 'a goldfish,' and there, sure enough, just below the murky surface, I could make out the dim reflection of an orange body. So there it was, Ascension's mud-dwelling mountain goldfish. I had lost my shoe and about a stone in perspiration, but I had conquered the mountain and sighted the fish. Now all I had to do was descend the mountain barefoot, a prospect made slightly less inviting by the jagged lava flow I would have to cross.

The goldfish were not, of course, native to Ascension. They had first been brought to the island by two Royal Marines. It must have been quite a trip. Could they have been carried all this way in a see-through plastic bag by some red-faced marine? While all his colleagues were busy packing tents and army rations into their packs, he would be gently holding the top of the bag in one hand and cradling the bottom with the other.

There was another creature that seemed to be entirely out of place atop a volcano in the Atlantic Ocean. Not some mud-caked, barefooted Englishman, but crabs, thousands of them, scuttling across the vegetation and even climbing trees. Now I must have missed out on that particular biology lesson, but I was always under the impression that crabs lived in or near water, not what must have been a week-long trek from the sea for these bright orange creatures.

In fact they are not shipwrecked crabs castaway on the mountain top, but a colony of land crabs. Although they are probably the earliest colonizers of the island, relatively little is known about them, except that they do make their way to the sea to lay their eggs, an epic journey for the orange crustacean.

At one time they had threatened to overrun the island. Their habit of digging holes in the ground made it virtually impossible to cultivate crops or gardens and the Royal Marines were called in. Their job was to exterminate the crabs, and they would be rewarded with a tot of rum for every ten pairs of claws delivered to their headquarters.

An hour and a half of 'oohs' and 'ahhhs' later I hobbled back to Johnny's Land-Rover. 'Hungry?' asked Johnny as he pulled a machete from the cab and wandered into the undergrowth. 'Mind your head,' he said as he sliced into a green trunk, sending the tree crashing to earth.

'Here you go,' he said, hacking off the stem of bananas and handing me a bunch. 'The fruit of Ascension,' he smiled as he placed the other bananas in the back of the car. 'I'll take them to the NASA station for the lads.'

Johnny had lived on the island for nearly fifteen years and was about as close as one gets to an indigenous inhabitant on Ascension, as the entire population is made up of transitory migrant workers, predominantly from St Helena.

He told me two stories that underline the global anonymity of Ascension. The first was that until a postcode was introduced for the island, nearly half the post had been misdelivered to Asunción, the capital of Paraguay in South America. The second story he told me was of the time he took his scout troop on a visit to Northern Ireland and England. During the trip, Johnny organized for the scouts to visit Downing Street and even wangled an audience with the prime minister, Tony Blair. The boys put on their best socks, buffed their toggles and made their way to No. 10, where they lined up for their introduction to Mr Blair, who upon hearing that they were from Ascension asked 'whereabouts in the Caribbean' it was. The boys were apparently horrified that their prime minister didn't even know where their country was.

The first and only time many people had heard of Ascension was when it was used as a vital staging-post during the 1982 Falklands War. With its secret military installations, only service personnel, government employees and those employed as contractors by companies on the island were permitted to visit. Even today the island is used mainly for communications, although the American military operate a surveillance station for the US Air Force. Cable and Wireless operate from Ascension, as does the BBC, which has its Atlantic Relay Station on the island. For most people, there's little reason to know about it, much less to visit.

Ascension was first discovered in 1501 by a Portuguese seafarer named João de Nova, who named it Concepción. It wasn't until two years later that another sailor, Alphonse D'Alberquerque, named and claimed it.

During the seventeenth century, ships called at the island to supply themselves with turtle meat and fresh water. In return they would leave goats behind with which future ships calling at the island could replenish their meat stores. Ships would also call at the island to leave letters, which would then be collected by ships heading in the same direction as the letters' destination. Haphazard, but certainly effective.

On 22 April 1701 William Dampier was shipwrecked on the island. Dampier was a mixture of pirate, adventurer, explorer and scientist. He was on his way back from an expedition in the southern Indian Ocean on behalf of the Admiralty when he was wrecked on Ascension's volcanic shores. His ship was lost, along with a fabled treasure which is still talked about and even hunted for today.

Dampier and his crew survived by following goat tracks to the island's drinking-hole, which is known today as Dampier's Drip. It was William Dampier who later captained the maritime expedition during which Alexander Selkirk asked to be left on the deserted island of Juan Fernández in the Pacific Ocean off the coast of Chile.

Selkirk stayed there for nearly four and a half years and is the inspiration for the most famous castaway of all time. His account of his years on the island was the inspiration for Daniel Defoe's *The Life and Strange Surprizing Adventures of Robinson Crusoe of York, Mariner*.

Dampier spent five weeks on Ascension, and the island's small museum still contains his diary. Other navigators who visited Ascension included Louis Antoine de Bougainville and James Cook, who landed on the island during his voyage round the world in 1775, on his way back from the Pacific having discovered the South Sandwich Islands and South Georgia.

The aridity of Ascension was the most likely reason why it remained uninhabited until Napoleon was sent to St Helena in exile in 1815. During the emperor's captivity on St Helena, a small British naval garrison was stationed on Ascension to deter the French, and the first settlement was established in the north-west of the island, the site of present-day Georgetown.

In later years a village was built at the foot of Green Mountain and named Two Boats. The original site was a stopping-place for sailors on their way to collect water from the mountain. It got its name from two longboats that had been placed there to provide shade for passers-by.

When Napoleon died in 1821, Ascension was not abandoned completely. The island had acquired a certain strategic importance as a support base for ships heading for the Orient and the Pacific. Neither the Suez nor the Panama canals had yet been built and the UK recognized the island's significance in the struggle against piracy and the slave trade.

The island became 'HMS *Ascension*', a 'Stone Sloop of War of the smaller class', and by the time of Napoleon's death Ascension had become an important victualling station and sanatorium for ships engaged in suppressing the slave trade around the west coast of Africa.

In 1823 the island was taken over by the Royal Marines and remained under their supervision until 1922, when it was made a dependency of St Helena. The island also became an important location for the Eastern Telegraph Company. Already by the end of the nineteenth century the ETC had started dealing with tele-communications via cable. The first cable was landed on the island in 1899, and with this Ascension became an important telecom-munications station. The cable went from Cornwall, via the Cape Verde Islands, Ascension and St Helena, to Cape Town, just in time for the start of the Boer War.

From 1922 until 1964, the Eastern Telegraph Company (it became Cable and Wireless in 1934) 'governed' Ascension, with senior managers handling the day-to-day operations of the island. Ascension became the centre of a spider's web, as cables radiated between there and Cape Town, Freetown in Sierra Leone, Pothcurno in Cornwall, Rio de Janeiro and Buenos Aires.

The island passed from the navy to the Commonwealth ministry, and in 1942 the United States government, by arrangement with His Majesty's government, built an airstrip on the island, Wideawake airfield. From 1943 to 1945 more than 25,000 planes made stopovers on the island on their way to the war in North Africa, the Middle

East and Europe. The US wartime base, holding as many as 4,000 servicemen at one time, was centred on Command Hill overlooking the runway. American troops left the island in 1947 and the airstrip fell into disuse until 1956, when an agreement was signed between Great Britain and the United States permitting the use of Ascension as a long-range testing ground for military missiles. A year later, the US Air Force presence was re-established and the airstrip enlarged. It is now an ICBM (intercontinental ballistic missile) and space missile tracking-station. During the Falklands War, Wideawake airfield became the busiest runway in the world, and it's arguable that without this mid-Atlantic asset the war could not have been won.

Ascension is now a dependency of St Helena, which is responsible for staffing the administrator's office, post office, savings bank and police detachment. The administrator is directly responsible to St Helena's governor.

Various companies keep the rest of the 1,000 inhabitants employed, the majority of whom are from St Helena. There are a further 200 British citizens and about 70 American nationals, who live on the island for anything from a few months to a few years, depending on contracts.

Georgetown is the capital of Ascension, though most of the island's inhabitants live within the four settlements outside George-town. Two Boats village is a residential area. Traveller's Hill is where the RAF contractors live and Cat Hill is the US base. The administrator's 'residency' is on Green Mountain.

After removing half of Green Mountain from my legs, regaining the use of my lava-bruised feet and improvising some footwear, I decided to head for the capital to sample Ascension's nightlife, starting with dinner at the Galley.

Ascension isn't famous for its culinary sophistication, but the Galley is the island's most popular eating-spot. This is a sort of cross between a soup kitchen, a school dining-room and a seaside café, and it seemed the island's nightlife begins early, as the Galley serves dinner from 5 p.m. to 6 p.m. only.

The Galley is a long, low building just opposite the single workers' quarters, and the room's 'centrepiece' was the three juice machines bubbling with abnormally bright neon liquids. They reminded me of the sort of thing you might find in a mad scientist's laboratory as he mixes his radioactive green and orange potions.

The building was decorated with what appeared to be old school tables and chairs with their rusty steel legs. The food itself was served from a metal cabinet, kept warm by a bright light that did nothing for the food's appearance. Macaroni cheese and chips was the order of the day, followed by a ready-bowled pudding – also wilting under a heat lamp – drowned in thick, yellow custard. All this could be washed down with a plastic cup of purple squash.

I felt like I was back at school as I collected my food from a dinner lady who reprimanded me for not booking my dinner in advance by signing my name in 'the book'. 'If your name's not in the book, you're not getting dinner,' she said, shaking her head in disdain at my ignorance of island etiquette. Eventually she relented on the understanding that I sign there and then for tomorrow's breakfast.

I wandered around the tables, with my tray in my hand, confronted with that age-old school dining-room dilemma. Who to sit with? I had only been on the island for a day, and I didn't recognize any faces. I blushed at the prospect of being turned away by the 'cool' lot.

'Excuse me, do you mind if I sit here?' I asked a smiley face.

'Sure,' he replied. I placed my dinner on the table and scraped a chair across the hard floor as I sat down.

The Galley is meant for the island's work force, almost all of whom are from St Helena and predominantly men, and the room was nearly full of hungry workers in their overalls, scratching their cutlery against the china bowls, eking out every last mouthful of sustenance.

There is no private ownership on Ascension. There are only employees who work for the five organizations that own the island. The group is called the Island Users' Group, and this consists of the

BBC, Cable and Wireless, CSO (a secret British agency used to 'listen in'), the RAF and the Americans.

'Have you been here long?' I asked my enforced dinner companion.

''Bout ten minutes,' he replied swigging on his purple squash.

'And what about on the island?' I pressed.

'Not so long,' he said, ''bout five years.'

What I soon discovered was that my dining companion, Josh, like the entire population of Ascension, was simply a transitory worker. The only meaningful question to ask a stranger is: 'Who do you work for?' Ascension Island employs the entire population, who by necessity are mainly young men. There are no old people on Ascension.

Josh explained that like most of the Saints on Ascension, he was there alone, supporting his family who lived back on St Helena. He lived in the singles' quarters across the road, and returned to his family in St Helena every few years. Ascension Island affords Saints the opportunity of high wages from the UK work sector with the advantage of a cheap cost of living, and while there is no private sector on Ascension and no private ownership of property, there is also no system of taxation.

But, as Josh explained over his mystery custard pudding, this was all about to change. He handed me a copy of the island's only weekly newspaper. 'NO TAXATION WITHOUT REPRES-ENTATION', screamed the headline of the *Ascension Times*, echoing the demand for democratic rights that started the American War of Independence more than two centuries ago.

The islanders, Josh explained, were up in arms and had decided to rally against the government decision to impose income tax, property tax and a tax on cigarettes and alcohol, without the provision of an island-elected council. They had even taken their battle to London. In a petition sent to the British Foreign Office, 300 islanders said, 'We, the undersigned, deplore the introduction of taxation without representation on Ascension and the failure of Ascension Island government and the British government to adequately consult, and take into account the view of, the people of Ascension.' They demanded that London and the local colonial government, under Administrator Fairhurst, 'introduce democratic representation without delay'.

The *Ascension Times* continued: '"We love Britain, and we love being British", said Lawson Henry, personnel director of Ascension Island Services, "but this colonial thing is shooting it down", he told reporters. "Power should be in the hands of the people," he added, "but the officials are terrified of losing control. If we don't like who is governing us, we want to be able to kick them out."'

Governor Hollamby runs Ascension from St Helena, and he had reported that the 1,000 islanders were not ready for democracy. 'There's not a lot of experience of governance among the most vociferous,' Mr Hollamby said in an interview. 'As they gain experience,' he added, 'they can take more responsibilities.'

Governors had consistently reminded me of headmasters throughout my tour of the Empire, and Hollamby's remarks could have been taken straight out of a school assembly. I had noticed how islanders always addressed the governors and their administrators, as 'sir'. I had also noticed how they would always stop what they were doing, practically bowing their heads in deference as he passed.

According to a two-year-old Foreign Office study, unless the government stepped in to help, Ascension faced a future in which its 'population would be reduced and the last semblance of community life would disappear and the island would become a single persons' work camp'. The report warned of discontent without democratic rights on the island. Given the history of Britain and her colonies, this seemed to be a statement of the blindingly obvious.

I said my goodbyes to Josh and, with a belly full of macaroni and squash, went off to explore the rest of what Georgetown had to offer.

Just beyond the supermarket there rises a huge, square, rather dilapidated building, one of the oldest on the island. It is built in the colonial style, two storeys high, and is surrounded by pillars and crowned with a small tower. This was once the headquarters of the garrison commander; now it is home to the island's only shoe shop, secondhand Sue Ryder clothes shop and a small hardware shop selling everything from 'I love Ascension' T-shirts to hammers and saws. The shoe shop was open for just two hours each week, on Tuesdays and Thursdays from 15.30 to 16.30.

The Sue Ryder opened only on Fridays between 17.00 and 18.00, and the hardware shop on Wednesdays and Saturdays from 16.30 to 18.00. The island's only petrol station was even more confusing, opening on Mondays and Wednesdays from 08.00 to 12.00, and on Tuesdays and Thursdays from 16.30 to 18.30. It could have been the same person doing the lot, closing one establishment before racing across town to open the next. Whatever the rationale behind it, it was a minefield for those preparing the week ahead, and particularly for visitors who lose their shoe atop a mountain on Saturday and who run out of petrol for their hire car on a Wednesday afternoon.

I climbed the stairs to the Exiles Club above the shops, hoping that I was on schedule and that I hadn't been expected to pre-book a pint. The club consists of a vast hall, with a balcony overlooking the harbour and the ocean beyond. Two fans hung lifeless from the high ceiling. The walls were decorated with sun-bleached photographs of the island. On two huge turtle shells hanging on the wall was a list of the British and American commanders of the island. A yellowing photograph of the Queen and Duke of Edinburgh on their wedding day smiled down from the whitewashed wall.

Some young children were sipping on cans of Coca-Cola, playing pool to the accompaniment of Madness, who were playing on the stereo. A man with a long white beard clutched his tot of whisky; his head drooped to one side, his back was hunched and he looked like he was about to pass out. The Saint barwoman was busy polishing glasses with a cloth.

As recently as the early nineties, access was strictly for British and Americans, and Saints were exiled from the Exiles. Today, although it is open to anyone, it is still difficult to visit, as it always seems to be closed. During my week on the island, I saw it open just twice.

The Volcano Club, or VC as it is known, is just a few miles away, but a world apart from the Exiles. As with much of life on Ascension, the island can be roughly divided into the American and the British sectors, and there is no greater display of cultural difference than the island's two 'clubs'.

While the Exiles Club is a sort of run-down tropical version of an English pub, the American VC is like some good ole boys' bar in the Midwest. It is much noisier and darker. Country and western music blared out while soldiers with their cropped hair and cowboys in their stetsons clutched bottles of Budweiser and snacked on hot dogs and tortilla chips. The bar was stocked with cans of Mountain Dew, root beer and bowls of tortillas. The walls were covered in ageing photographs of rockets leaving Cape Canaveral and Ascension from space, and there were a number of signed photographs of astronauts.

The more time I spent on Ascension, the more I became aware of the broad divide between the US and the UK sections. Half the cars on the island were old right-hand drive Ford Escorts and Capris, while the other half were left-hand drive Dodge trucks and Buicks. The island has a cricket pitch and a baseball field. The US military supermarket has shelves bulging with Lucky Charms and Oreo cookies, while the British market is stacked with Walker's crisps and Findus Chicken Kievs.

With a tummy suffering from the combination of macaroni, custard and Budweiser, I decided it was time to call it a night.

My next Ascension experience was to visit gossip central, Georgetown's coffee shop, open, of course, just twice a week – on Mondays and Fridays from 09.00 to 13.00 – though it seemed half the island came for a cup of tea, cake and some tittle-tattle.

The coffee shop was between the police station and the prison and consisted of a small wooden building with a fenced-off pen to keep the donkeys out, in which there were a number of plastic chairs and tables. The floor was the ubiquitous volcanic ash.

I spent the morning sipping on St Helenian coffee and watching life on Ascension go by. Two German fishermen were meeting to discuss the potential of bringing their game-fishing outfit from West Africa to the island. Some FCO officials who had just flown in from England and were still in their pinstripes were meeting with Adam the tax man. Johnny's granny was sipping on a cuppa and even Governor Hollamby's administrator and number two on the island, Fairhurst, popped in for a chat and a cup of char, as did one of the island's uniformed bobbies.

The general chat revolved around the impending tax, but I soon learned from Joan the tea lady that tax wasn't the only thing being introduced to the island that raised temperatures. Compulsory castration was also being introduced, for the donkeys.

Probably first introduced by the old Royal Marine garrison, the donkeys have roamed Ascension for donkey's years. They were originally used to transport water from Dampier's Drip to Georgetown, but today they are largely feral, except for a particularly friendly city donkey known as Fred with a penchant for digestive biscuits, and for attempting congress with Paddy the golden retriever.

The Ascension Island Society for the Prevention of Cruelty to Animals had been established to monitor and control the feral donkey population on the island, and apart from the proposal to give contraceptives to the females, it had been decided that the most humane way of controlling the herd was by castrating some of the males, a decision that had got some of the islanders up in arms. 'NO CASTRATION WITHOUT REPRESENTATION' exclaimed a homemade poster that soon appeared in the window of an anti-castration campaigner.

Donkeys are just one of the hazards you can encounter on Ascension's roads. Driving on the island should be simple as there are no traffic lights, no roundabouts and no motorways, and the island speed limit is just 40 m.p.h. But what it lacks in traffic, it makes up for in animal obstacles: donkeys, sheep and the land crabs all seem to use the roads too, and they provide constant obstacles to island drivers. Wary of all this, I set out in my hire car to explore some of the island's more intriguing-sounding destinations.

Ascension's landscape is littered with place names that refer to the island's rich history, but without an indigenous population it is difficult to establish the provenance of many of the names. Certainly the island's bleak volcanic landscape is probably responsible for inspiring such places as the Devil's Cauldron, the Devil's Ashpit, the Devil's Riding School and the Devil's Inkpot. Other names, such as the Gallows and Dead Man's Beach, Benin City, Pan-Am Beach, Cricket Valley and the Broken Tooth live-firing area, tell of the island's slightly more contemporary history.

From One Boat the road splits left to Pyramid Point and English Bay. The road passes Ascension's only golf course, which is in the *Guinness Book of Records* as the worst golf course on the whole planet. It isn't hard to see why, as it is nothing more than a dusty plain devoid of any trees or vegetation, scattered with sharp stones and surrounded by a sea of black lava.

I parked as close to the sea as I could get and got out to walk. English Bay, on the island's north coast, must rival Ascension's golf course as one of the most unusual holiday spots in the world. The bay is home to one of the most beautiful beaches on the island, with its long, white, sandy stretch dipping gently into the warm turquoise waters. But it isn't called English Bay for nothing, and this mid-Atlantic paradise is also home to the BBC South Atlantic Relay Station, and to the power station and desalination plant which supplies most of the island's electricity and domestic water, and the island's fuel tanks.

An enormous golfball aerial marks the edge of the bay, and a series of huge pylons follow the shoreline behind it. These were the BBC aerials. One islander told me that the signal is so strong at English Bay that you can lie on the beach and listen to the World Service in the air waves as they leak from the transmitter. I had even been told of one sunbather who claimed to have seen streaks of light emanating from the cables.

Comfortless Cove, round the headland to the west, is one of the few places on the island where it is safe to swim. It was originally called Sydney before the name was changed to Comfort Cove. From the 1830s the inlet was used for landing crew members from the ships working off the west coast of Africa who had contracted yellow fever. The cove was used as a quarantine station and the island's garrison would supply provisions for the ill. Many died from the disease and the cove was renamed Comfortless Cove, as an indication of the misery experienced there. Victims are buried in a small cemetery just inland from the cove. Instead of stones, graves are marked by sun-bleached pieces of driftwood. The cove was also used as the landing-point for the transatlantic telephone lines when they were laid at the turn of the century. There is still the small landing-strip from which the cables were winched ashore, and a small hut still furnished with a table and even an old dial telephone.

I spent the afternoon sunbathing on the sandy beach and swimming in the warm waters. A number of sunburnt soldiers were also enjoying the sunshine, swigging on cans of lager, their camouflage uniforms neatly folded next to their matching green towels. For no reason I could fathom the telephone in the small hut kept ringing. Each time I answered the phone I could hear distant voices over the crackling line — faraway conversations, unaware they had an audience on Ascension. This was the island's raison d'être, and now I was at it too.

I had arranged to visit the BBC relay station. The Beeb had established an Atlantic relay station on the island in 1966 to improve coverage of short-wave broadcasts to Africa and South America. As I drove up to the relay station I saw the familiar trademark letters still emblazoned across the side of the building, their colour faded by the fierce island sun. They seemed out of place in such an un-British environment. At one stage this was part of the BBC's operational portfolio and no different from TV Centre or Broadcasting House, and Ascension itself, including the power station and desalination plant, were all run from the BBC's HQ at White City.

In 1997, however, the BBC appointed a private contractor, Merlin Communications International, to operate its Ascension facilities and today the relay station has a considerably less significant role to play, used predominantly for World Service transmissions to West Africa.

I was thrilled at how basic the facilities were. Huge wooden cupboards containing pumps and bellows like some medieval sorcerer's workshop were busy transmitting *The Archers* to Africa. The whole station looked more like my old school science lab than a crucial relay station.

The eastern side of the island is remarkably different from the rest. This is the side exposed to the tropical wind which brings humidity to the land. A road here was built by NASA to lead to its centre for the study of outer space and for the Apollo expeditions which first took man to the moon. The centre was built in 1965 and it closed in 1989, when it was deemed unnecessary. It was now home to Johnny's scout troop. Only Johnny could convert a space station into a boy scouts' den. How many children get to play in old NASA space stations? Two palm trees on either side of the road act like an archway at the entrance. Grass has started to sprout in the untended car park. The building itself was vast. Some of the windows were broken and the paint was flaking and peeling.

Inside, light fittings dangle from the ceiling and the air is damp and musty. The walls are still covered with old posters and stickers from various space missions. Dozens of rooms lead off each corridor that runs up and down the side of the deserted hall, and it was these rooms that Johnny had converted into dormitories. Each room contained half a dozen metal foldaway beds with thin mattresses.

The history of this building still hangs heavy in the air. The foundations of the huge aerials that tracked man's first mission to the moon remain like monuments to the importance of this centre. I could almost hear the buzz of radios in the air as I wandered around the derelict building. Today the scouts have repainted one side of the hut in bright colours, and Johnny is even installing a chemical loo and a water tank for them.

The space connection has not quite vanished from the island because, although NASA have long since given up permanent residence, the European Space Agency still owns the Ariane tracking station, which is to the east of the island. Johnny probably has designs on that too.

That evening I had been invited to his house for a celebratory St Patrick's Day dinner. His house was at the edge of town, next to Clarence Bay. It was a roomy single storey building furnished largely with plastic garden furniture. The floors were covered in white tiles that gave the house a cool feel even in the balmy evening.

Johnny's guests were already sipping gin and tonics when I arrived. His mother was over visiting him from Northern Ireland. Shubash – Shub, as he is known to everyone – is the island's doctor, and was there with his Zambian wife Raxa. Jacqui and Adam Hensham had both recently moved to the island from London. Jacqui now worked for the island's Turtle Conservation, while Adam, who had previously worked for Price Waterhouse, had been sent to the island to help implement the unpopular tax system, quite a responsibility for a thirty-something. It was a diverse group of people, but one that reflects the eclectic nature of Ascension's population.

Johnny had prepared a big bowl of spaghetti bolognese which we washed down with large bowls of vanilla ice cream. 'How did you get that?' chorused the guests in genuine astonishment at Johnny's ability to get the impossible. I had e-mailed Johnny before I left England asking if there was anything I could bring with me. He had sent a list that included rope, cheese and ice cream. The island was currently experiencing one of its frequent shortages, and while cheese had become a staple, the absence of ice cream had caused near anarchy in the island's supermarket.

Sadly, I decided that the ice cream wouldn't survive the journey, so was astonished to find myself sat on the Tristar next to a soldier who was travelling with a shopping bag full of fresh milk, cream and three pints of chocolate chip ice cream.

The evening's conversation was dominated by talk of the impending taxes, for which Adam had been responsible. Johnny was slightly more upbeat than most: 'We want to open the island to tourism,' he explained, 'and the only way we can increase tourism is by improving the island's infrastructure.'

Bound up with the tax issue for him was that of private owner-ship. Many people, including Johnny, had concluded that with the introduction of a taxation system, islanders would have to be given the right to buy their property, something Johnny had been itching to do for years.

I was again struck by the islanders' affinity with and love for this bleak volcanic island, and as with the Falkland Islands became aware of a simmering rift between the military, who see and use the island as a work place, and the civilian workers, who speak of the island as their 'home'. Raxa and Shub's daughter was visiting Ascension from the UK. She had been educated at a British boarding-school and was currently studying at Southampton University. She reminded me of Charlie, my university friend who had been so obsessed with the island.

She explained that her entire university thesis was about Ascen-sion Island, and that as well as returning to the island for every holiday, she was also planning on taking a year out from university to spend more time there. I imagined her walls in halls also being adorned with maps and memorabilia of her island paradise.

Throughout the evening I noticed Paddy snooping around the beach next to Johnny's house. Every so often he would return licking his lips. 'It's them walking Frey Bentos,' smiled Johnny, 'he just can't resist them.' He licked his lips. 'Crunchy on the outside, soft in the middle,' he joked.

These walking pies were one of the island's most well-known and revered inhabitants, the green sea turtles. Before the island was inhabited, the beaches served as the main breeding ground for the Atlantic population of green turtles owing to the lack of predators.

I once spent a year on the Mosquito Coast of Honduras and Nicaragua in Central America. I went there when I was nineteen and ended up working on a turtle conservation project with an American Peace Corps volunteer named Bonnie and an American anthropologist called Mark. I spent nearly six months living on the remote and rugged Atlantic coast of Honduras monitoring and at times collecting newly hatched eggs to prevent them being poached by locals, who favoured them as a delicacy.

I had never tired of watching the enormous turtles haul themselves up the beach before slowly and laboriously digging their nests, using their flippers as shovels, and laying up to 150 ping pong ball-sized eggs. Sometimes we would collect the eggs into buckets and rebury them elsewhere. The turtles leave enormous 'tractor' tracks up and down the beach from where they have hauled their weighty shells. These tracks are like following footprints for the poachers and we had decided that the clutches stood a much better chance if we moved them somewhere else. I used to feel like a father when I watched them hatch from the nest I had redug for them. I even used to help some along in the hope that my little clutch of green Fogle turtles would beat the odds and make it to adulthood.

Each year the male and female turtles migrate from Brazil to Ascension, more than 1,250 miles away. Scientists have long studied how they could travel over such a vast distance and still end up on the same tiny beach on an island that is little more than a pin prick in the South Atlantic. How they navigate is still not entirely understood but it is thought to be a combination of smell and magnetic orientation.

Green turtles are found nesting on many tropical and sub-tropical beaches around the world. However, the green turtles that nest on Ascension are the largest of their species, at about six feet in length and weighing up to 550 pounds.

The arrival of man on Ascension dramatically lengthened the odds of the turtles making it to adulthood, as sailors realized the nutritional usefulness of such a creature. The turtles would be captured and held in the turtle ponds which were built in 1829. They would be held here until ships arrived, on to which they would be loaded to provide fresh meat for the sailors. The turtles would be placed on their backs, unable to right themselves, in the ship's hold, where they could survive for many months with a minimum of care.

Turtle soup also became a delicacy for the aristocratic, and Ascension's turtles would be shipped to London for the Lord Mayor and the Admiral of the Fleet. Today the turtles are heavily protected. Though they still suffer predation from birds, cats and even crabs. Not to mention a golden retriever called Paddy.

After dinner, I went for a wander along Long Beach. Given that green turtles have been estimated to live for between sixty and a hundred years, I was looking for some familiar faces. 'My' turtles would be nearly eight years old, I thought, as I wandered past dozens of laying turtles. The sky was peppered with stars that gently illuminated the turtles' prehistoric faces. As I walked up and down the beach, hundreds of baby turtles were making their bid for freedom by rushing towards the Atlantic surf.

That night as I lay in my bed listening out for the buzz of the mosquitos, I was startled by the telephone ringing. I picked up the receiver, only to hear the familiar distant crackling voices I had heard down at Comfortless Cove. I eventually fell asleep only to dream that one of 'my' turtles from the Mosquito Coast was trying to call me from a telephone paybox on some remote island where he had got lost. Typical Fogle trait, I thought.

Next morning Johnny had arranged for me to climb one of the letterbox walks. The idea of letterboxes is not a new one, as in the seventeenth century outward-bound ships would leave messages on the island for the next ship to take home. The letterbox walks had been devised in much the same way when, in 1913, the first letterbox, a green tin box, was placed at what is now known as Letterbox, on the most easterly point of the island.

Today there are more than eighteen scattered around the island, each with a pad of ink and a hand stamp as proof that visitors made it. Johnny and his god daughter Danielle were keen to take me to White Hill letterbox on the eastern shore of the island, overlooking one of Ascension's sub-islands, Boatswain Bird Island.

Ascension Island used to be home to one of the largest seabird colonies in the tropical Atlantic, with up to 30 million boobies, terns and frigatebirds nesting there. The introduction of cats in 1815 and the arrival of man, who harvested the birds, their eggs and their guano, reduced that number to about 400,000 today, most of which live on Boatswain Bird Island.

I could hear and smell Bird Island long before I could see it. The island is a huge rock just off the east coast of Ascension. It is flat-topped sheer rock about a quarter of a mile long and some 300 feet high. The island is iced white from the guano that smothers the black volcanic rock.

Although landing on the island is prohibited, Johnny had once visited as part of an RSPB study. He told me that the smell and the sound are almost unbearable, and that he had ponged of guano for weeks after.

Danielle, Johnny and Paddy all stormed ahead as I struggled with the heat and the mountain scree that kept slipping from beneath my feet. I had learned from the Green Mountain fiasco and had purchased some brand-new walking-boots from the island's shoe shop. (Tuesdays and Thursdays 15.30–16.30.)

On my last evening on Ascension, Adam the tax man had invited me fishing.

The harbour jetty itself has the essential crane used for hoisting cargo containers ashore, and a fisherman's work area, which includes a large table for gutting and preparing fresh fish. The wall behind is tiled with the fins of tuna saved as mementos and nailed up like some morbid shrine.

A flock of tiny rowing-boats were leashed to the jetty railing like a pack of dogs tied outside a shop by their walker. These are used by the islanders to reach their fishing- and sailing-boats moored to buoys further out in the bay. In the distance was the tanker, the *Maersk*, that supplies the island with fuel and which has a dual role as one of the island's evacuation craft in the event of a volcanic eruption. In the heat, gas and lava of an exploding island I could think of better escape vessels than a petrol tanker. At such times perhaps one's not fussy.

A gaggle of children were busy jumping into the warm water

from the jetty wall. They would then use a guiding rope to hoick themselves from the sea and up the slippery steps before dive-bombing into the water again. Paddy also came down to join them, swimming in circles trying to catch the swarms of black fish that teased him by nibbling at his toes.

When Adam the taxman had finished number-crunching for the day we were to meet Buffalo, one of the island's migrant Saint Helenian workers. We were going hunting for tuna.

We descended the steep steps to the water and boarded the tiny dinghy that would transport us to Buffalo's fishing-boat that was anchored out in the harbour. The dinghy was barely big enough for the three of us, and water lapped over its sides.

Once safely aboard the fishing-boat we followed Ascension's shoreline as the setting sun illuminated her slopes orange and bronze. The sky was clear except for the permanent cloud that shrouded the peak of Green Mountain in a white veil. She looked like a dollop of mint ice cream covered in a puff of whipped cream.

Ascension Island is a rocky peak on the mid-Atlantic ridge. She stands proud and isolated above the water, her steep cliffs dropping to the ocean floor many thousands of feet below. Buffalo explained that the best depth for tuna-fishing was at 500 feet or more. You didn't need to travel far from the shore before the sea bed had fallen away sufficiently.

Buffalo picked up a small anchor and dropped it over the side. Several yards of chain snaked into the murky depths followed by more than a hundred yards of thick rope. He then handed me a fish about the same size as I normally go fishing for, which I attached to a thick hook that would have done the eponymous Captain proud. I dropped my line into the darkness below.

The peace and solitude as we bobbed up and down on the gentle swell thousands of miles from any mainland came from our true isolation, the island our only link with civilization and security. She appeared even more barren and bleak from the water. The surf licked at frozen lava that spilt into the Atlantic waters. The setting sun silhouetted her outline and painted the sky above her with streaks of colour, like a half-finished painting.

Adam passed us each a can of Guinness. The click as we opened the cans seemed destructive and I wondered how far the sound would carry out here.

For several hours we sat patiently as the lights on Ascension intensified in the gathering dusk. She wasn't a pretty island, but as we sat out here, listening to the world, the sight of her was comforting.

Buffalo had lived on Ascension for nearly as long as Johnny, but he was getting ready to return to his home island of St Helena in just a few months' time. I asked him why he was leaving Ascension after so many years. ''Cause St Helena is my home,' he said taking a swig from his can.

'Doesn't Ascension now feel like home after so many years?' I asked.

'Nope,' he smiled.

'Why not?' I continued.

''Cause nowhere's like St Helena,' he replied. 'Ascension's too dry.'

As well as the rift between begrudging military and non-military on the island, there appeared to be a further sub-division within the civilian sector: roughly, those St Helenians who come to work on Ascension because they have to for financial reasons, and the rest of the expat community, many of whom consider Ascension to be their own undiscovered island utopia.

We hadn't had so much as a kiss from a fish since we lowered our lines several hours before. I became impatient and started fiddling with the line. If I pulled, I could feel the weight of the bait and the hundreds of yards of line that streaked below. I pulled at the line and in a moment of absent-minded stupidity I wrapped it round my forefinger. I must have held it there for several seconds before Buffalo asked me to hold his rod while he manoeuvred the boat. I released the line from my finger and as I stretched across the boat, I felt my rod snatch hard against my palm.

Its tip bent hard into the water as line screamed from the reel at an Olympic pace. Guinness flew as I struggled to balance the two rods and a can of Ireland's finest. For a couple of seconds, chaos reigned over our small fishing-boat as Buffalo rugby-tackled the rod and attempted to throw on the brake. The whizzing noise from the reel seemed to drown all other sounds. And then as quickly as it all began, there was silence. The fish had its snog and left my bait to it. It had been using her. Bastard, I thought.

It was only then that it dawned on me how close I had come to having my fingers sliced clean off as if by cheese wire. Had the fish struck before I was asked to help Buffalo it would have been very messy indeed.

The sun set into the Atlantic Ocean and after several hours we decided to concede victory to the tuna and return to harbour. It was then that I got to observe again one of the greatest attributes of island life – resourcefulness.

One hundred yards of line and an anchor would have taken us most of the evening to haul in by hand, but Buffalo had devised a brilliantly simple device using things he had found washed up on the beach. He had attached a piece of rope to a large yellow fishing float. He then looped the rope around the anchor cable and tied it to the other end of the float.

I was intrigued as Buffalo started the engine and began to edge slowly towards the shore with the anchor still in the water. Slowly the anchor line threaded itself through the loop, as the float acted as a sort of aquatic lever, and Buffalo pulled up the slack, which he neatly coiled in the corner of the boat, and fifteen minutes later the anchor lay cradled below the fishing float. 'Genius,' I said to Buffalo as he pulled the anchor aboard and headed for Georgetown.

I spent my last day on Ascension trying to visit the places I had missed. I explored the island's museum, where I found Mrs Fairhurst busy photocopying and stapling together the island newspaper, the *Ascension Times*. The thousand weekly copies are all photocopied and stapled by hand. I visited the American baseball park and played football with the children at Two Boats school. The more I visited, the more I was struck by the transitory nature of life on the island.

'Are you out to watch Miss Isle tonight?' asked a young Saint on his bicycle.

I hadn't heard that the island was holding a beauty pageant. 'Where will it be?' I replied, not one to spurn the opportunity of an evening of beautiful women.

The young boy scrunched his face up as if I had just asked where fish live. 'The sky,' he guffawed pointing upwards. 'Sometimes you can see the afterburner,' he added with excitement before pushing his bike off and doing a nifty little wheelie next to a pissed-off-looking donkey.

I was thoroughly confused. Ascension was strange, but now it seemed to be rubbing off on the children. Only later, in the island's supermarket, did I understand what he meant.

The island has three supermarkets. The US military supermarket, the British NAAFI and Georgetown's supermarket, the only one open to 'civilians', called the Ascension Island Commercial Services Shop (or AICSS in Ascension parlance), which stocks everything from year-old magazines to the mind-boggling selection of Walker's crisps and soft drinks which dominated the shop. Roughly half the products were from the UK, the rest from South Africa.

The island was just a week away from the implementation of taxation. For the first time in the island's history, duty would be payable on tobacco and alcohol, and the locals weren't taking any chances. I saw one Saint loading twenty crates of beer into his pick-up truck, to beat the levy; in fact the shop was practically dry from the last-minute pre-tax rush.

'I see *Pathfinder*'s back in town,' said an elderly Saint woman paying for her goods.

'Yeah, missiles coming in tonight,' replied the cashier.

'Oh,' she said. 'When will you get more ice cream?'

'On Thursday's RAF Tristar.'

My supermarket conversations have always been limited to: 'Do you have a reward card?' 'No.' 'That will be £89.63 pence, please.'

But not on Ascension. Here they were talking about missiles and an ice cream shortage about to be rectified by the Royal Air Force.

I had misheard the young boy on the bicycle; he hadn't said 'Miss Isle' but 'missile'. I wasn't sure which sounded more exciting.

The USS *Pathfinder* is based in Florida and she is deployed to

Ascension each time the island is used for missile practice by the United States. I had watched her anchor off Georgetown the day before. She had seemed unremarkable except for the large white satellite dish attached to her stern. Missiles from the continental USA are fired to land as close to Ascension as is considered reasonable, while the USS *Pathfinder* is responsible for tracking their trajectory with her enormous satellite dish, and totting up the score in this giant game of darts.

But even though the knowledge that the missile is deliberately offset by a careful percentage to prevent a bullseye is not entirely reassuring, I was still pleased I'd be catching the show.

That evening – my last on the island – I had been invited to visit the administrator, Geoffrey Fairhurst, and his wife up at the residence on Green Mountain. The residence lies almost at the summit. At one stage it had been the island's sanatorium, the mountain hospital where sick soldiers and sailors went to recover in the cooler climate.

The building itself is a low, square, one-storey house with grey stone walls. A long gravel drive led to the front door. The administrator's old Rover was already parked in the drive when I arrived. I was met at the door by one of their St Helenian staff, who led me through the house to the garden, where Mr and Mrs Fairhurst were sipping tea.

The sun was still high in the late-afternoon sky as I stepped out on to their manicured lawn. The back of the house was draped in ivy and the garden borders were a rainbow of colours from the vibrant flowers that illuminated the garden. I could have been in Surrey except for the dramatic view that stretched beyond.

The edge of the garden simply fell away to reveal the black volcanic landscape of the island over 500 yards below, and beyond the rugged lava flows the Atlantic Ocean sparkled a dozen hues of blue. Like a camera lens trying to focus, my eyes struggled to adapt to the extraordinary view. The garden positively glowed in the sunlight. It was as out of place as the kind of desert oasis that you expect to see in films.

As I sat in this peculiar English garden, the volcanoscape stretching out below, a bright orange crab scuttled across the neatly manicured lawn, clutching a flower in its pincer.

'Have you enjoyed the island?' asked the administrator.

'Loved it,' I exclaimed.

'Yes, we're rather fond of it too,' he said handing me a glass. 'In fact we're thinking of extending my contract,' he smiled. 'I am due to retire soon, and I would like to retire here,' he explained.

Ascension Island certainly seemed to have an effect on those who had lived there. I thought about my university friend Charlie and his island shrine, and of Johnny who would be king, and of all the islanders who would come up to me as I wandered around Georgetown: 'Have you been up Green Mountain?' 'What about the wind turbines?' 'Have you visited English Bay?' 'Isn't Comfortless Cove beautiful?'

I had been charmed by the island and her eccentricities, and so it seemed rather appropriate that I should spend my last evening on Ascension Island sitting on an English lawn sipping a gin and tonic with HH the administrator and his wife, watching a missile as it streaked across the starry sky and disappeared somewhere into the horizon. I told you Ascension was strange.

Epilogue

'I'll meet you h'outside Harvey Nichols,' explained James in his distinctive accent. I was arranging to meet James 'Jimmy' Glass, Tristan da Cunha's chief islander, who was visiting London with his wife as part of his world lobster sales tour.

It was an incongruous place to catch up. The last time I had seen him was nearly a year earlier on the tiny South Atlantic island. Jimmy didn't strike me as the Harvey Nichols sort.

'Sorry we're late,' apologized my girlfriend, who was astonished to find them waiting patiently on Sloane Street, even though we were more than an hour late. 'Not to worry,' smiled James with an infectious chuckle, 'we are used to waiting. An hour is nothing, we usually wait a year,' he winked. My girlfriend's eyes bulged.

James and his wife would be away from the island for several months as they visited various restaurants and fish dealers across the world in an attempt to strengthen their markets around the globe, and secure their island's future. They hoped they would be able to return to Tristan da Cunha aboard HMS *Endurance*.

The Glasses looked terribly out of place in the trendy fifth-floor bar. Their eyes betrayed their unease. They looked alert and vaguely threatened as we sat amid the crowd of champagne-swilling, pin-striped bankers bellowing about their latest million-pound deals.

A lot had happened since my voyage to Tristan da Cunha all those months ago. I had taken the best part of a year travelling nearly 100,000 miles, spanning three oceans and three continents to visit six tiny islands with a combined population smaller than an English village. All my years of daydreaming had finally become reality.

The islands were no longer pin pricks on my old wall map, but images, smells and sounds ingrained for ever in my subconscious, each one its own unique ingredient. I may have failed to discover a new island of my own, like the medical officer aboard HMS *Endurance*, but I had unravelled a childhood mystery and successfully made the journeys to all the islands.

I had learned that although the British government has always guaranteed to respect the right to self-determination of its overseas territories, these remote islands remain part of the UK not because they necessarily want to but because they *have* to. Geographic, economic and social isolation mean that many of the islands would not and could not exist without financial assistance from the UK.

But the Gibraltar fiasco of 2002, in which the British government entered talks with Spain over the future of the overseas territory despite a local referendum overwhelmingly against any deal, has thrown doubt over the future of all the UK's overseas territories. Never have these remote islanders' lives and homes seemed so finely balanced and fragile.

I had been largely touched by the islanders' unfailing generosity, and warmed by their humility and pride. I had witnessed the many different facets and symptoms of island life, from idealism and resourcefulness to the gossiping, loneliness and insecurity endemic to small island communities.

And yet each time I returned from one of my Teatime adventures, I was always overwhelmed by the same feelings of remoteness and detachment from what I had come home to, the same feelings I had after returning to reality from my year on Taransay.

While these islands had become such a significant part of my life I soon realized I was of very little importance to them. In the Teatime Islands life went on.

The British Indian Ocean Territories were once again in the news as Diego Garcia became a prison for Iraq's most wanted, in the aftermath of the second Gulf war.

St Helena was still waiting for her airport, and despite a report in *The Times* that DFID and the St Helena government were still looking for tenders for the project, Shelco remained as optimistic and defiant as ever, and Jo Terry and his wife continue their island vigil.

Ascension finally held a referendum for 'democracy', in which the people voted overwhelmingly for an island council with control of the island's budget. Elections were held at the end of 2002, in which twelve people stood for the council, from which seven were elected. One of whom was, of course, Johnny Hobson.

According to the most recent reports the council has been able to meet only a few times since the elections, but the provision of a new government house and council chamber should ensure increased activity. I couldn't help but wonder what sort of opening hours they would operate.

As well as being elected councillor, Johnny had succeeded in buying the island's only hotel and renovating it. The Obsidian Hotel now has its own pub, the Anchor Inn, and a restaurant to rival the Galley, the Sunset Bistro. The German fishermen had also hit success when their embryonic fishing venture's first client landed a 1,500 lb blue marlin. Ascension's donkeys remain 'undoctored'.

And as for Pitcairn, Operation Unique continues its lengthy course. Charges have been made against the nine islanders, but the case awaits the decision of Governor Fell as to when, how and where the men will be tried. In the meantime, the island remains suspended in limbo, as indeed it has been for the four years since the case began.

However, administrative changes on the tiny Pacific island have added half a dozen new inhabitants to the island's minuscule population. Pitcairn now has a permanent 'governor's representative', the first of which is Jenny Lock, a career diplomat with the rather unusual task of living with the islanders for a year. She won't be too lonely though, as joining her will be some social workers and a permanent policeman, who will undoubtedly qualify for the title of the 'world's most remote beat'.

Charles Veley completed the Travellers' Century Club list in Priština, Kosovo, making him the fastest and youngest person ever to complete it. He continues his world record attempt and according to his last missive he was in Seoul en route for Beijing for meetings with the Chinese government to discuss getting to the notoriously difficult Paracel Islands in the South China Sea.

The Teatime Islands finally had faces and even characters for me, each with its own unique individualism, born of a unique history, geography and society. The islands had elicited every emotion in me: the Falklands had excited me, Ascension intrigued me, the British Indian Ocean Territories saddened me, Pitcairn disappointed me, St Helena heartened me, and Tristan da Cunha had humbled me.

It was strange sitting with Tristan's chief islander in Central London, but suddenly I understood. It all became clear. We may not have been on an island in the physical sense, but our minds and spirits were. Like so many islophiles before me, I had been bewitched and enchanted by these islands and their communities. Their wind and tides beat through my body with invisible force. I thought back to Rachel Field's island poem:

> I don't know why and I can't say how
> Such a change upon me came,
> But I've slept on many an island
> And I'll never be the same.

'To Tristan,' I proposed, holding my glass aloft.

James chuckled and I sat back in my chair and dreamed of penguins.

Bibliography

Kenneth Bain, *St Helena, the Island, Her People and Their Ship*, Wilton 65, 1993

Ian Ball, *Pitcairn: Children of the Bounty*, Gollancz, 1973

Dea Birkett, *Serpent in Paradise*, Picador, 1997

Julia Blackburn, *The Emperor's Last Island: A Journey to St Helena*, Secker and Warburg, 1991 (Minerva, 1992)

Mary Cawkell, *The History of the Falkland Islands*, Anthony Nelson, 2001

Thurston Clarke, *Islomania: A Journey among the Last Real Islands*, Abacus, 2002

Klaus Dodds, *Pink Ice: Britain and the South Atlantic Empire*, I. B. Tauris, 2002

Arne Falk-Ronne, *Back to Tristan*, Allen and Unwin, 1967

Sergio Ghione, *Turtle Island: A Journey to Britain's Oddest Colony*, Allen Lane, 2002

Philip Gosse, *St Helena 1502–1938*, Anthony Nelson, 1990

Duff Hart-Davis, *Ascension: The Story of a South Atlantic Island*, Constable, 1972

Barbara Hodgson, *Hippolyte's Island: An Illustrated Novel*, Chronicle Books, 2001

Lucy Irvine, *Castaway*, Gollancz, 1983 (Penguin Books, 1984; Corgi, 1999)

Donald S. Johnson, *Phantom Islands of the Atlantic: The Legends of Seven Lands That Never Were*, Souvenir Press, 1997

Trevor Lummis, *Life and Death in Eden: Pitcairn Island and the 'Bounty' Mutineers*, Gollancz, 1999 (Phoenix, 2000)

Mark McCrum, *Castaway*, Ebury Books, 2001

Harry Ritchie, *The Last Pink Bits: Travels through the Remnants of the British Empire*, Hodder and Stoughton, 1996 (Sceptre, 1997)

Diana Souhami, *Selkirk's Island*, Weidenfeld and Nicolson, 2001 (Phoenix, 2003)

Sue Steiner, *St Helena, Ascension and Tristan da Cunha*, Bradt Travel
    Guides, 2002

Debbie Summers, *The Falkland Islands*, Falklands Conservation, 2001

Leslie Thomas, *My World of Islands: A Voyage to Paradise*, Michael Joseph,
    1983 (Mandarin, 1995)

William Wagstaff, *Falkland Islands*, Bradt Travel Guides, 2001

Simon Winchester, *Diego Garcia*, in *Granta Magazine*, No. 73

—, *Outposts: Journeys to the Surviving Relics of the British Empire*, Hodder
    and Stoughton, 1985 (Penguin Books, 2003)

Louise B. Young, *Islands: Portraits of Miniature Worlds*, W. H. Freeman,
    1999

Index